COMMUNITY MOBILISATION
METHODS AND MODELS

COMMUNITY MOBILISATION
METHODS AND MODELS

Edited by
Dr. R.R. Prasad
Professor & Head
Centre for Equity & Social Development
National Institute of Rural Development & Panchayati Raj
(NIRD & PR)
Hyderabad (A.P.)
(INDIA)

DPH

DISCOVERY PUBLISHING HOUSE PVT. LTD.
NEW DELHI-110 002

Published by:

Tilak Wasan

DISCOVERY PUBLISHING HOUSE PVT. LTD.

4383/4B, Ansari Road, Darya Ganj

New Delhi - 110 002 (India)

Phone : +91-11-23279245, 43596064-65

Fax : +91-11-23253475

E-mail : discoverypublishinghouse@gmail.com

sales@discoverypublishinggroup.com

website : www.discoverypublishinggroup.com

***First Edition:* 2015**

ISBN: 978-93-5056-739-5

Community Mobilisation: ***Methods and Models***

Printed at:

Infinity Imaging Systems

Delhi

PREFACE

Bringing people together to effect change is one of the most important elements of problem-solving in a democracy. If sustainable development leading to elimination of poverty has to be ushered in, governments of the developing nations world will have to take a lead role in fostering a framework of grassroots institutions of the people through community mobilisation. Through mobilisation, people can organize themselves to take action collectively by developing their own plan and strategy for recovery rather than being imposed from outside.

For this purpose, methods and models that would help them to take decisions regarding their own development need to be understood so that the communities can plan, implement and evaluate their own actions. This book would strengthen their understanding of the key concepts related to community mobilisation in local development planning, and to create a common vision of how the most vulnerable in rural communities can be empowered through mobilisation. The book would also provide clear guidance on how a process of community mobilisation can be facilitated step-by-step, including advice on what tools can be used and demonstrate how, where, and when the process of community mobilisation can be integrated and made complimentary to the planning and budgeting processes. It is based on the assumption that the development of communities and individuals should reflect a commitment to social justice and an equitable sharing of the benefits of development.

This book presents the results of an extensive review of articles in peer-reviewed publications, journals and books on community mobilisation. The author also reviewed relevant gray literature and project documents from organizations working in the community mobilisation in the field. Readers of this book may include the staff and associates of NGOs engaged in community development in rural areas, individual activists and community mobilisers, particularly those working directly with the most vulnerable groups, elected and appointed officials in Local Government institutions.

The author has drawn upon and summarised comments and stories from many contributors and would like to express great appreciation to all of them.

R.R. PRASAD

Contents

1 Community Participation and Community Mobilisation

INTRODUCTION

There are many paths to development. Different paths to development, nevertheless, converge in an assumption that improvement in living conditions are not brought about from above by some outside agency but by the people themselves taking an active part in their development. It is, therefore, generally agreed that if progress is to be achieved, it cannot be imposed from outside and must be based on small locally based and sustainable initiatives. The strategy for empowering the poor should be embedded in the grassroots where the under developed masses, so far reliant on informal organizations for their survival, are provided with formal access to the state through their own organizations.

Wignaraja and Sirivardana (2000:232) contended that throughout the last fifty years of development response, planners and policy-makers assumed that the State would provide the lead role in formulating and implementing enabling policies for poverty alleviation. Sub-sequently, the focus then shifted to development activities of locally rooted micro-development organizations with a view to encouraging participation of the poor in development. People's participation in development assumed importance because in the past the rural poor were rarely consulted in development planning and usually had no active role in development activities. FAO (1997) in its report 'Participation in practise: Lessons from the FAO People's Participation Programme' emphasised that "uunless the rural poor are given the means to participate fully in development, they will continue to be excluded from its benefits". Wignaraja and Sirivardana (2000:233) are of the view that in the past ten to fifteen years, a sufficient body of experience has emerged which demonstrates that where the poor participate as subjects and not objects of the development process, it is possible to generate growth, human development and equity.

Rural transformation is an ongoing process and requires active communities, vibrant leadership and strong institutions to ensure that 'transformation' is sustained and the communities strive towards it with or without the presence of an external catalyst. Rationale for involving communities is based on the premise that sense of 'ownership' of the developmental initiatives by the local people instills confidence, sustains the momentum and ensures success. Sense of ownership is defined as the community's feeling/belief that the problem/issue and/or programme belong to them and they have a commitment to the programme. How intensively and extensively the people are involved in defining the issue or programme, the planning process and the implementation, will affect the sense of ownership. "Ownership develops when partners play a key role in formulating and implementing a project and understand the benefits of participation. The recognition by each partner that he will be better able to achieve his own goals by collaborating and helping his partners reach their respective goals is the best way to ensure partners are committed for the long haul" (Kraemer (1993:23). Figueroa *et al.* (2002:32) have argued that even though an external agent may help determine the needs/programme goals, and guide the implementation process, the community should be heavily involved so that a sense of ownership can develop. The gain of creating a sense of ownership is that it reinforces what people learn and encourages them to integrate the shared learning into related situations. This in turn, feeds back into strengthening other social-change outcomes such as: 'sense of collective efficacy'.

People's participation as a concept was formulated in the mid-1970s, in response to the growing awareness that the various approaches then employed for rural development, such as community development, integrated rural development or basic needs did not often lead to significant rural development and especially poverty reduction, largely, as was then thought, because there was little involvement in development projects of those undergoing 'development', and particularly the poor. At the World Conference on Agrarian Reform and Rural Development (WCARRD), held in Rome in 1979, the international community identified the reason for this failure – the lack of active participation of the poor in programmes designed, supposedly, to assist them (FAO, 1997).

WCARRD declared that participation by rural people in the institutions that govern their lives is a basic human right. If rural development was to realize its potential, the Conference said, disadvantaged rural people had to be organized and actively involved in designing policies and programmes and in controlling social and economic institutions. WCARRD saw a close link between participation and voluntary, autonomous and democratic organizations representing the poor. It called on development agencies to work in close cooperation with organizations of intended beneficiaries, and proposed that assistance be channeled through small farmer and peasant groups (FAO, 1997).

A participatory approach advocates actively involving 'the public' in decision-making processes, whereby the relevant 'public' depends upon the topic being addressed. The public can be average citizens, the stakeholders of a particular project or policy, experts and even members of government and private industry. Participatory decision-making is not only desired and demanded by citizens who wish to play a more active role in the governance of their society. Regional, national and local governments, development agencies and NGOs, scientists and companies are also increasingly eager to reap the benefits of actively engaging in decision-making processes diverse perspectives and those who will be affected by policies.

Effective and meaningful public involvement is seen as essential to:

- Enable high quality and democratic governance.
- Strengthen civil capacity.
- Develop and deliver programmes effectively and efficiently build public confidence and trust in decisions.
- Generate a greater understanding of public issues, concerns, priorities and solutions.
- Build broader support for programmes and initiatives.
- Increase mutual learning through the sharing of information, data and experiences.
- Ensure that decisions and policies incorporate knowledge and expertise that otherwise might be overlooked.
- Reflect a wider range of public concerns and values in decision-making.
- Rapidly identify possible controversial aspects of an issue and help bring together different points of view to achieve consensus in a collaborative manner.

So far all development interventions have been supply-driven. As a result expected results could not be achieved and the people did not come up to play any active role to sustain those. For that reason now attempts are being made to make all development programmes demand-driven. For a demand driven development process community participation is a pre-requisite.

In recent times, methods to improve management of centrally planned programmes, endeavors to generate critical political will to provide appropriate direction and support to development programmes, and efforts to involve communities as decision-makers and implementers of their own development have received considerable attention.

The pivotal role of people's participation in development is now re-emerging in economic and social development thinking. The strategy for sustainable development includes

Characteristics of Supply-Driven and Demand-Driven Development Programme

Supply-driven development	Demand-driven development
• Centrally decided • Dependant on availability of resource • People's need is not emphasized • Possibility of quick implementation • Absence of community participation	• Decided by the concerned people • Possibility of mobilizing and availing resource • Based on people's need • Slow implementation • Full community participation
• Management and maintenance is hampered • Resource mobilisation is hampered • Does not sustain • Environment is degraded	• Effective management and maintenance • Proper mobilisation and use of resource • Sustainability • Ecological balance

a 'people-centred' approach that will improve the poor's access to productive assets, allow them to participate in designing and implementing development programmes, and foster their involvement in institutions from village to national level (FAO 1997). People-centred development also means full community participation at both decision-making and implementation levels.

Efforts to reduce rural poverty in the past also tended to focus on increasing the income and food security of rural poor people. Increasingly, there has been a greater emphasis on the human and social factors that cause poverty. This broader understanding of the factors affecting poverty in rural areas has been reflected in many rural development project designs since the mid-1990s. Project design stressed peoples' participation and empowerment, enhanced social capital, demand-driven development and a community-driven development approach.

The IFAD's Rural Poverty Portal (http://www.ruralpovertyportal.org/) mentions that community-driven development (CDD) involves a degree of devolution of responsibility to communities for managing their development, including the design and implementation of projects. This requires that the communities themselves have the capacity to assume responsibility. It also requires a culture of public administration that views communities as development partners in their own right, rather than as simply recipients of benefits through public expenditure. The extent to which communities can shape their own development priorities within a project context defines the extent to which the project is applying a community-driven development approach.

Community-Driven Development (CDD)

CDD is a relatively new approach to rural development. Community-driven development (CDD) recognizes that poor people are prime actors in the development process, not targets of externally designed poverty reduction efforts. In CDD, control of decisions and resources rests with community groups, who may often work in partnership with demand-responsive support organizations and service providers, including elected local governments, the private sector, non-governmental organizations (NGOs), and central government agencies. CDD can increase the effectiveness, efficiency, and sustainability of projects or programmes, making them more pro-poor and responsive to local priorities. Other objectives include developing capacity, building social and human capital, facilitating community and individual empowerment, deepening democracy, improving governance, and strengthening human rights.

A central feature of the approach is its attempt to place the community at the heart of the development process. The main principles of CDD are:

- To place control and resources in the hands of the community.
- To view poor people as themselves assets and partners in development.
- To build-on existing institutions.

The process of focusing on the community and its role in development leads to an emphasis being placed upon local empowerment and capacity-building within the community.

The four core features of CDD (Binswanger and Aiyar 2003) include:

(i) *Real Participation and Empowerment*: Including devolution of authority and resources, community co-financing, local participation in all stages of project design, and availability of technical assistance and facilitation from higher administrative levels.

(ii) *Accountability*: Horizontal and downward to peers, not just upward to central levels.

(iii) *Technical Soundness*: Context-specificity; designing in phases; ensuring full participation; administrative, fiscal, and political decentralization; full utilization of local capacities; use of clear field-tested manuals and tools for each actor; provision of technical advisory services.

(iv) *Sustainability*: Fiscal, asset, environmental, and social.

Why Community-Driven Development?

Poor and marginalized people have often been viewed as the target of poverty reduction efforts. Community Driven Development (CDD) approaches turn this perception on its head, and treat poor people and their institutions as assets and partners in the search for sustainable solutions to development challenges. CDD - broadly defined - is an approach that gives control over planning decisions and investment resources to community groups and local governments. CDD programmes operate on the principles of local empowerment, participatory governance, demand-responsiveness, administrative autonomy, greater downward accountability, and enhanced local capacity. Experience has shown that given clear rules of the game, access to information and appropriate capacity and financial support, poor men and women can effectively organize in order to identify community priorities and address local problems, by working in partnership with local governments and other supportive institutions (Alkire *et al.* 2001).

Community-driven development is indelible in the development landscape. It is increasingly visible in the policy design of many governments, non-governmental organizations, and multilateral institutions and features in important debates involving democracy, governance, institutions, and decentralization. This has philosophical and instrumentalist underpinnings, with participation as both means and end. Participatory or community-driven development is advocated on the basis that, among other advantages, it can reduce information problems for development planners and beneficiaries, increase the resources available to poor people, and strengthen the capacity for collective action among poor and other marginalized societal groups.

Community-driven development (CDD) gives control of decisions and resources to community groups. CDD treats poor people as assets and partners in the development process, building on their institutions and resources. Support to CDD usually includes strengthening and financing inclusive community groups, facilitating community access to information, and promoting an enabling environment through policy and institutional reform. Experience demonstrates that by directly relying on poor people to drive development activities, CDD has the potential to make poverty reduction efforts more responsive to demands, more inclusive, more sustainable, and more cost-effective than traditional centrally led programmes. CDD fills a critical gap in poverty reduction efforts, achieving immediate and lasting results at the grassroots level and complementing market economy and government-run programmes. With these powerful attributes, CDD can play an important role in strategies to reduce poverty.

CDD gives control of decisions and resources to community groups. These groups often work in partnership with demand-responsive support organizations and service providers, including elected local governments, the private sector, NGOs, and central government agencies. CDD is a way to provide social and infrastructure services, organize economic activity and resource management, empower poor people, improve governance, and enhance security of the poorest. Support to CDD usually includes:

- Strengthening and financing accountable and inclusive community groups or CBOs.

- Facilitating community access to information through a variety of media, and increasingly through information technology.
- Forging functional links between CBOs and formal institutions and creating an enabling environment through appropriate policy and institutional reform, often including decentralization reform, promotion of a conducive legal and regulatory framework, development of sound sector policies, and fostering of responsive sector institutions and private service providers.

According to the Voices of the Poor study (Narayan and others 2000), based on interviews with 60,000 poor people in 60 countries, poor people demand a development process driven by their communities. When the poor were asked to indicate what might make the greatest difference in their lives, they responded: *(a)* organizations of their own so they can negotiate with government, traders, and NGOs; *(b)* direct assistance through community-driven programmes so they can shape their own destinies; and *(c)* local ownership of funds, so they can end corruption. They want NGOs and governments to be accountable to them.

CDD is an effective mechanism for poverty reduction, complementing market – and state-run activities by achieving immediate and lasting results at the grassroots level. Experience has shown that CDD can enhance sustainability and make poverty reduction efforts more responsive to demand. CDD has also been shown to increase the efficiency and effectiveness of poverty reduction efforts. Because it works at the local level, CDD has the potential to occur simultaneously in a very large number of communities, thus achieving far-reaching poverty impact. Finally, well-designed CDD programmes are inclusive of poor and vulnerable groups, build positive social capital, and give them greater voice both in their community and with government entities.

CDD Complements Market and Public Sector Activities

Experience has shown that policies aimed at promoting national economic competitiveness and state-run public investment programmes are essential but insufficient for poverty reduction. These policies and programmes often do not benefit everyone, and benefits often take years to trickle down. CDD offers the opportunity to fill this critical gap by achieving immediate and lasting results at the grassroots level.

The market alone cannot provide all essential services and goods for poverty reduction – it often provides insufficient public goods (for example, roads, quality education, and health care for poor people) while overharvesting common pool goods (for example, forests, watersheds, and fishery resources). Although national state-run programmes focused on investing in human and physical capital have the potential to redress some of these imbalances, accumulated experience has shown that central government programmes are often slow to deliver basic services and are often ineffective in reaching poor people. Market-and state-run activities can be effectively complemented by community-driven solutions that engage CBOs, local governments, NGOs, and the private sector. By using CDD approaches and local actors to provide key goods and services, governments can support immediate poverty reduction by efficiently building human and physical assets at the local level.

CDD Enhances Sustainability

CDD can make services responsive to demand expressed by poor men and women and as a result can enhance sustainability. As consumers, community members are the most legitimate, informed, and reliable source of information about their own priorities. Community-developed facilities such as: health centres, schools, and water supply systems tend to have higher utilization rates and are better maintained than when investment decisions are made by actors outside the community. Experience also demonstrates that demand is better articulated when communities contribute to investment costs and control investment choices. A water supply study of 1,875 households in rural communities in six countries (Benin, Bolivia, Honduras, Indonesia, Pakistan, and Uganda) suggests that water system sustainability is significantly higher when communities control key investment decisions and when they pay part of the investment costs, ensuring that they get what they want and are willing to pay for (Sara and Katz 1997).

CDD Improves Efficiency and Effectiveness

Studies and practical experience suggest that CDD can improve the effectiveness and efficiency of services in many sectors and contexts. Examples of these benefits for infrastructure, education, micro finance, and natural resource management are given below.

- *Infrastructure:* Community management of development investments usually results in lower costs and more productively employed assets. Studies of community-organized irrigation systems in Asia, for example, have repeatedly found that systems constructed and operated by the farmers themselves, often without much external assistance, generate a higher level of agricultural productivity than more modern systems constructed by government agencies with substantial external assistance (Lam 1998; Tang 1992). A recent study in Zambia compares CBO-managed and contractor-managed approaches to developing school infrastructure programmes. Unit costs under the contractor approach were more than twice as high as under the CBO approach. Similarly, a recent study in South Africa shows that when CBOs are responsible for all aspects of the project (design, management, and monitoring), costs per beneficiary are less than half than when the CBOs are not decision-makers (Adato and others 1999).
- *Education:* There is empirical evidence that community management and accountability can improve education outcomes (Jimenez and Sawada 1998). Greater parental involvement in children's education can inspire children to attend school and put pressure on providers to deliver better services. Communities that oversee school management are also more willing to assist in financing. Preliminary results from the Philippines show that community-managed primary schools have lower costs while holding enrollment and quality constant (Jimenez and Paqueo 1996).

- *Group-based Micro Finance:* Evidence suggests that certain models of both individual and group-based micro finance can extend the reach of financial services and achieve high repayment rates. Some micro finance programmes rely on local groups that, because they know community members' characters and economic activities, can provide peer pressure. Group-based programmes tend to do particularly well where the screening and monitoring costs of credit are too high for the lender and when the group approach reduces the cost of information gathering and creates incentives at the local level (Adams, Graham, and von Pischke 1984).
- *Natural Resource Management:* Several countries have moved from state to community management of natural resources, mainly as a result of poor outcomes under state-led programmes. The joint forest management programme in the Indian state of Andra Pradesh shows how community management can increase the effectiveness of services (Venkatamaran and Falconer 1999). More than 5,000 CBOs have rejuvenated more than 1.2 million hectares of degraded forest in the state. Degraded forests have sprung back to life, timber smuggling has almost stopped, and cattle grazing is under control. Village labour is more gainfully employed and out-migration has declined. Soil conservation has saved local water resources.

CDD Allows Poverty Reduction Efforts to be Taken to Scale

Because CDD devolves responsibilities and resources to the local level, activities can occur simultaneously in a large number of communities without being constrained by a central bureaucracy. When poor communities are trusted to drive development and are given appropriate information, support, and clear rules, a system can be put in place not to provide for poor people, but to facilitate their active and ongoing role in rolling out poverty reduction efforts.

CDD Makes Development more Inclusive of the Interests of Poor People and Vulnerable Groups

Representative CBOs can provide voice and empowerment to groups that are typically excluded from the development process. The interests of women, indigenous groups, ethnic minorities, the disabled, and people with AIDS might not be effectively expressed through standard political and economic structures. If these minority groups are actively involved in CBOs, they will help make development processes more inclusive. Inclusion also requires that scarce public resources be targeted to groups that most need them. In the absence of reliable information to allow means testing (such as for household income), involving communities directly in the targeting process can improve efforts to target the poorest and most marginal individuals and groups. For example, parent-teacher associations might be in the best position to determine which children should receive tuition or school lunch subsidies, as shown in a recent study of a targeted school enrollment subsidy programme in Bangladesh (Ravallion 1999).

CDD Empowers Poor People, Builds Social Capital, and Strengthens Governance

CDD empowers poor people. The objective of development is not merely to increase incomes or to improve poverty indicators, but also to expand people's real freedoms. These are the choices people make between different valuable beings and doings, such as being nourished, being educated, participating in public debate, or being free to walk about without shame (Sen 1999). This analysis is reflected in the *World Development Report 2000/2001* (World Bank 2000), which identifies empowerment as one of the three elements of poverty reduction.

Targeted community-driven approaches devolve control and decision-making to poor women and men, which empowers them immediately and directly. While clear rules, transparency, and accountability are important safeguards to prevent corruption or the capture of community resources by elites, the speed and directness with which CDD empowers poor people is rarely matched by other institutional frameworks for poverty reduction.

Control over decisions and resources can also give communities the opportunity to build social capital (defined as the ability of individuals to secure benefits as a result of membership in social networks) by expanding the depth and range of their networks. This kind of network expansion, which is critical for long-term growth and development, also has positive short-term effects on welfare and risk exposure. Several studies conducted in Bolivia, Burkina Faso, Indonesia, and Tanzania found that social capital has a positive effect on household welfare (as measured by per capita consumption), and that the effect was several times greater than that of human capital alone (Grootaert 1999a; Grootaert and Narayan 2000; Grootaert, Oh, and Swamy 1999). The creation of networks and social capital also helps to reduce household exposure to risk. Poor individuals and households manage risk in many ways, including offering reciprocal self-help, participating in local organizations, and building linkages with people outside their social networks. For example, rotating savings and credit associations in Bolivia, Peru, Guatemala, and Indonesia are a means by which people save and lend among themselves on the basis of reciprocity and mutual trust. Development strategies that strengthen CBOs and build social capital can also strengthen the safety net for poor people and reduce their exposure to risk.

Finally, strengthening local associations that are inclusive can increase poor people's voice in local political processes and governance. In Bangladesh, for example, leaders of community groups formed and strengthened with the help of NGOs are increasingly being elected to leadership roles in local government bodies.

CDD Creates Alternative Institutional Arrangements

Where CDD arrangements are appropriate, governments can consider a range of institutional options to support CBOs. Local or municipal government, the private sector, civil society, and central government or central funds can provide critical support to CDD. Although there are many variations regarding the exact roles of each player, three broad sets of arrangements have emerged:

- Partnerships between CBOs and elected local or municipal governments.
- Partnerships between CBOs and private support organizations (NGOs or private firms).
- Direct partnerships between CBOs and central government or a central fund, including other, higher-level governments and funds, for example, states or provinces in federal systems.

Participation and Community Empowerment

To effectively address issues of sustainability and equity, people centred and people controlled development is evolving as an alternative approach. The focus of current development efforts is, thus, heavily tilted in favour of building institutional capacity through participation and local self-reliance leading to empowerment. The notion of 'people's participation' is now widely recognized as a basic operational principle of development programmes and projects. Participation has come to be recognized as an absolute imperative for development. Some even argue that development, in fact, is participation. There is nothing more basic to the development process than participation. Over the last ten years, participation by the people has become a buzzword in the development community. Chinese philosopher Lau Tse embodies the essence of the participatory approach to community development in a poem.

"Go and meet your people, live and stay with them, love them, work with them. Begin with what they have, plan and develop from what they know, and in the end, when the work is over, they will say: 'We did it ourselves".

Participation is a process of empowering the community to be able to solve their own problems through equal partnership, transparency, power-sharing, shared responsibility and co-operation.

The Principles of Participation

The long-term objective of using participatory approaches is to improve the capacity (empowerment) of everybody who directly or indirectly participates in the programme or project, through their involvement in decision-making and follow-up activities.

The principles of participation are:

- *Inclusion*: Of all people, or representatives of all groups who will be affected by the results of a decision or a process - for example a development project.
- *Equal Partnership*: Recognising that every person has skill, ability and initiative and has equal right to participate in the process regardless of their status.
- *Transparency*: All participants must help to create a climate conducive to open communication and building dialogue.
- *Sharing Power:* Authority and power must be balanced evenly between all stakeholders to avoid the domination of one party.
- *Sharing Responsibility*: Similarly, all stakeholders have equal responsibility for decisions that are made, and each should have clear responsibilities within each process.
- *Empowerment*: Participants with special skills should be encouraged to take responsibility for tasks within their speciality, but should also encourage others to also be involved to promote mutual learning and empowerment.
- *Co-operation*: Co-operation is very important; sharing everybody's strength reduces everybody's weaknesses.

Advantages of Community Participation

Few people now dispute that participatory approaches to organizational development and management and community empowerment provide a powerful combination for sustainable development. There is a considerable body of literature documenting the beneficial impact of participatory approaches in community level projects, particularly in terms of greater sustainability. Typical statements of impact are as follows:

- The programme and its implementation gets tuned to the existing social, economic, and cultural context hence meeting the community's needs.
- It creates a sense of belonging and responsibility for stakeholders in planning and implementing the

programme so that the impact of the programme as well as the programme itself are more sustainable.

- The requirement to give everybody a role in the process, especially in terms of decision-making and responsibility, results in the empowerment of everybody involved.
- Implementation activities become more objective and flexible according to specific conditions.
- Greater transparency due to disbursement of information and authority.
- The implementation of the project or programme is more focused on the community's needs.

The FAO (1997) has pointed out that for governments and development agencies, people's participation through small groups offers distinct advantages which, among others, include:

- *Economies of Scale:* The high cost of providing development services to scattered, small scale producers is a major constraint on poverty-oriented programmes. Participatory groups constitute a grassroots 'receiving system' that allows development agencies to reduce the unit delivery or transaction costs of their services, thus broadening their impact.
- *Higher Productivity*: Given access to resources and a guarantee that they will share fully in the benefits of their efforts, the poor become more receptive to new technologies and services, and achieve higher levels of production and income. This helps to build net cash surpluses that strengthen the groups' economic base and contribute to rural capital formation.
- *Reduced Costs and Increased Efficiency*: The poor's contribution to project planning and implementation represent savings that reduce project costs. The poor also contribute their knowledge of local conditions, facilitating the diagnosis of environmental, social and institutional constraints, as well as the search for solutions.
- *Participation can Ensure Effective Utilisation of Available Resources*: The people and other agents work in tandem

towards achieving their objectives. The local people take responsibility of various activities. All these improve the efficiency and make the project more cost-effective.

- *Building of Democratic Organizations*: The limited size and informality of small groups is suited to the poor's scarce organizational experience and low literacy levels. Moreover, the small group environment is ideal for the diffusion of collective decision-making and leadership skills, which can be used in the subsequent development of inter-group federations.
- *Sustainability*: Participatory development leads to increased self-reliance among the poor and the establishment of a network of self-sustaining rural organizations. This carries important benefits: the greater efficiency of development services stimulates economic growth in rural areas and broadens domestic markets, thus favouring balanced national development; politically, participatory approaches provide opportunities for the poor to contribute constructively to development.
- *Effectiveness:* Lack of people's involvement has been seen as one of the major causes of failure of most projects. People's participation can make the projects more effective by providing them say in deciding the objectives, strategy and participating in implementation there by ensuring effective utilisation of the local resources.
- *Self-reliance:* A major criticism of many development interventions has been that they create a kind of dependence syndrome. However, if the local resources – both human and material are utilised, the realisation grows that may problem have local solutions. With active involvement of the local people, it is not only possible to break the mentality of dependence but also increase the local people awareness, confidence and control. In fact, the involvement in decision-making, implementation and monitoring develops human resource, which can enable them to participate at other levels.

Coverage

Despite professed target groups and attempts to cover the weaker sections, most projects have been found lacking in this aspect. The benefits are cornered off by the elite and powerful. People's participation can be a potent way of ensuring the benefits to the target group. Further, the cost effective operations can ensure that resources are available for wider coverage of the disadvantaged rural people.

Sustainability

Most of the externally assisted projects fail to sustain the level of activity once support or inputs are diminished or withdrawn. People's participation is regarded as an essential pre-requisite for continuity of the activities. The involvement of local people and utilisation of local resource becomes essential for sustainability.

Community Participation and Community Mobilisation

Of late great success has been achieved around the world in the programmes like: immunization, eradicating illiteracy, empowerment of the weak and the underprivileged, creating self managed institutions of the poor etc. One of the key elements responsible for this success has been the concept of community mobilisation, the process of bringing together all feasible and practical inter-sectoral social allies to raise people's awareness of and demand for a particular development programme, to assist in the delivery of resources and services and to strengthen community participation for sustainability and self-reliance. Human history is dotted with examples of massive efforts to mobilize different human societies to achieve some set goals.

Experience has shown that, given clear rules of the game, access to information, and appropriate support, poor men and women can be effectively mobilised and organized to provide goods and services that meet their immediate priorities. Not only do poor communities have greater capacity than generally recognized, they also have the most to gain from making good use of resources targeted at poverty reduction (Alkire *et al.* 2001).

For poverty eradication to be meaningful to the poor, it must be holistic. Effective poverty alleviation strategies therefore should have significant collective and mobilizing dimensions. Community mobilisation provides a suitable framework for holism in development, first by catering to the needs and aspirations of the poor; and, second, by seeking to engineer social change on the basis of self-reliance. It capitalizes on people's energies and commitments, on available resources, and on situations that can help move a group of people to achieve a common purpose, and understand why it matters to them. Community mobilisation is an important resource in developing countries that can create a positive forward energy and supplement the modest financial resources of the State.

There is a symbiotic relationship between community mobilisation and development process. Community mobilisation lies at the root of genuine development. It gives impetus to the necessary changes that must occur before development - whether social, political or economic - can be realised.

Community mobilisation is the cornerstone of participatory approaches in rural development and poverty alleviation programmes. It is a powerful instrument in decentralization policies and programmes aimed at strengthening human and institutional resources development at local level. Community mobilisation strengthens participation of rural poor in local decision-making, improves their access to social and production services and efficiency in the use of locally available financial resources, and enhances opportunities for asset-building by the poorest of the poor.

The concept of community mobilisation emerged from the recognition that a genuine participatory approach to development is essential for success and sustainability. Civil society participation in development efforts is therefore increasingly recognized by development agencies and governments as essential for promoting good governance - improving responsiveness of national policies and programmes to citizens' needs and ensuring transparency and accountability in policy-making and implementation processes. Genuine participation of citizens however, goes beyond dialogue with or contracting a few non-governmental organizations. It must engage all citizens (women and men, in their various capacities, socio-economic status, affiliations and locations) beyond elections to active participation in making-decisions that affect their lives. Engaging people to participate effectively in development processes which in turn depends on the efforts to create institutional mechanisms that promote participation; particularly for the people who are oppressed, suppressed and are disadvantaged in the society.

One of the important arguments about community mobilisation is that it reduces poverty as it enables poor people to carry out a number of functions themselves to improve their socio-economic situations, provides opportunity to form their own organizations for promoting their development through their own efforts and participating actively in decision-making processes that improves their living standards.

In its broadest sense, community mobilisation is a dynamic, participatory process of empowering weak and alienated groups at the individual, community and institutional levels for their sustainable socio-cultural, economic and political advancement; the sustained nature of the outcome – whether in livelihoods, literacy or any other realm – brings about change in the existing power structure that mitigates poverty, reduces the risks of social conflict and encourages smooth transitions in the community or society in which the effort takes place. This community mobilisation process is iterative with each action contributing to further actions which collectively and synergistically contribute to ever increasing improvements and changes to the issue at hand. At the individual level, people may experience immediate psychological empowerment – increases in self-respect, self-esteem or self-confidence and capacity – that evolves from collective action. At the community level, this empowerment allows individuals and groups to mobilize themselves towards the goals of socio-economic and political change that they themselves define.

Development involves change, and change involves complex interaction among groups in different segments of society who hold different attitudes, values and interests. Changes made within one group affect other groups. Isolated attempts to involve various groups are not enough. There is a need to tackle these complex tasks in a broader strategic framework. Training and applied research in mobilization work for development are necessary. If sustainable development leading to elimination of poverty has to be ushered in, governments of the third world will have to take a lead role in fostering a framework of grassroots institutions of the people through community mobilisation.

2 COMMUNITY MOBILISATION
MEANING AND CONCEPT

"Never doubt that a small group of thoughtful citizens can change the world. Indeed, it is the only thing that ever has."

Margaret Mead

INTRODUCTION

Among key factors that make a development programme succeed, community participation is vital. Community mobilization is a broad scale movement to elicit people's participation in achieving a specific development goal through self-reliant efforts. Community mobilization enhances participation of rural poor in local governance and is the cornerstone of participatory approaches in rural development and poverty alleviation programmes. It is the process of bringing together or empowering members of the community from various sectors to raise awareness on and demand for a particular development programme. It facilitates change and development taking into account the felt needs of the community and leads to community organization. It is a powerful instrument in decentralization policies and programmes aimed at strengthening human and institutional resources development at local level. Therefore, while essentially aiming to give ownership to the community, community mobilisation strengthens the capacity of women and men to address their needs in a socially, economically, and ecologically sustainable manner. It organizes people at the grassroots' level to carry out self-help activities that help to influence and change policies and programmes. Embodying the principles of participatory approaches, economic empowerment, community organization, and local governance, it provides a basic framework that helps systemise and make the mobilisation process more effective.

Community mobilisation works on the basic premise that poverty is a form of social, political and psychological disempowerment and occurs when people lack access to social base of power and productive wealth. Thus enhancing people's access to the social power reinforces their political power too, and an increase in productive wealth leads to improved livelihood. When people are socially empowered the atmosphere is conducive for them to group together into organizations. These organizations, through capital generating and skill enhancement activities, work for collective benefit of the community.

Meaning of Mobilisation

Isabel Carter in the book 'Mobilising the community: A PILLARS Guide' has argued that people often think of 'development' as something that comes from outside the local area. If life is hard and there are few facilities for health, education or economic development, people may have little hope for the future. They may wait for 'outsiders' to come and take action. Waiting for change to be brought into the community by outsiders may take a very long time indeed. It may also not bring the changes that people long to see. However, it may be possible for a small committed group within a community to bring about real changes for the better on their own. This is called 'mobilising' argues Isabel Carter.

A few persons assume that if they go to a community and organize a group so that it has some structure or form (*e.g.*, has a chair person, treasurer, secretary and vice chair), and that the group says it is ready for action, that they have 'mobilized' a group. Not necessarily. The word 'mobilize,' has the word 'mobile' in it. That means movement, or action. A mobiliser has not mobilized a group just by organizing it into some sort of structure. It has to engage in some action before it can be said to be mobilized. Community mobilisation should result not just in the creation of some groups, but should result in community-based organizations that engage in effective communal action.

Mobilisation is the act of assembling and making both troops and supplies ready for war. The word *mobilisation* was first used, in a military context, in order to describe the preparation of the Prussian army during the 1850s and 1860s. Mobilisation theories and techniques have continuously changed from then till today. The process of bringing people in a community together to work towards a common goal is called community mobilization. A community that is mobilized well is able to work together to address a specific and well-publicized issue that would result in improvement in their lives.

'Mobilisation', which is often used as a synonym for collective empowerment, connotes both action (*i.e.,* people being involved in doing things) and organization. The concept of mobilisation was first used to refer to the shifting of the control of resources form private-civilian to public-military purposes. More recently, it has been applied to a society's deliberate increase in the control of a variety of assets, such as: new nations' mobilisation of economic resources for development. According to Jenkins (1983:533) "*mobilisation is the process by which a group secures collective control over the resources needed for collective action*. The major issues, therefore, are the resources controlled by the group prior to mobilisation efforts, the processes by which the group pools resources and directs these towards social change and the extent to which outsiders increase the pool of resources". Jenkins (1983) is of the opinion that little agreement exists on the types of resources that are significant. Several analysts have offered classificatory schemes based upon the usefulness of particular resources in controlling the actions of targets (*e.g.,* Etzioni 1968:388-89: Gamson 1968:100-5). In this vein, Rogers (1974) has distinguished *instrumental resources* used in actual influence attempts from *infra-resources* that condition the use of instrumental resources. Similarly, Jenkins (1982a) has distinguished *power resources* that provide the means for controlling the actions of targets from *mobilizing resources* such as facilities that provide for mobilizing power resources. Mobilisation is essentially *(i)* attitudinal commitment to action; and *(ii)* a means of translating this commitment into action on observed behaviour. This is a composite process involving several stages: *(a)* the existence of values and goals requiring mobilisation; *(b)* action on the part of leaders, elite or institutions seeking to mobilize individuals and groups; *(c)* the institutional and collective means of achieving this mobilisation; *(d)* the symbols and references by which these values, goals and norms are communicated to and understood as well as internalized by individuals involved in mobilisation (Nettle 1967: 32-33).

The problem with schemes based on uses, however, is that most resources have multiple uses. Any scheme that ignores the intrinsic features of resources is therefore of limited value. In response, most analysts have simply listed the assets that are frequently mobilized by movements (*e.g.*, McCarthy and Zald's (1977) money, facilities, labour, and legitimacy: or Tilly's (1978:69) land, labour, capital, and technical expertise). Freeman (1979:172-5) has offered a more useful scheme, distinguishing *tangible assets* such as: money, facilities, and means of communication from the *intangible* or 'human' assets that form the central basis for movements. Intangible assets include both specialised resources such as organizing and legal skills, and the unspecialized labour of supporters.

Mobilisation is the process, argues Barua (2001), by which energy that is latent from the viewpoint of the acting unit is made available for collective action. A more mobilised unit can get more done collectively either by increasing the number of goals it realizes or by increasing the intensity with which it pursues those goals it is already realizing. Barua feels that it is essential in this discussion to maintain the differences among sub-units, units and supra-units, because mobilisation of one entity often entails the de-mobilisation of some others. She refers to the process by which a unit gains significantly in the control of assets it previously did not control as mobilisation. By definition, it entails a decline in the assets controlled by sub-units, the supra-unit of which the unit is a member, or external unit, unless the assets whose control the units gained are newly produced ones. A mere increase in the assets of members, sub-units, or even of the unit itself does not mean that mobilisation has occurred, though it increases the mobilisation potential. The change in the capacity to control and to use assets is what a significant.

Mobilisation is, by definition according to Barua (2001), both a process of change (in the control of structure) and a changing process. Mobilisation is also conceived as the process by which potentials are brought closer to actualization; the raw material is processed to provide the societal energy to fuel the pursuit of societal goals, and energy locked in other entities is made available.

What is Social Mobilisation?

Social mobilisation is an approach and tool that enables people to organize for collective action, by pooling resources and building solidarity required to resolve common problems and work towards community advancement. It is a process that empowers women and men to organize their own democratically self-governing groups or community organizations which enable them to initiate and control their own personal and communal development, as opposed to mere participation in an initiative designed by the government or an external organization.

The social mobilisation process encourages people to work together by sharing common interests for the development of their own community. Social mobilisation involves planned actions to reach, influence and involve all relevant segments and sectors of society to reach a common goal. One of the major gains of the social mobilisation is that people develop a habit of making a decision on consensus basis.

Social mobilisation involves planned actions and sustained processes to reach, influence, and involve all relevant segments of society across all sectors from the national to the community level to create an environment that results in positive behaviour change. Social mobilisation is a multifaceted, multilevel, community-based, sustained effort to address an identified community need. It begins with community members, preferably from different groups, planning and engaging in projects to address the need; derives its strength from its diversity of members and its decentralized and more sustainable nature; takes time and persistence in building connections, mobilizing people, and supporting them as they organize into groups; and facilitates change by mobilizing and empowering people and groups to do projects to meet the identified need. As defined by UNICEF, social mobilisation is a broad scale movement to engage people's participation in achieving a specific development goal through self-reliant efforts.

Social mobilisation is a dynamic, long-term process in which stakeholders use a number of strategies, such as: policy advocacy and social marketing, to make sustainable changes in the community. At its heart, a social mobilisation movement seeks societal change. Because of these differences, changes made within one of these groups do not necessarily lead to changes throughout the society. To bring about systemic change for girls' education, for example, community members must do many things, such as: *(i)* build a common awareness across society of the need for girl's education; *(ii)* convince people of (change beliefs about) the value of girls' education; *(iii)* remove societal barriers to instituting girls' education; and *(iv)* find support and resources for making changes.

Social mobilisation takes vertical programmes, often 'owned' by particular departments of government, and makes them more horizontal. This is achieved by involving a broad alliance in the planning process at the national level by attempting to continually decentralize the planning process. Through devolution, even to the grassroots level where possible, greater ownership and sustainability will be achieved. Social mobilisation, argues Reddy (2001), means the process in which major clusters of old social, economic and psychological commitments are eroded or broken and people become available for new patterns of socialization and behaviour.

Social mobilisation involves planned actions and processes to reach, influence, and involve all relevant segments of society across all sectors from the national to the community level, in order to create an enabling environment and effect positive behaviour and social change. The spark that ignites the process of social mobilisation – the original catalyst for change – can come from the grassroots or the national level. The important thing is that this catalyst – an individual, a group of individuals, or an institution – facilitates a process in which ultimately power is shared with a wider, more diverse group of stakeholders. For genuine change to occur, it is important that those most directly affected by the change be integrally involved in the process of determining the nature of the change.

Social mobilisation embraces other behaviour change strategies and skills including advocacy, community mobilisation, social marketing, and behaviour change communication. All of these strategies can be used in a social mobilisation movement to promote conscientization, a state of critical consciousness as defined by the Brazilian educator Paulo Freire (1973) and ultimately link the hands of those having less power, voice, and resources with those who have more. The process is not adversarial. It is collaborative. It is about transformation. It is about fostering momentum for positive change in support of gender equity, as well as reproductive and human rights.

Defining Social Mobilisation

Social mobilisation is a methodology for making the poor contribute to economic growth. Rana (2001) is of the opinion that "social mobilisation provides a non-violent way out of the morass of deprivation, alienation, insecurity, political graft, and corruption experienced relentlessly over the past fifty years of development and democracy". Social mobilisation, according to Rana (1995a:5), may be defined as "the process of enabling the poor, marginalised and disenfranchised segments of society to build and manage their own organizations and thereby participate in decisions affecting their day-to-day lives through the use of their own creativity". Deutsch (1961) states that social mobilisation is a name given to an overall process of change which happens to substantial parts of human population in countries which are moving from traditional to modern ways of life. This specific process of change, he says, affects residence, occupation, social setting, associates, institutions, roles and ways of acting, demands and capabilities. Later, Deutsch gave a rather short hand definition of his concept of social mobilisation as "the process in which major clusters of old social, economic, and psychological commitments are eroded or broken and people become available for new patterns of socialisations and behaviour".

Jerry Gana (1989) argues, "social mobilisation is the process of pooling together, harnessing, actualizing and utilising potential human resources for the purpose of development. It is a process whereby human beings are made aware of the resources at their disposal, and are also motivated and energised to collectively utilise such resources for the improvement of their spiritual and material conditions of living." Social mobilisation, argues Ikoiwak (1989), in fact, is an essential surgical operation for the removal or virulent tissues of underdevelopment in a polity. These malignant tissues are old or traditional economic, social, institutional, administrative, cultural systems.

Social mobilisation, according to Cohen (1969), can also be defined as "a process of engaging a large number of people in joint action for achieving societal goals through self-reliant efforts. Its immediate expected outcomes are the mobilisation of all possible resources and the sustained adoption/utilisation of appropriate policies, technologies or services through the modification of attitudes and behaviour of various social actors". According to Amarsinghe (2001) social mobilisation "is a process of organizing the target groups to take initiatives and assert themselves". It seeks to make people more aware of the resources available to them, to raise their consciousness and to give them the motivation to undertake development activities for their own betterment in the long-run social mobilisation aims at empowering people to demand and generate the satisfaction of their needs.

What is Community Mobilisation?

'Social Mobilisation' is commonly considered to be an important dimension of capacity, organization and institution building, particularly when relating to disadvantaged people. Social mobilisation may occur at all levels. Most often, however, the term is used for activities in local communities, although not necessarily confined to such communities. When thus confined, the process is commonly referred to as *community mobilisation*. This may involve whole communities or be limited to sections of communities (for instance, land-less people or groups of particularly poor women).

Community Development is the process of social change. Community mobilisation is the pivot for people-centred development process. Community mobilisation applies to the way in which people can be encouraged and motivated to participate in programme activities. Community mobilisation is helping communities be aware of an issue and take action. Community mobilisation is the process of stimulating, encouraging and guiding members of the community in the community development process. Community mobilisation is also a capacity-building process through which community individuals, groups, or organizations plan, carry out, and evaluate activities on a participatory and sustained basis to improve their socio-economic conditions either on their own initiative or stimulated by others. The Community mobilisation approach builds on the community's capacities, skills and assets, instead of the community's problems.

Expanding on this definition somewhat, we can list the key tasks involved in most successful community mobilisation efforts. In general, community mobilisation involves:

- Developing an ongoing dialogue between community members regarding developmental issues.
- Creating or strengthening community organizations aimed at improving living conditions.

- Assisting in creating an environment in which individuals can empower themselves to address their own and their community's developmental needs.
- Promoting community members' participation in ways that recognize diversity and equity, particularly of those who are most affected by the poverty.
- Working in partnership with community members in all phases of a project to create locally appropriate responses to development needs.
- Identifying and supporting the creative potential of communities to develop a variety of strategies and approaches to living conditions.
- Assisting in linking communities with external resources (*e.g.*, organizations, funding, technical assistance) to aid them in their efforts to living conditions.
- Committing enough time to work with communities, or with a partner who works with them, to accomplish the above. Normally, this process is not suitable for short-term projects of less than two years.

The inter-relationship between community mobilisation and social mobilisation needs to be clarified. For some social mobilisation seems to cover mostly social movements initiated from the top in which persuasion and/or 'manipulation' techniques are used to reach objectives on a massive and rapid scale. Conversely, community mobilisation for participation is often viewed as spontaneous movements initiated form the grassroots, which take the form of self-help and small-scale projects. Avoiding this simplistic and counterproductive dichotomy, Cohen (1969) argues that community mobilisation and social mobilisation can be made unified parts of the same process of social change so that ultimately community mobilisation is viewed as the community component of the national development process.

The process of bringing people in a community together to work towards a common goal is also called community mobilisation. A community that is mobilized well is able to work together to address a specific and well-publicized issue that would result in improvement in their lives. Organizational skills are essential to achieve this. This involves people working together to solve problems, to keep their leaders accountable and to participate meaningfully in their community. Grassroots communities can benefit if they are active in promoting their interests.

Why Community Mobilisation?

Community mobilisation should be promoted to strengthen problem-solving capacities on poor people. Community mobilisation addresses the top and the bottom level to strengthen the capacities and capabilities of local communities and of service providers. Linking communities to services is the challenge!

Community mobilisation aims at:

- Making people aware of their own potential.
- Encouraging them to sustainably use their resources.
- Improving self-help capacities (the ability to act) and capabilities (the knowledge how to act).
- Enhancing local governance.
- Facilitating the integration into the local market economy.

The basic idea is to strengthen the problem-solving and functional capabilities of community-based organizations (CBOs), in formal local groups and vulnerable families 'on the job'. While they are taking over tasks and responsibilities in their projects they develop confidence and capacities. Community groups are supported to take charge of their resources and the decision on how these are to be used. They are made aware about the system of service providers that include the state, NGOs and the private sector and how these can serve village development. One of the main aims of community mobilisation in the longer term is to close the gap between service providers and people and establish constructive dialogue and working relationships. Local communities become partner in-stead of recipients. The system of service providers that include the state, NGOs and the private sector.

Community Mobilisation is Successful if,

- Villagers are more confident to demand services from the State, NGOs and the private sector. They themselves are more responsible and capable of handling own projects. Their capacity to contribute to and to pay for services, increases.
- Service providers are capacitated to respond adequately to the demands from the village level.

In the longer run, community mobilisation aims at enhancing local governance. Good local governance means that citizens trust the public administration and the state legislation. To promote development and governance, community mobilisation needs to address and balance three concerns.

- *Asset-based Support:* Resource-poor, vulnerable households may be unable to cope with a sudden shock and need temporary support to overcome an acute crisis. Community mobilisation supports vulnerable households with development packages for income generation and social integration in particular.
- *Capacity Building:* Institutional development and capacity building is the core. Community mobilisation assists in the organizational development of state and non-governmental partner institutions, strengthens social net works at the local level and encourages transparent and accountable community institutions. Furthermore, community mobilisation seeks to link the corporate sector (*e.g.*, banks) to the village economy.
- *Local Governance:* Community mobilisation creates the demand for institutional accountability and responsibility from office bearers of government institutions, as well as from NGOs. This helps to establish local governance: People have trust in the work and decisions of office bearers.

Community mobilisation creates incentives at different levels to improve self-organization and services. The principles and attitudes promoted by community mobilisation enhance problem-solving capabilities and promote mutual recognition between state institutions, NGOs and villagers who work jointly in implementing projects.

Why do People get Involved in Community Mobilisation?

- To grow, survive, self-actualization.
- To improve their existing conditions and quality of life.
- To challenge the status quo.
- To increase their capacity to deal with socio-economic problems.
- To promote their vision for themselves and/or society.

Reasons for Actions of Communities

- To grow and survive.
- To gain access to resources.
- To gain skills and expertise.
- Need satisfaction.
- Distribution/Allocation of power.
- Adaptation to change.

Mobilisation Needs

- Concerned citizens willing to work toward change.
- Emerging leaders to inspire and guide the effort.
- A common community vision of the results.
- People who respect individual group efforts, but support the common goal.
- Recognition and encouragement for involvement.
- Plans to reduce 'at-risk' situations for the coalition.
- Leaders who encourage, build, develop strategies, and share both work and recognition.
- Awareness of human-relations impact on group action.
- Time.

Community Mobilisation: The Main Theoretical Considerations

The concept of mobilisation answers the analytic question: what is the source of the energy for societal action? As the libido is 'mobilised' by the various mechanisms of the personality to energize its actions and the work of these mechanisms, so are the assets of member sub-units, unused from the unit's viewpoint, made available-through the processes of mobilisation-to 'energize' (or cover the 'costs') of the actions and controls of the unit.

Maximum unit-mobilisation, however, does not assure maximum realization of the goals of the mobilizing unit because some of these goals tend best to be served by activities of the sub-units; hence, these sub-units must retain some of the assets and manpower. To some degree, these statements about the relations between unit and sub-unit actions (or performances) also hold for the controlling processes: sub-units' overlayers control the activities in the service of some unit-goals. But, Barua (2001) suggests, if a unit's goals are to be realized to a high degree, the ratio of unit-controls over sub-units' controls needs to be higher than the ratio of unit-activities over sub-units' activities, because unit-goals are realized to a greater extent if some of the sub-units' activities are controlled by the unit rather than by the sub-units. The realization of unit-goals is expected to be greater if, in addition, the relations among the sub-units are in part regulated by the unit and not determined only by the existing bonds among the sub-units, their relative power, their unregulated interaction, or other 'ongoing' processes. Thus, the high realization of unit-goals requires that unit-mobilisaton provide assets for both unit-activities and for unit-controls, but especially for the later. The other theoretical considerations related to community mobilisation are:

To Mobilize is to Collectivize

The transformation that mobilisation entails collectivization - not necessarily of ownership but of effective control. The assets themselves may remain in their original locations and need not necessarily be directly transferred to or used by a controlling elite or organization. It is, rather, the unit's capacity to control the use of the assets - including those held by the sub-units – that is increased. For example, to the degree that corporations can be instructed to follow government-set 'guidelines', a gain in the national level of mobilisation is achieved. Or, more indirectly, by issuing large sums of money a state can gain control of the assets of the assets of some member-collectivities without orders being issued to or even requests being made of the collectivities.

Whatever the form of mobilisation, whether it be direct or indirect, the process entails a shift of control and/or a shift of the usage of assets, except when the newly available assets come from external sources. Since the ratio of the assets used by a societal unit over the assets used by the sub-units increases, mobilisation makes the societal unit into less private, more public, and, hence politically intensive.

Mobilisation as a Control Concept

Mobilisation, like decision-making, social planning, and other related concepts, implies a collective actor who is capable of controlling societal processes, at least to some degree, and is not merely subject to them. Thus, mobilisation is viewed as a drive which is, at least in part, deliberately initiated, directed, and terminated, and not as a by-product or as a compilation of the decisions of myriad micro-units. This is not to imply that mobilisation has no unanticipated consequences or that the actor's controlling overlayer is in full or even in considerable command of the fluctuations of the process; however, there is the assumption of a voluntary element, represented by one or more sub-units-such as a government, as organizational leadership, or a regional council-which are steering the process. That is, the societal change involved is, in part, intended.

Mobilisation as a Changing Force

The theory of societal guidance differs most from other theories in contemporary social science in that it sees the mobilisation drives of collectivities and societies as a major source of their own transformations and of the transformations of their relations of other societal units. As a societal unit mobilizes, it tends to change its own structure and boundaries and the structure of the supra-unit of which it is a member. For instance, the drive of West European societies to overcome the disintegrative and depleting effects of World War II entailed both internal transformation and the initiation of a trans-national community. De-Stalinization, a process of demobilisation, not only altered the internal structures of East European communist societal but also de-unified the bloc and made it less like an empire and somewhat more like a commonwealth. To stress the importance of mobilisation as a transforming force is not to underplay the roles of new ideas, of changes in the means of production, or of forces in the societal environment as sources of societal change. But these are, to varying degrees, extra-societal. The most central intra-societal source of change, as we see it, is the successful drive on the part of one or more collectivities or of the society at large to mobilise new internal or external sources of energy. Most other intra-societal changes in this direction tend to establish the conditions, which provide the prerequisites for increases in the unit's activities.

Marx argued that history is propelled by inter-class struggle; we hold that the acting units are often collectivities whose primary base is not shared economic interests but shared values and statuses, especially ethnic ones, and that the relationships among collectivities are various mixes of conflict and cooperation and not only 'struggles'. Even more importantly, the struggle that is most significant for the explanation of societal change, of history, is one which is internal to each collectively (and society). This is the struggle to mobilize under the given conditions and for the purpose of changing them; it occurs between the mobilisers and the unmobilised in one and the same collectivity (or a society). Were all the members of a collectivity (or a society) to mobilize all of their assets and themselves in support of a line of collective action, it would be as if all the latent energy locked in a pound of material were released and transformed into power; it would propel the collectivity into the highest levels of activeness and alter the societal map. Of course, mobilisation drives are themselves affected by external conditions. Lower collectivities find it more difficult to mobilise than collectivities, which rank higher in the societal structure.

Before the discussion can be advanced, two points related to the differences between the internal (unit; sub-unit) and the external (inter-unit and unit: supra-unit) aspects of the process must be noted. *First*, the mobilisation of a unit - as a process of change - may be solely internal (limited to the mobilisaton of sub-unit assets to unit controls), or it may also be external, drawing on the assets of other units or supra-units. *Second*, while mobilisation may be aimed at a variety of goals, viewed as a changing process the most relevant distinctions are between changing structure and changing boundaries between changing the structure or boundaries of the mobilizing unit (self-change), of other units, or of the relations of the actors to each other.

The Holistic vs. Targeted Approach to Community Mobilisation

In general, community mobilisation agencies (CMAs) follow either a targeted model by organizing a particular group of people (*e.g.*, the poor, *Dalits*, women) or a holistic model by organizing people without any differentiation. Both models have drawn on similar principles of mobilizing groups, but have reached beyond specific manifestations of poverty such as income, literacy, health and sanitation, while also working towards a wider representation of society. The modalities of these agencies reveal that the holistic or broad-based approach achieved greater consideration than the targeted approach in launching project activities. The agencies supported by government bodies and banks/cooperatives tend to emphasize the targeted approach. The joint ventures of NGOs and government organizations, however, are increasingly stressing the holistic approach to community mobilisation. CMAs working under the umbrella of NGOs are almost equally divided between the two models.

Preconditions for Mobilization

How and under what conditions the rural people can be mobilized for active 'participation' in the rural development programmes? Moulik (1977) argues that the objective conditions which will enhance the possibility of mobilizing and organizing the rural people is the prevalence of dissatisfaction among them about the existing situations, – a reaction to inequalities either in the land tenure situation or the social structure or the inequalities of opportunities to utilize resources and technology and particularly to the growth of such inequalities. Other factors, which facilitate conscientisation of the rural people in the process of creating preconditions for mobilization for participation in the rural development programmes, are:

- The increasingly important role education and other forms of Contract and acquaintance with the world that differs considerably from the traditional frame of reference.
- Better communication by road and modern means of transport with urban areas.
- The industrialisation process give many rural people the chance to participate in urban life and new forms of organization and such people returning to their villages where the potential for new forms of organization and solidarity increased.

Provoked Participation and Mobilization

Whatever preconditions there may be for mobilizing rural masses for active support for development programmes, Moulik (1977) argues that little will happen if they do not realise their position and believe that something can be done about it. 'Class-consciousness' in the Marxian sense is rarely found among the rural mass but this does not mean that there is complete lack of clarity. What is lacking is Paulo Friere's conscientisation or politicization - a process in which socio-psychological factors play purposeful role in mobilizing and organizing themselves around a development programme meant for their own benefit. This last mentioned essential process of mobilizing rural people happens most often than not by what is known as provoked participation. By 'provoked participation', Moulik meant that better understanding of the existing objective conditions and the possibilities of changing them are stimulated among the rural mass, mostly through the influence of outsiders (external source) and rarely through a charismatic leader from within the community (internal source). Among the external source there are the examples of field-workers of Paulo Friere's Conscientizacao prograrmne in Brazil, political party cadres in China, Vietnam and Indonesia. The social workers, extension agents; other government development agents, Missionaries, voluntary agencies, urban-based organizers, teachers end students, and various specially organized institutions are also the examples of outside stimulators. On the other hand, there are several successful instances of mobilization of rural masses as a result of the almost accidental presence of a charismatic leadership among the rural mass itself: Emiliano Zapata in Mexico, Luis Taruc of Philippines and Jose Rojas of Bolivia are cases in point. But unfortunately such phenomenon of charismatic leadership from within the rural communities is extremely rare to happen and it is not necessary to wait until such things happen. Hence, the importance of provoked mobilization from outsiders or external sources, which can and do perform similar functions as the local charismatic leaders. Since it is not possible to wait indefinitely for the appearance of local charismatic leader to mobilize rural people and also because it is not possible to replicate or repeat the charismatic local leadership in various socio-political situations, it becomes necessary to depend on external sources for provoked participation.

Implementation of Intervention Techniques

Moulik (1977) argues that in order to mobilize rural people in support of the development programmes, it is important to select the intervention techniques. There are two basic approaches of implementing intervention techniques: *(i)* Harmony Model and *(ii)* Conflict Model. The basic assumption in the harmony model is that all different interests at the community or regional level can be developed simultaneously. In other words, ideologically this model assumes too optimistically that development can take place and mobilization of the masses is possible without profound social conflict. As in the community development programme in India, this model assumes that the rural people want and can sustain economic progress themselves as soon as they have been shown its advantages and that the changes must and will come about democratically and through voluntary participation, that is, in response to the 'felt needs' of the villagers. It is also believed in this model that innovations, - be they technological, institutional and structural, can be introduced in a rural community through proper extension and service activities over a period of time utilizing established local, leaders, influential people and progressive farmers. A large majority of the rural people may not participate in this innovation-introduction programme, but through democratic influence, demonstration and percolation effects over a period of time the majority can be mobilized to support this programme. All in all, the major assumption in harmony model is of *status quo* orientation of the social system in which a technological change is certainly favoured but without change of the social and political structure. This does not mean that this approach of harmony model as enunciated in community development programmes cannot stimulate rural people's awareness and readiness for action in support of the rural development programmes. It has been increasingly realised that the potential conflict and confrontation can be the most effective mobilizing force for provoking participation of rural people in support of development progrtarmnes.

What is this conflict model? The basic assumption in this model is that the rural poor can be provoked and mobilized only when they are extremely discontented and excited about any concrete event or a situation signifying the potentiality of an acute conflict. In order to identify the potential conflict situation, an organized effort is needed to first evaluate the class contradictions prevailing in the system. Having identified the potential conflict situation, deliberate escalating actions are to be undertaken first through a conscientisation programme. This is basically an educational and politicization process utilising certain elements of the rural life and culture (*e.g.*, folk tales, village history, present and past land tenure system, jokes and tales etc.,) which are essentially considered as 'counterpoints' to the 'culture of repression' in which the rural poor live. These counterpoints make the rural poor aware of their position in the society, their rights and in a sense make them class-conscious. Once this happens it becomes relatively easy to organize and mobilise the rural people for the action programme to follow. The very existence of a negative reference group in the form of landlords, rich peasants, money lenders, merchants, urban exploiters, corrupt bureaucrat and officials and all the host of various exploitative elements in the existing structure fosters a solidarity and cohesiveness among the rural poor, which helps to form their own representative interest group or association. And this interest group or association becomes the mouthpiece for voicing resentment in the open and organize actions to remedy the situation.

The conflict model essentially begins with the structural interventions because in most situations the potential point of conflict lies in the existing socio-economic structure, particularly, in the developing Asian/African countries. The issues such as security of tenancy, better tenancy legislation, sharecropping arrangements which are more favourable to tenants, and eventually land reform as the final demand are the conflicting situations usually utilised in the conflict model. There are also important issues which can be utilised for conflict model such as exploitation by moneylenders and merchants, exploitation by higher castes, control over service institutions such as cooperatives, health and educational institutions and other developmental agencies for favourable terms for credit, marketing and supply of essential agricultural and other inputs, bargaining for favourable wage-rates, and exclusive employment programme for the rural poor. One can go on adding to the list. The important point is to mobilize and organize the relevant groups whose interests are to be served in the model. For example, on the issue of land reform, only the small landholders, the tenants, and the landless labourers should represent in the organization of the interest group or the association. Obviously, efforts will be made by the traditional rural rich and elite to resist and suppress the growth of such threatening associations and various legal and illegal measures may be taken to scuttle their demand, which in effect will further escalate the process of conflict and accelerate the process of conscientisation and mobilization.

For the leaders or the stimulators, it is always advantageous to take up the specific and concrete cases of abuses, or excesses or grievances. To start with only such steps are undertaken within the existing framework of the law. Petitions are made to the competent authority in the government or in the court, mass meetings are held to rally support for the petition. In most cases initial strategies of action are purposely made non-violent or a form of disobedience in the form of strike or demonstrations culminating into a symbolic direct action, such as, occupation of land in the case of land reform issues. These actions are undertaken in order to make it clear to the authority or to the vested interest group the seriousness of the demand.

It is extremely facilitating for the mobilization process if the authority or the government is tolerant and tacitly approve the demands for gaining strength for the rural masses. In the process of activating conflict model, if some demands are fulfilled and benefits accrued to the participant group, the mobilization get an added momentum with the taste of success. On the other hand, if the main initial demands are fulfilled there is the possibility of losing interest on the part of the participants in continuing mobilization unless various other related issues and actions are brought into focus simultaneously. Similarly, a continued frustration in the fulfillment of demands may leave the participants embittered and resigned to the old situation, which can only be counteracted by renewed process of 'conscientisation' process. Believers of armed revolution may at this stage like the rural masses be equipped with weapons to defend themselves and their rights.

Instruments and Principles of Community Mobilisation

The instruments, principles and attitudes of community mobilisation need to be fully integrated into the work of partner institutions, such as: government departments, NGOs and local leaders. This can be done through training, mainstreaming of best practices and joint learning 'on the job'.

- *Dialogue:* Community mobilisation establishes dialogue between all relevant persons and institutions. Dialogue is the basis for confidence, trust and thus development. Dialogue means open communication with all partners involved in the project cycle.
- *Capacity Building:* Community mobilisation aims at unfolding the capabilities and capacities of local partners and service providers. One explicit aim of any project is to increase the ability of partners to handle such projects with less assistance in the future.
- *Social Responsibility:* In communities, some have more than others. Community mobilisation demands that the elite care about the more vulnerable in the villages. Vulnerable families are to be integrated into the community.
- *Transparency and Accountability:* Every villager has the right to know about the technical procedures, the financial flows and the project progress. Therefore it would be desirable to sign contracts, select beneficiaries in an open process, and encourage documentation process in a project book and thus open avenue for an exchange of information.
- *Sustainability:* Community mobilisation demands local responsibility, commitment and contributions to initiate ownership among those who benefit from the project. This is expected to improve the likelihood that those persons who benefit will take care of their project in future.
- *Gender:* Men, women, young and old people within a village experience different conditions and have different needs and capabilities, which have to be addressed and taken care of.
- *Do no Harm:* Community mobilization during a conflict situation, such as a civil war, has to take the dimension of conflict into consideration. Do we increase existing tensions within and across communities? What is our role as development professionals in the conflict? What response could we expect towards our action from the conflict parties? In a conflict situation, it is important to remember that dialogue and transparency promote a

certain degree of confidence and reduce friction among communities and also between service providers, communities and social/community mobilisers.

Key Action Steps in Community Mobilization

Specific action steps are useful in conducting community mobilization in an effective manner. Many of these steps need to be applied repeatedly or on a periodic basis.

Learning about Community Composition, Organization, and Leadership

An essential first step is to learn about community composition, organization, and leadership not only at present but also in the recent past and the more distant past. Comparing these time frames helps to show traditional structures and to identify changes in demographics, leadership patterns, and sub-groups that could create tensions, increase conflict, and influence protection issues. Also, the time frames can help people reflect on whether they are moving in the right direction or have forgotten their traditions and former vision of how communities should be. These time frames can each be explored in the context of a timeline that also identifies major events in the wider political and social arena. How far back to go is a matter of judgment. In Afghanistan, it would be useful to explore at least one time period before the Soviet invasion.

Learning about Community Power Structures

Defined broadly, power is the ability to have influence in moving towards a goal. In this sense, Gandhi had great power even though he was not an official leader. Similarly, many people have power because they influence public opinion – these are called opinion leaders. Others have power because they serve as gatekeepers whom outsiders must convince or win over if their projects and ideas are to take root in the community.

A useful starting point in assessing community power structures is to identify not only people in obvious or official positions of power (*e.g.*, commanders, shura members) but also the people in the community who are influential or who are change agents. These may be people who wield influence in different domains – education, religion, security, health, etc. Also, for each sub-group, there tend to be particular leaders, either informal or formal. For example, women's groups and youth groups tend to have identifiable leaders or members who are seen as spokespeople for their sub-group.

Learning about community power structures – power mapping – is like identifying levers that one can use subsequently to mobilize particular groups. If religious authority is needed to support work on a particular child protection issue, then one needs to know who are the key religious authorities and influence agents. Also, if important child protection issues become apparent in health posts and clinics, it is vital to know who are the key leaders on health issues who could help gain support for child protection initiatives.

Assessing and Building Inclusion

As community patterns evolve and change, it is vital to keep track of who is excluded and to work for their inclusion in community planning and action. Usually, each village has 'key informants' – people who know a lot about the community – who think about issues of social justice and who care deeply about the rights of each individual. If such a person can be identified, he or she can probably provide a quick overview of who is typically marginalized and left out of community activities and why. Another way to identify who is excluded is to go visit families from some of the groups that tend to be excluded in most communities – those having people with disabilities, the poorest households, etc. This approach has the advantage of hearing directly the voice of marginalized people, which helps to empower them. By asking whether they participate, why or why not, and would they like to participate more, one gains insight into their situation. Also, their statements of desire to participate more adds a different perspective to commonly heard 'stories' that community leaders frequently tell, such as: "They don't want to participate because they are too poor and have no time for meetings."

Facilitating Child and Youth Participation

Particularly in a child protection programme, the leadership and full participation of children and youth is a fundamental element of community mobilization. One way to do this is to engage children and youth in spreading key messages about protection issues, health, and related issues through means such as community drama. Also, children are frequently the best motivators of community engagement and action. It would be thus useful to conduct dialogues either with the community or with particular sub-groups in which children tell the story of particular children and ask the group they are addressing for their help in addressing the children's needs.

Developing a Mobilization Strategy

Effective community mobilization requires having an appropriate mobilization strategy. A weak but widely used mobilization strategy is to conduct a general community meeting or series of meetings that motivates some people to take action on a particular issue. This strategy is limited because those who choose to get involved may represent only a small subset of the community. Key sub-groups that have relevant expertise or perspective may be completely excluded, and the people who seem so highly motivated may have little influence with these key groups. Also, there is a risk that the same people in the village will dominate the discussion whenever an NGO arrives, presenting themselves as leaders who speak for everyone. Many villagers may resent these 'power grabbers' or 'self-promoters' and may withdraw from the discussions. The result can be disempowerment of most people rather than the community empowerment that is sought.

Appropriate mobilization strategies are guided by several criteria: activation of diverse and appropriate subgroups, inclusiveness, progressive realization of goals, and intrinsic motivation. These are outlined as action points below.

- *Activate Diverse Sub-groups:* In mobilizing a community on child protection issues, it is necessary to activate all the relevant groups – girls, women, men, boys, teachers, and so forth. This requires working through the leaders of the various sub-groups and asking them to spread key messages and to invite participation in their respective networks. If a particular project goal is to influence behaviour of a particular group such as mothers or teachers, then it is particularly important to activate the sub-groups who are most relevant (for example, women and education leaders).

- *Be Inclusive*: If community mobilization is to activate everyone, respect everyone's rights, and meet the interests of all, it must be an inclusive process.
- *Start Small and Work up*: Community mobilization efforts often fail because the planners attempt to accomplish too much at once. To stay motivated, local people need to make discernible progress, accomplishing smaller goals before taking on the larger goals. In practice, it is valuable to take a phased approach in which groups first achieve smaller, attainable goals, increasing their motivation to take on larger goals. Otherwise, people tend to become frustrated and to give up.
- *Promote Intrinsic Motivation*: A key to community mobilization is to stimulate people's volunteer spirit of doing things because they help the entire community, building on intrinsic motivation rather than external rewards. When external rewards such as payments are introduced, some people participate because they want the reward. When the rewards are no longer provided, their activity ends, with the result that the project becomes unsustainable. To be sustainable, people have to believe in the inherent value of the project, own it and take it as their own, and work because it gives them satisfaction and meaning.

Some Uses of Community Mobilisation

Community mobilisation as an innovative policy of a government can be employed to effect social and economic reforms. Huttington (1968) sees such reforms as those affecting changes in traditional values and behaviour patterns, the expansion of communication and education, the broadening of loyalties from family, village and tribe to nation. It embraces secularization of public life, rationalization of authority structures, the promotion of functionally specific organizations, the substitution of achievement criteria for ascriptive ones, and the equitable distribution of material and symbolic resources.

On another score, community mobilisation can be employed in liberating people from oppressive social relations such as feudalism (Rahman 1980). Equally applicable, Rahman (1980) further argues, in this case is the use of community mobilisation in liberation from oppressive political relations. If the oppression borders on exploitation which is sustained by dominance – dependence relations, that is, the exploited depending on the resources and goodwill of the exploiter for livelihood, liberation may initially increase material hardship. To sustain the struggle, the oppressed needs a good combination of material and mental staying power.

Community mobilisation implies serving a collective purpose. It involves motivating and inspiring a large number of people into action. Without an 'organic unity of consciousness' of the people – both the leaders and the followers – the process runs the risk of failure. Mobilisation, even if inner – urge oriented, may not be spontaneous. It requires an *organizational medium* for its stimulation. This organization medium may be a collective or 'a centre of gravity in development effort'. Rahman (1980) defines a collective as an association of individuals who posses a sense of identity with the association, so that the collective interest (as defined collectively by an agreed procedure) registers emotionally in the consciousness of its members as part of their 'individual' interest. Successful mobilisation requires that the correct choice of collectives, whether the family, the village community or the nation, be made and used for specific tasks of mobilisation.

Social mobilisation can be used to achieve self-reliance within a collective like a village or a country. In its fundamental sense, self-reliance is defined as a state of mind that regards one's own mental and material resources as the primary stock to draw on in the pursuit of one's objectives and finds emotional fulfillment not only in achieving the objectives as such but also in the very fact of having achieved them primarily by using one's own resources. Self-reliant mobilisation requires deep emotional identification of the people's concern with a collective chosen for such purpose. Besides, the collective must control all necessary resources which can provide the material basis of self-reliance.

Community mobilisation acts as a catalyst for organizing the members of a community to take group action by sharing their problems and seeking their own solutions by pooling their own resources, obtaining external help and participating actively in the decision-making processes that shape their lives as individuals and as members of households and the local polity. The process helps people move from the passive status of welfare recipients to that of citizens who possess vital knowledge of their communities and localities and therefore know best how to effect - and direct – change at the local level. Unlike social engineering attempts by external experts from above – often paternalistic and usually unsustainable – social mobilisation processes place the values, priorities and agency of citizens at the grassroots level at the centre of development efforts.

As a vehicle of organizational capacity building, community mobilisation functions primarily as a mechanism of empowerment. While capacity building usually refers to knowledge transfers to individuals or groups, community mobilisation enables people to fuse what they themselves know with external information and techniques so as to carry out particular activities. For disadvantaged groups in particular, this transformation increases their power relative to that of other groups in their socio-economic and political environments. Empowerment in this sense is thus an outcome of both the capacity building of people and a reform of the rules and practices that oppress them.

The scope of community mobilisation reaches well beyond pooled savings, training effort, literacy or hygiene campaigns or even choices concerning basic livelihood opportunities. It concerns not only improving project performance by making claims on external resources but also demands accountability from powers that be. In itself, it educates citizens politically in the art of governance and the pursuit of rights and civic roles.

3 ORGANIZING AND MOBILISING RURAL POOR

"The best way to find yourself is to lose yourself in the service of others."

Mahatma Gandhi

Community organizing explicitly seeks to build the power-base of the poor so they can affect and change the public policies and private market forces that create and sustain social and economic inequality.

Henry Allen, Hyams Foundation

INTRODUCTION

Voicelessness and powerlessness are two elements that characterize poor people's exclusion. Poor people seldom find themselves in a situation where they can express their views or get involved in decision-making processes. Enabling poor families to lift themselves out of the pit of powerlessness is a fundamental factor needed to alleviate poverty. Poverty is a condition of hunger, low income and lack of services. It is also a condition of vulnerability, exclusion and powerlessness – the erosion of people's capability to have their voices heard. Voicelessness is particularly acute for the rural poor, who account for a majority, some three quarters, of the 1.2 billion people living on less than one dollar per day. Among the poor, women are particularly disadvantaged, having significantly less access than men do to knowledge, assets and services. These inequalities affect the ability of women not only in their social role, but also in their economic role, which is crucial in the rural economy. More generally, the rural poor, and women in particular, rarely control the conditions that determine their livelihoods. For many rural people – small holders, landless wage labourers and sharecroppers, small entrepreneurs, nomadic pastoralists, artisanal fishermen and women, indigenous peoples, ethnic minorities and members of scheduled castes – powerlessness is experienced as an inability to influence decisions affecting their lives, negotiate better terms of trade, and make governmental and non-governmental organizations (NGOs) accountable to them. It is intimately linked to weak local governance. Powerlessness is an effect of poverty. It is also one of its most important causes (IFAD 2003).

It is difficult to bring about sustainable socio-economic changes in the situation of the poor people. The forces against the poor are so many and the social system so biased in favour of the rich that it will not respond to the demands of the poor people. As atomised and isolated individuals, the poor are too weak, powerless and lack the capacity to take individual initiatives to improve their conditions. They often tend to accept the status quo as their fate. Human creativity lies dormant in people who live in poverty and derivation. Mainstream development processes not only bypass the atomised poor but sometimes harm them by making them victims rather than beneficiaries of development.

Poor people have no voice because they have no organization. One person working alone may feel unable to do much to change their situation. They may have no confidence to make changes, take action or speak out. A group of people who share the same situation, commitment and values, however, can achieve a great deal. Through working together and supporting each other they can take practical action. This can help build their confidence in themselves as a force for change. Together they may feel able to ask outsiders for advice or help. Together they can be strong. While many groups come together around specific issues, and organize to confront those issues, it is generally argued that emphasis should be given first on building of an organization and, only then, focusing on specific issues. Building a strong, lasting and staffed organization alters the relations of power. Once such an organization exists, people on the 'other side' must always consider the organization when making-decisions. An organization gives people a way of expressing their group needs in a way that cannot be ignored. People remain poor not so much because of lack of resources but rather because of the lack of organized strength to get access to resources. Understanding better the strengths and weaknesses of the poor in terms of their ability to utilize whatever resources they possess is essential for enhancing their power.

Organization is the thread out of which the fabric of development is woven. Organization is an important means of overcoming such disabilities resulting from atomization and isolation. In a broad sense, the purpose of an organization is to provide a continuing mechanism for the pursuit of the interests of its members as collectively identified by them (Tilakaratna 2005). Poor people have no voice because they have no organization. In the society, the various forces that work against the poor are highly organized. To overcome the constraints and effectively use the space, that is, to be empowered, it is necessary for poor people to organize themselves (World Bank 2002). Similarly, it is argued by the IFAD (2003) that enabling the rural poor and their organizations to influence institutions (including rules, laws, regulations) and policies of relevance to rural poverty reduction requires strengthening the capacity of the rural poor and their organizations. Concretely this implies institutional transformation: developing and strengthening the organizations of the poor to confront the issues they define as critical; increasing access to knowledge so that poor people can grasp opportunities and overcome obstacles; expanding the influence that the poor exert over public policy and institutions, including local and national governments; and enhancing their bargaining power in the marketplace (IFAD 2003). The IFAD further argues that organized groups and communities are more likely to have their voices heard and their demands met. When membership-based groups federate at higher levels, they can gain voice and representation in policy dialogue and decisions that affect their well-being. Therefore, the poor need, first and foremost, to be provided the chance to build individual and collective capabilities to gain access to economic opportunities and basic social services and infrastructure. Enhancing the human and social capital base of the rural poor will enable them to interact with those wielding power on a more equitable and informed basis, and thus negotiate more effectively on issues that affect their well-being. The development of organizations that empower the poor, and the rules and policies that secure sustainable access for the poor to assets such as land and water, to technology, finance and other services and to efficient markets, and allow the poor to participate in decision-making is central to more rapid rural development and poverty reduction.

Organizations of the Poor

Since time immemorial, groups and communities have organized to take care of themselves. Local organizational capacity refers to the ability of people to work together, organize themselves, and mobilize resources to solve problems of common interest. Often outside the reach of formal systems, poor people turn to each other for support and strength to solve their everyday problems. Poor people's organizations are often informal, as in the case of a group of women who lend each other money or rice. They may also be formal, with or without legal registration, as in the case of farmers' groups or neighborhood clubs.

Organized communities are more likely to have their voices heard and their demands met than communities with little organization. Poor people's membership-based organizations may be highly effective in meeting survival needs, but they are constrained by limited resources and technical knowledge. In addition, they often lack bridging and linking social capital, that is, they may not be connected to other groups unlike themselves or to the resources of civil society or the state. It is only when groups connect with each other across communities and form networks or associations-eventually becoming large federations with a regional or national presence-that they begin to influence government decision making and gain collective bargaining power with suppliers of raw materials, buyers, and financiers.

Organization simply means the creation of organs as instruments of action (Tilakaratna 2005). When groups of people having common interest feel the urge to further those interests they will be stimulated to create their own organs as instruments of action. Organizations of the poor are, accordingly, organs created by the poor who have become conscious of their deprivation and feel the urge to ameliorate their conditions, which means to overcome dehumanising poverty and to enhance their social and economic status.

Organization is essentially a means of empowering the poor to enable them to deal with the problems and issues of their poverty. Individually poor people cannot overcome powerlessness, collectively, they can. Their strength is in organization. Organization is the thread out of which the fabric of development is woven. Organization is a tremendous creative power. An organization gives people a way of expressing their group needs in a way that cannot be ignored. Building a strong, lasting and staffed organization alters the relations of power. Once such an organization exists, people on the 'other side' must always consider the organization when making-decisions. Organizations at one stage of development give rise to institutions at a later stage (Jacobs and Asokan 1997).

Organization is a power of the human mind. Mind has the capacity to relate and combine individual acts to form systems that can be repeated over and over again to accomplish the maximum results with the least investment of time, energy and resources. Systems are miniature organizations. Social organizations are collections of systems coordinated in space and time to achieve specific results. The introduction of organization elevates action from the physical to the mental level. A market is a simple form of organization to bring together buyers and sellers at a particular place and specific time for purchase or exchange of goods with less expenditure of time and energy. The more advanced the organization, the greater its capacity to channel social energies efficiently to achieve greater results. The development of retailing from the small family-owned corner store to the modern department store to the mail order catalog and the Internet illustrate the impact of increasingly sophisticated organization on any field of activity.

The development of organization in society takes place both in the horizontal and vertical plane. It spreads horizontally at each level to cover the entire society with its systems. It rises vertically to achieve higher levels of complexity and higher standards of performance. The horizontal expansion of organization increases its reach and extends its access. The vertical elevation of organization raises its skills, efficiency and productivity. Social organizations are a natural outgrowth and projection of emerging energy, knowledge, skills and values in the society. They are at once the means and the expression of society's development.

Like the individual and the organization, societies develop by effectively directing and channeling their energies by continuously increasing the organizational efficiency with which they execute every type of activity. As skills direct the energies of the individual and systems direct the energies of the organization, organizations direct the energies of the society. Organizations constitute the skills of society. These social systems are of many types, both formal and informal. They cover the actions and interactions within and between every field of social activity. A comparison of any two countries at different levels of development will reveal significant differences in the level and sophistication of the systems they employ to carry out activities. The effectiveness of organization is determined by its authority, complexity, and capacity for coordination and integration with social needs.

Organization is the mechanism by which the surplus energy in society is harnessed, mobilized, directed and channeled to produce greater results. Organization derives energy from being integrated with the society in which it functions. The energy of the society comes from its needs and aspirations. This energy pervades the social organizations established to meet these needs. The more finely the organization is tuned to fulfill underlying social aspirations, the greater the energy flowing through it. The will of the society changes over time as old attitudes and goals are replaced with new ones. Organizations that adapt to these changes continue to thrive. Those that remain fixed in the past mold decline, become ineffective and are eventually discarded or fade away.

Development involves the emergence in society of organizations that reflect the aspirations of the society and are fashioned in consonance with its cultural values and ways of life. The imposition or blind imitation of external models of organization may result in artificial forms of organization that at best partially channel the social energies for development. Japan developed rapidly because it possessed the knack for adapting and molding Western institutions to its own social and cultural context.

Authority of Organizations

Organization derives productive power from authority. What distinguishes an organized social collective from a mob? The organized collective mobilizes and directs the energies and capacities of people in a controlled manner to carry out purposeful activities, whereas the mob unleashes pent-up energies in an uncontrolled manner for destruction. The capacity to control and govern human energies is an essential characteristic of all organizations.

The first human collectives most probably consisted of bands of hunters working together to obtain food and protect the members of the group. Formation of a hunting collective required the identification of a leader who could direct the actions of the group, give instructions and enforce discipline. The primary qualifications for leadership were physical strength and fighting prowess, that is, the capacity to physically enforce authority over other members of the group. Authority was essential to maintain order and discipline within the group regarding the sharing of food and work responsibilities as well as to demand courageous self-sacrifice of members in times of war. The greater the strength of the leader, the greater is the stability, internal order and fighting capacity of the group. The maturation of the hunting group into an army involved a further development of organization. The military leader appointed a hierarchy of officers, each empowered with specific limits of authority. Strict obedience to those in command and unquestioned execution of instructions endowed the organized army with far greater strength.

Organizations derive power from internal authority and discipline. Western society's reverence for freedom and individual liberty has sometimes eclipsed the vital role of authority in social organization. Without it, no organization and no society can exist or function for a moment. The greater the authority under which individuals function, the greater will be the accomplishment. As society progressed from the primitive fighting group to more advanced forms of human collective, the center of authority gradually shifted from the military to other centers in society. Religious, academic, administrative, political and commercial centers of power became increasingly important. The distribution of authority may have diluted the absolute authority of the military leader, but it enormously enhanced the overall exercise of authority in society. Whereas the military leader was primarily concerned with the exercise of authority to preserve peace and to conquer in war, these new centers of power exercised authority over what people believed, worshipped, taught their children, grew, produced, consumed, how they worked together and settled disputes, where they traded or traveled, what they could own, buy or sell. This more organized society acquired infinitely greater capacity to increase the productivity of its members (Jacobs and Asokan 1997).

Complexity of Organization

One of the primary powers of organization that make it so productive is the division of labour. Specialization of function enables people with specific endowments to do what they do best. It also enables individuals to acquire a narrow set of skills rather than trying to learn how to perform every activity for themselves. Whether for a family, a company or a society, the result of this specialization is an enormous enhancement in overall efficiency.

Division of labour enables organizations to carry out vast numbers of different activities simultaneously. The greater the number of individual functions it performs, the more complex the organization. The more complex the organization, the greater its productive potential. Complexity is also enhanced by increasing the number of levels in the organizational hierarchy and the extent of co-ordination and integration it achieves with other organizations and activities in the same field and in other fields. Organizational complexity is powerfully enhanced by coordination between two or more separate systems or organizations. Co-ordination between buyers and sellers gives rise to the commodity exchange and the stock exchange. Co-ordination between purchasing, production and sales systems made possible the enormous improvements in efficiency and speed of delivery that have been achieved by just-in-time inventory management. Co-ordination of reservation, ticketing and routing systems between competing airline companies has increased the volume and reduced the cost of air travel by providing travelers with easier, more frequent connections between different airlines. Co-ordination is even more powerful when it is between distinctly different types of organizations. Co-ordination between biotechnology and agriculture created the technology of the Green Revolution. Co-ordination between universities and business has aided the development and commercialization of today's computers. Coordination between computers and telecommunication systems gave birth to the Internet. The US space programme that placed a man on the moon in less than ten years was the product of one of the most complex efforts at co-ordination ever attempted, involving cooperation between more than 400,000 people in thousands of different public and private scientific, commercial and governmental agencies.

Poor people's organizations, groups, and networks, working with others, can mobilize resources to improve individual health, education, and security of assets. Working through representative organizations, poor people can express their preferences, exercise voice, and hold governments and state service providers accountable for providing quality services in education, health, water, sanitation, agriculture, or other areas. Collective action through poor people's membership-based organizations can also improve access to business development and financial services, and to new markets where people can buy needed items and sell their produce. These collective capabilities that allow poor people to mobilize and organize to solve-problems have not yet been systematically included in strategies to reduce poverty.

The poor people should have the capacity to organize themselves at the local level. Local organizational capacity refers to the ability of people to work together, organize themselves, and mobilize resources to solve problems of common interest. For poor people, the capacity to organize and mobilize to solve problems is a critical collective capability that helps them overcome problems of limited resources and marginalization in society (World Bank 2002).

Community Organization

In order to translate the principles of community development effectively into practice for the attainment of socio-economic and environmentally sound development, the formation of Local Community Organization at the micro-level is vital for the whole process to follow at the meso-level. Such organizations are local institutions to decide, plan, implement and manage activities in the light of the principles formulated for the comprehensive community development. These institutions may be a mass coalition of village, or Muhalla, or an interest group, or a group of like minded people for promotion of the group interest in the principles of co-operation and democracy.

Such organizations can be created around a single activity of common interest of the community and it can be nurtured over the time by development activities. It is easy to organize but to keep them organized in not an easy task for the social organizers and the community members themselves. This is the point where the need for developing local, representative NGOs is seriously felt, as the SOs of external NGOs would not be able to stay with the communities for ever to keep them organized. Moreover, they will remain organized if it continues to convey benefits to its members through local set up. Otherwise they will get dissolved with the phasing out of external programme (Jan 2001).

Necessary Conditions for Social Organization

The necessary conditions for initiating and sustaining the participatory institutional development process at grass root level, according to Jan (2001) are:

- It is important to emphasise that great care must be taken to ensure that these measures complement or build upon locally existing institutions and organizations rather than replace them. Problems of acceptance often occur when introducing completely new forms of organizations. Yet, the simple transformation or modernisation of 'traditional organizations' can also be problematic.
- Field experience showed that it is most helpful if the SOs assist as catalysts in group development and in linking groups to government/NGO services. Community leader or social organizers role is that of an advisor strengthening the groups' leadership, organizational and planning capacity, a participatory trainer, teaching basic problem-solving and technical skills, and a link person facilitating communication between the groups and government/NGOS development services. Once groups reach maturity, community leader or social organizers withdraw from the groups.
- Financial support (government or external project) is necessary for financing training of support staff and providing seed money, and/or financial topping-ups to self-mobilised savings, and/or loans.

Organizational Leadership and Vulnerability

Empirical evidences have shown that the larger and more established an organization becomes, the more likely it is to be dominated by a minority, whether these leaders were richer members or the formerly poor now ascendant over their brethren. While strong leadership can make an organization more powerful and more effective, it tends increasingly to serve the interests of a minority rather than those of its majority. This tendency is stronger in organizations whose members are less well endowed with power resources, being economically poorer and having less education and lower social status. Leaders can be kept accountable to members through internal electoral competition.

The history of organizations involved in rural development with poverty reduction as a goal is not so dismal. Takeover by the rich and domination of the poor in organizations is not inevitable (Esman and Uphoff, 1984; Krishna *et al.* 1997). However, the 'iron law' is not easily alloyed and remains a warning for everyone. The odds favor eventual oligarchic rule and an eclipse of internal democracy. Procedures for internal democracy, accountability and transparency are even more important in organizations of, by and for the poor. 10 This is consistent with Wade's analysis (1988) of Indian irrigation systems. He found less collective action in larger command areas, but these were public sector systems in which an irrigation bureaucracy would assure water at least to the head of a canal. Richer, more 'powerful' head-end farmers could benefit from non-maintenance of the canal and ensuing maldistribution of water. In Nepal, head-enders needed the co-operation and assistance of tailenders to make sure that water from the river reached the command area.

'Committees of vigilance' overseeing and balancing executive leadership are increasingly found, for example, in Latin American organizations at the grassroots. However, such measures should not hamstring or immobilize leadership, since initiative and even boldness are needed for effectiveness on behalf of the interests of the poor. Building and maintaining consensus behind the purposes and strategies of an organization is compatible with, indeed a prerequisite for, strong leadership.

Other factors being equal, the level and effectiveness of organization determines the strength of a group, agency or community. Let us use a foot ball team as an example. If you have two football teams, with the same number of individuals, the same range of skills, physical condition, and technology (*e.g.*, quality of shoes), they would be equal. Let us say one team is not organized; there is no division of labour, no co-ordination, no recognisable social structure. The other team is organized, has a coach with authority, has different roles for goalie, defence, left and right wings, centre forward, and other division of labour. Different team members have different roles and practice playing in an integrated manner (*e.g.*, passing the football). In this case it is easy to see that the second team is more powerful, has more strength and capacity than the first one, even though their other characteristics are equal. Better organization makes better capacity (Bartle 2004).

The Role of Cognitive Factors

In analyzing organizational potentials and processes for benefiting the poor, enhancing their ability to achieve their needs and wants, it is easier to focus on structural factors – roles, rules, precedents and procedures – things that can be observed and changed by decisions and actions. I have myself focused on these through most of my career as a social scientist concerned with rural development and poverty reduction. They are more amenable to intervention or purposeful construction. Moreover, they are terribly important for the poor themselves, to achieve and maintain effectiveness and accountability.

However, Uphoff (1996) feels that he has become increasingly cognizant of the more subjective dimensions of organizational performance, things loosely characterized as norms, values, attitudes and beliefs. In my own experience of introducing local organizations for improving irrigation management, working with farmers considered to be among the poorest in Sri Lanka and Nepal, I have found that one needs to look beyond structural elements of organization and to appreciate the effects of cognitive elements, even if these are harder to identify or affect.

This appreciation, stemming from practical engagement in poverty reduction efforts, has informed my approach to social capital (Uphoff 1999, Uphoff and Wijayaratna, 2000; Krishna and Uphoff, 2002). I think this distinction could be usefully integrated into all of our social science analyses because it makes explicit the complementary sources and impetuses of human activity that occurs in groups of any scale:

- Incentives and patterns that arise from individual consciousness and intentions.
- Those that are 'second-order' realities, constructed from shared ideas and aspirations.

This distinction is one that permeates all of Weber's analysis of economic and social organization, though it is not always expressed so summarily. Further discussion here is not needed or appropriate since we are at this stage exploring how we can reliably and realistically measure 'empowerment' so that this concept can be used to guide policy and practice that will enable the poor to improve their conditions and futures.

This effort represents an advance upon earlier concerns with 'basic needs' not because these were not worthy and beneficial, but because they remained essentially paternalistic and did not address human needs and potentials in their fullest sense. Meeting basic needs provides a foundation for improving the prospects of the poor, but we need to venture onto less material and less tangible terrain if we are to mobilize World Bank and other efforts for realizing broader objectives of human development.

Societal Space for Organized Actions by the Poor

By space is meant the extent to which the right of association for the poor is respected and safeguarded by governmental legislation, policies and practices. In other words: What is the freedom available for the poor to form into independent organizations of their making without the fear of repression?

Currently, the most important method available for the poor to organize and enjoy legal status is to form co-operatives under Co-operative Law. However, the co-operative movement (with the possible exception of the thrift and credit co-operative societies) has in general failed to provide an effective organizational mechanism for the poor. At present most of the organized groups of the poor in the country operate informally - they lack legal status.

Hence, one positive action that the government can take is the enactment of supportive legislation to facilitate the organization of the poor and to give such organizations legal status. In regard to rural workers, the International Labour Organization's ILO Rural Workers Organization Convention and Recommendation (No. 141 and 145 of 1975) provide the rationale and guidelines for the enactment of the necessary legislation. In this Convention, the term rural worker has been defined to include any person engaged in agriculture, handicrafts or related occupation in a rural area whether as a wage earner or as a self-employed person such as a tenant, sharecropper or small owner-occupier provided that they work the land themselves with the help of their family labour or with the help of occasional outside labour.

Besides legislation, government policies and practices are a key determinant of the space available for the poor to form independent organizations of their own. The main issue here is whether there is a political will to permit free association for the poor. Organization of the poor results in a diffusion of power. Organized people operate as pressure groups on the political and administrative system. A conducive framework and an environment for the organization of the poor can be created only if there is a political will and commitment at the highest levels.

Activities of an Organization

The activities of an organization of the poor can vary substantially depending on the nature of the socio-economic context in which it operates, the specific interests that a particular group seeks to pursue, and the level of consciousness attained by the members of the group concerned. According to Tilakaratna (2005), we may summarize the potential activities under four categories namely:

1. Defensive actions.
2. Assertive actions.
3. Constructive actions.
4. Transformative actions.

- *Defensive Actions*: Are basically aimed at protecting the existing sources, means and conditions of living against erosion or encroachment by actions of other interest groups or the government. They represent collective actions initiated by the poor to prevent deterioration in their customary mode of living, which may result from a proposed project, policy shift or other external intervention.

- *Assertive Actions*: Refer to assertion by the poor of their economic and social rights available to them under governmental legislation, policies and programmes as well as what they collectively consider to be their legitimate entitlements.
- *Constructive Actions:* Refer to development projects of a self-help nature initiated by groups of poor using primarily their own resources. Instead of waiting for the government to deliver their needs, organized groups could initiate actions to satisfy their group needs for certain services by mobilizing their own resources with supplementary assistance from outside. The activities generated through such means can take a variety of forms such as:
  - *Infrastructural Works*: Feeder roads, simple irrigation works, school buildings and similar physical structures.
  - *Economic Projects:* Such as: consumer goods stores, schemes for collective marketing, cultivation of new crops or animal husbandry, and diversification of economic activity by the setting up of small industries.
  - *Social Development Activities*: Such as: drinking water wells, housing improvements, health and sanitation programmes, pre-schools and community centres, and finally.
  - *Cultural and Other Activities*: Such as: festivals, drama, sports and religious activities.

In this way, organizations can serve as an instrument to mobilise people's own resources for projects, which could satisfy a wide variety of people's needs.

- *Transformative Actions:* Represent innovative and creative initiatives of organized groups of poor with a relatively high level of consciousness. Such groups will attempt to explore and experiment with development styles, which represent alternatives to the mainstream development processes.

The above listing of possible actions clearly shows the potential available for the poor to launch a process of self-development through organized initiatives. Organizations enable the poor to mobilise their own resources as well as assert their right to a legitimate share of social resources. The activities of any particular organization may represent one or more of the above categories, often some combination of the above.

Community Organization *vs.* Organizations of the Poor

Many of the things needed to meet the needs and wants of the poor require collective action for:

- Establishing and maintaining a clean village water supply.
- Banding together to purchase raw materials in bulk at lower price for making handicrafts and to gain access to more favorable markets through group marketing, thereby also reducing the time spent on selling products individually.
- Improving local sanitation to reduce diarrhoeal and other diseases that are unnecessarily endemic among the poor (improving hygiene would be more of an individual effort).
- Deterring police, moneylenders and other local power figures from victimizing petty vendors, day laborers, unmarried women, lower castes and other vulnerable groups.

Many of the constraints, injustices and indignities identified as particular burdens of the poor require not just individual or public sector action but actions by the poor themselves. Empowerment of the poor thus can be promoted through some combination of:

- Direct enhancement of their respective assets and capabilities so that they have a higher probability of achieve what they need and desire through their own efforts – a 'private' approach to empowerment of the poor.
- Establishing assets and capabilities at higher levels of decision-making and activity that lead to the same or similar outcomes, *i.e.*, enhancing the abilities of the poor

to get what they need and want. This latter is a 'collective' strategy of empowerment, important because the first can never be sufficient to meet all of the needs and wants of the poor. Also, this is often needed to protect gains made through the first approach.

Roles and Functions of an Organization

For people to become organized and act collectively, they need to have some recognized roles, formal or informal, along with supporting rules, precedents and procedures for enabling them to perform four basic functions that are essential for any organization and collective action:

- Decision-making.
- Resource mobilization and management.
- Communication and co-ordination.
- Conflict resolution (Uphoff 1986).

Collective action of any sort, whether through legally established local government bodies, through formally constituted organizations such as: co-operatives, or through informal sets of actors who have on-going social relationships and common purposes, will require performance of these four functions. To build up capacities of the poor to utilize their limited resources more effectively to achieve goals and benefits on their own behalf, one of the basic strategies for empowerment that goes beyond individual and household units and aims will be either *(a) strengthening* such roles, rules, precedents and procedures where they already exist, or *(b) establishing* them where they do not.

Functions and responsibilities of the local organizations, their salient features, and threats, according to Jan (2001) include:

- Mobilise saving to provide credit to the community members and promote local economic activity for income generation.
- Take-up social projects in order to create harmony and mutual understanding among the people.
- Arrange reclamation and development of land and irrigation facilities and other productive physical infrastructures and their regular maintenance.

- Supply agriculture inputs and other requisite of the community.
- Arrange and participate in developing human skills.
- Sponsor and supervise schemes of primary health with special emphasis on sanitation, conservation, cleanliness and portable drinking water.
- Encourage primary education and adult literacy.
- Co-ordinate and co-operate with other departments and organizations.

Salient Features of an Exemplary Community Organization

- The members of a local organization have a clear understanding about the concept of self-help and self-reliance through community development and its own duties and responsibilities within a community organization.
- The members of a community organization have collective and participatory approach towards the solution of their common problems.
- They believe that all are for one and one is for all – and have a sense of ewe – feeling and collective belonging.
- The community organizations try to promote the common interest of its members and to facilitate them in the attainment of their needs. Minority benefits should be considered minor and secondary factors by community organization.
- Regular meetings and savings is a regular business of the community organization in order to promote the habit of thrift and savings among the members and to generate capital for self-financing.
- Community organizations have the spirit of self-management, self-help and self-reliance.
- The community organizations are free of all political and sectarian issues and its sole objective should be the promotion of socio-economic interest of its members. They, however, must make the community members aware of their right to vote and their understanding as to how they can effectively exercise this right.

- The office bearers are devoted and dedicated leaders and sincere to develop their communities.
- The community organization initiates some socio-economic activities from time to time from their own resources.
- It establishes links with other institutions and agencies for the comprehensive village development.

Threats to Community Organizations

- *Resistance:* Community organizations can encounter active and passive resistance from many sources, like: local elite, political leaders, religious leaders and in some cases may be area administrators. To avoid such resistance the programme should have an equitable and supportive role for all walks of life and for all governmental and non-governmental organizations in the area. The community workers would have to use all organizational tactics to deal with all such people during his interaction and motivational visits.
- *Sub-ordination:* Some time the community organization is dominated by the prosperous farmers, merchants and other businessmen and the organization is converted to the services of vested interest people and not the whole community. Moreover, in some cases the main cause of the damage or effectiveness of a community organization may be leadership; and today's leadership might become tomorrow's oligarch to use the local organization for his own vested interest. The factor, which leads to dominate, is the lack of managerial skills between the leaders and the followers. The major measures for controlling dominance is the training of members of the local organization in participation, decision-making and other organized activities. Regular follow-up, general conferences of the representatives; papers on different activities and on performance of the local organization and its wider distribution or reading in the general meetings can improve such situations.
- *In-effectiveness:* Community organization might become ineffective to its members in due course to time. This is

mainly due to lack of skills in organization development, accounts and planning work. The other reasons include no risk taking nature of the rural people and uncertainties surrounding the rural life. The community worker will have to train the office bearers in particular and general members in book-keeping, organizational work and resource mobilisation from the community itself through their leaders. Fund raising through donation, and saving will considerably improve the effectiveness of a local organization. Similarly, follow-ups by the social organizers are also helpful in keeping the community organization effective.

- *Mal-practices:* Dishonesty and lack of dedication are the common problems for the survival of a community organization. Some time individuals use community organization for their own interest or for the interest of his friends and family, which diminishes the collective interest of its members. Sometimes the funds are miss-appropriated and used for the above purpose. Smaller groups, regular meetings and simplification of the procedure can overcome the mal-practices. In the smaller groups, there is more interaction and all members know each other through their names, faces and performance and such cases there is more group pressure to handle the funds honestly.

Similarly, general body meeting makes the representation more effective and prevents misappropriation. Simple bookkeeping procedures can enable the community members to understand the financial position of community organization and their own liabilities. The important point for the sustainability of an organization is to encourage and reinforce members commitment to their organization and to their sense of responsibility toward the organization.

Levels of Collective Action

It should be understood that there are levels of decision-making and activity beyond the individual and household levels. Several levels often get grouped loosely (and unusefully) as 'local,' (Uphoff 1986a). This shows how three levels could be distinguished at which collective action is possible – and for the poor, desirable.

The group level, at which people associate according to common characteristics and interests to promote common interests, as farmers or fishermen, as women or men, as youths, as members of an ethnic or religious group, as speakers of a common language, etc.

The community level, determined by people's residential patterns, such that neighbors living in some proximity join together to protect and advance shared interests.

The locality level, representing a set of communities that have ongoing patterns of interaction and cooperation, based on proximity, common-pool natural resources, exchange of labor, a central market, shared religion or ethnicity, or other interests.

For empowering the poor, the first level of collective action has many advantages because it is more homogeneous, based on members having shared characteristics. Organizations for the poor that are smaller and more homogeneous can be more easily utilized by the poor to advance their interests. It is an important question whether community and locality organizations be designed or given incentives so that they make net contributions to empowerment of the poor, not expecting them to be totally devoted to this purpose. If so, resources besides those of the poor will be mobilized to improve the livelihoods and help attain the needs and wants of the poor. This may not always be feasible, but as an empowerment strategy, it deserves consideration. How can the poor get community and locality organizations – through their decision-making, resource mobilization, communication, and conflict resolution – to take seriously the problems created by poverty and to redress these imbalances? Allies from higher levels, whether units of government or external institutions like NGOs, can assist in encouraging such efforts, but they cannot dictate the internal dynamics of community or locality organizations (Ostrom 1990). Possibly the poor will represent an important (swing) voting block, so that leadership from the richer majority will need to attend to problems of poorer members. If voting power does not count, the latter can be more easily ignored; thus ballots can be one source of empowerment. The most reliable means to give the poor some leverage, even if they constitute a minority, is to have activities where the better-off majority benefit from the participation of the poor, or incur some costs from their non-participation.

Case studies of organizational form evolved by the poor in different socio-economic contexts reveal that organizations have operated best when they are rooted in small grassroots groups (as the base) which have as members persons with more or less similar economic interests and linked together to be able to operate as larger entities (a federation/ association/forum) where necessary. The small groups at the base (generally not more than about 20 to 25 member households) are the operational entities dealing directly with matters relating to economic matters (savings, credit, production, employment, etc.,) while the inter-group federations will deal with certain problems and issues common to all groups, which may be a larger issue, which no individual group can handle or simply co-ordination of activity. Small groups are organized first, for example on a block-by-block or small neighborhood-by-small-neighborhood basis. Once the small groups have met and worked successfully together on issues, they are brought together into a larger community-wide organization.

What is a Group?

A group is not just a collection of people who come together for sometime, for example, passengers on a bus may be together for several hours, but they are not 'group'. Why? It is because these people are not doing any common task, they have not collectively decided to do anything together. They are together only once. No one is exercising any leadership over the bus passengers.

A Collection of People will be called a GROUP if:

- They come together to work for a common purpose.

- There is a conscious membership – members know they are members, and others who are not members, know they are not. Membership criteria and responsibilities, as well as rights are known.
- The members meet regularly.
- There is identified leadership, whether there is one leader or several. The group recognises the leadership, and the leaders 'lead'.
- The members take collective action, and carry out decided-upon plans. A collection of people that doesn't do anything is not a group.
- They have decided on some rules and procedures for their being together and working together. These rules may be formally written down, or they may be only commonly understood.
- The people who come together have a common interest. No purposeful dialogue can take place until the members have a common interest.
- The members have a common understanding of their reason for meeting, of themselves as members.
- The size is big enough and small enough to allow members to interact and participate. In terms of what 'feels like a group' and what is a minimum size for effective collective work together, it can be said that when five or more persons get together regularly, meet and talk to each other, it is 'a group'.

The Culture of a Strong Group

The culture of the group is determined by the attitudes and customs established by practice by the group members. The culture of the groups of poor women should be dynamic, alive, marked by:

- A strong feeling of Unity.
- Freedom of expression of ideas and feelings.
- Respect for others.
- Democratic decision-making.
- Equality in the commonality of group membership.
- Each person Taken Seriously, each important.

In such a group, each member feels important, valued, powerful and the group provides a base of security. It is from such a base that the poor people can feel 'empowered' and work together to change their world.

Forming Groups of the Rural Poor

The formation of self-help groups of the rural poor is the first step in a long-term institution building process. Groups are formed around activities designed to satisfy the priority needs of the intended participants. Group membership offers the poor a number of advantages:

- *Groups are Starting-bases for Development Activities*. By pooling their capital, labour and other resources, members are able to carry out profitable self-help activities which, if undertaken by individuals, would involve greater risk and effort.
- *Groups are Efficient Receiving Mechanisms*. Well trained and motivated groups offer government and NGO development agencies cost savings in the delivery of inputs, services and facilities.
- *Groups are Learning Laboratories*. Members learn from their group promoter, and from each other, such skills as managing group enterprises, articulating, discussing and solving-problems, and keeping accounts.
- *Groups Help Empower the Rural Poor*. Groups provide the poor with an effective instrument for participation in local decision-making, helping them to co-operate more fully in the development of their communities and to exert pressure, where necessary, to improve their conditions.

Forming Small, Homogeneous Groups

For forming small and homogenous groups, one should first make an inventory of all existing forms of people's groups organizations within the proposed action area. These groups and organizations may be traditional or more modern types, such as farmer associations, co-operatives and trade unions.

The question is whether or not these organizations genuinely represent the interests of the rural poor. Co-operatives are often too large and their structures too hierarchical to be effective vehicles for participatory development. Similarly, traditional tribal or community groupings are often managed in a top-down fashion and may provide limited opportunities for participatory learning and decision-making. If the inventory indicates that participatory groups are lacking, efforts should be made to promote their formation among the poor people. Four essential guidelines should be followed:

- *Groups should be small*: The optimum number of members is between eight and 15. Small groups facilitate dialogue between members, have greater economic flexibility, and are less likely to be dominated by management elites or break down into factions.
- *Groups should be Homogeneous*: Members should live under similar economic conditions and have close social affinity. Homogeneity reduces conflict at group level: members with similar backgrounds are more likely to trust each other and accept joint liability for their activities.
- *Groups should be Formed Around Viable Starter Income-Raising Activities*: Income-raising activities are crucial to group development because they generate assets that help build financial self-reliance.
- *Groups should be Voluntary and Self-governing*: Participants should decide who will join the groups, who will lead them, what rules they will follow, and what activities they will undertake. Decisions should be taken by consensus or majority vote.
- *Prior to Beginning Group Formation, Household Survey should be Conducted:* With the local population to identify homogeneity factors, poverty levels, priority needs and criteria for group membership. The objectives of the project and its focus on the poor should be openly discussed and the villagers involved in selection of criteria for participation in the groups.

Formation of viable and stable groups requires patience and, in most cases, a period of from two to six months. Both overly rapid formation and overly long delays, which may dampen the interest of potential group members, should be avoided.

Power of the group is built up in a step-by-step approach, which includes both recruitment and achievement. Small groups are organized first, for example on a block-by-block or small neighborhood-by-small-neighborhood basis. Once the small groups have met and worked successfully together on issues, they are brought together into a larger community-wide organization. The larger group thus has an infrastructure as well as experience.

The groups begin with small, 'winnable' issues. The newly organized group is rarely ready to take on City Hall – yet. Taking on a task too big is likely to be ineffective and lead to the demoralization of the group, encouraging a 'See, I told you so' response, as members move back to resignation to intolerable or unjust conditions. The organizers must put a strong emphasis on helping the group choose 'winnable issues' with which to begin.

Inter-Group Federations

Once groups have established a sound economic base, one should promotes their consolidation into local-level inter-group federations. It does this because small groups usually become stronger and more efficient when horizontally and vertically linked. Inter-group federations promote solidarity and economies of scale both in group activities and delivery of development services, and enable members to develop a broad base for action. In addition, development of local - and, eventually, regional and national - structures can stimulate the formation of more groups. An inter-group federation represents its constituent groups and is not an executive body: it must be accountable to all group members. It should have a facilitating, co-ordinating and educational role and become a source of technical assistance, economies of scale and guidance.

Inter-group federations may be legalized as pre-co-operatives or federations in order to obtain more recognition, legal status, services and facilities. They may also link themselves to participatory, rural poor-oriented cooperatives or other people's organizations. Linking federations to existing organizations not only facilitates delivery of development services and facilities, but also the consolidation of group plans into multi-group or federation plans that can be matched with area and regional development plans through local coordination committees. Thus, a two-way planning process can be developed. Through inter-group activities and federations of groups, the poor become increasingly self-confident and recognized by their wider community. They obtain organizational power and may eventually be represented in local government bodies.

Case studies of organizational form evolved by the poor in different socio-economic contexts reveal that organizations have operated best when they are rooted in small grassroots groups (as the base) which have as members persons with more or less similar economic interests and linked together to be able to operate as larger entities (a federation/association/forum) where necessary. The small groups at the base (generally not more than about 20 to 25 member households) are the operational entities dealing directly with matters relating to economic matters (savings, credit, production, employment, etc.,) while the inter-group federations will deal with certain problems and issues common to all groups, which may be a larger issue, which no individual group can handle or simply co-ordination of activity (Tilakaratna 2005).

Stages of Team Formation

According to Jan (2000), social organizers need a sound understanding of community organization dynamics in order to be of real help when working for their team building. Like all good teams, the community organizations have an especially challenging task in the early stages of their development. Five stages of development have been identified:

Stage 1: Forming

In which the members of the village organization (VO) meet one another and begin exploring their roles in the team, their relationship with one another as team members, and ideas about how the team will operate. Even if the team members already know each other, if they are just beginning to work in this team, the forming stage still occurs. This stage is generally characterized by uncertainty: members' tentative sharing of information and ideas, polite exploration of options, and careful scrutiny of other members of the VO.

Stage 2: Storming

In which members of the VO begin to understand their differences, encounter divergent ideas about their task, their roles, and the processes by which they will do their work. This stage is generally characterized by disharmony: competition of individuals, ideas, and approaches; conflict among members about differences; frustration about the lack of cohesion; sectionalising of the team into differing camps, and threat of the community organization breaking down.

Stage 3: Norming

In which the members of the VO begin to recognize a common interest in the team and its task, develop common goals for the team, clarify roles of individuals within the team, and develop strategies for working together smoothly. This stage is generally characterized by optimism: relationships in the team deepen, tensions ease, members' concerns are resolved, and the team's task and process are clarified, the formation of a team is underway.

Stage 4: Performing

In which the members of the VO work productively to achieve their goals and carry out their work. This stage is generally characterized by productivity: a sense of progress and achievement on the part of the team develops, bonds are formed between members, and enthusiasm and creativity for the team's work are high.

Stage 5: Adjourning

This is the real testing time in which members of temporarily established VOs, having completed their task, prepare to disband. This stage is generally characterized by reluctance to part. The VOs where the team spirit is alive, after completion of one project, the team members review their experiences together, evaluate their accomplishments, and restart the process for a new development project and also arrange to stay in touch.

Group Leader

A good leader should provide a stable base for a group, should be able to inspire group members to take action, should be able to keep the group united, should have the confidence to speak out if things go wrong and should always be open to new ideas. However, leaders should also be people who are always ready to listen, especially before making-decisions. People often choose strong individuals with influence and wealth as group leaders. Sometimes this may be the right choice, but sometimes these individuals lead the group in the way they want, rather than the way most of the members want. A quieter person who listens well, may prove to be a good leader, especially if they are really committed to the group's well-being.

What Makes a Good Leader?

There are three kinds of leadership:

1. *Leaders who Command:* They make decisions on behalf of the group and allow little or no discussion with group members. In times of trouble, this may be necessary but in other situations it is unlikely to encourage the group to grow in confidence and skills.
2. *Leaders who Consult*: These leaders encourage discussion about situations and goals and then make a decision on behalf of the group.
3. *Leaders who Enable:* They set certain limits but within these limits encourage and enable members to gain confidence in discussing and analysing their situation and in making their own decisions.

How to Choose Leaders?

- Discuss the purpose of the group. What kind of leadership style will be needed? What particular knowledge and skills might be helpful? The likelihood is that there will be no-one in the group who will make a perfect leader, but there may be someone who could develop into a good leader.
- Take time to consider who should be nominated, based on all that has been discussed.

- If a vote is needed to allow members to choose between two leaders, decide how this can be done to allow each person to vote privately without being under any pressure. What is happening in the drawing below?

Setting Aims and Objectives

A new group must take time to carefully agree on the purpose of the group. Most groups come together because members all have an interest in a similar idea. This is usually the main 'aim' of the group. However, they should first meet with others in the community to discuss the needs, then agree on exactly how they plan to work together, what their priorities are and how they can work together effectively to reach their aim. It is usually a mistake to set lots of objectives. Discuss what you hope to see happening in the future. Then try to decide on just a few key objectives.

Planning Activities with the Five Finger Method

The Tearfund International Learning Zone (2005) has suggested the five ginger method for planning activities. Once a group has agreed its objectives it can begin to take action. For successful activities, it is always helpful to first plan them carefully and put them in order of priority. The Five Finger Questions are a very good way of planning:

Planning Activities with the Five Finger Method

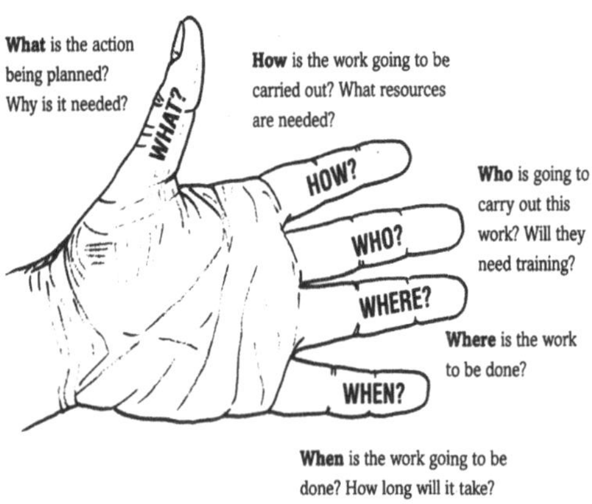

What is Organizing?

One of the most important and most overlooked development assets is the capacity of poor people to mobilize and organize for collective action. Because community organizing is the foundation for mobilizing local human resources, community organizations and leaders are needed to take on the responsibility and authority for management and development activities. The community is always listed as a target for social mobilization, along with policy-makers and political leaders, planners, media practioners, businessmen and civic leaders, religious groups, government technical agencies, NGOs, field-workers and volunteers. By that term is meant, usually, a single village, a district, a town, a city, a province, a region, a nation or nearer home, an atoll or island where the other social mobilization targets live. Hence, community refers to the basic population, the people themselves, or certain groups in a geographic area which must be reached with information/ message/appeal and encouraged to act in concert towards some developmental ends, *i.e.,* immunization campaigns, weighing of pre-schoolers, home gardening, mangrove replanting, preparing a community plan, identifying common problems, deciding on priority projects, etc.

In this context, community organizing refers to that process or methodology for motivating people to act as a group towards some developmental goals or objectives, which may include improving the overall health situation, reducing the number of malnourished children over time, increasing the number of home gardens or pits, building more latrines, immunizing more children, helping the island council build an office, road, school building, etc. Social mobilization has two components: Institution Development and Economic Development. The underlying assumption in the social mobilization process is that people get organized to work together if they live in close proximity and share common interests for community development. The foremost requirement in the institutional development process is that people organize themselves into community organizations

(COs). A CO is created around activities of averring importance to most of the villagers, whose continuing economic interests are best served by organizing themselves as a group. Active participation is sought from all households, without any restrictions or discriminations. This is essential for the whole society to move together in consensus and to build community-level social capital. When individuals organize themselves into broad-based groups, they have the leverage with which to address and tackle problems that they alone could not have done.

Lessons from Geese

A flock of geese, flying in a V-formation, provides important lessons in organizing. A goose flock can fly up to 1,000 miles without resting; whereas a single goose is exhausted after flying about 500 miles. The geese flying in the back utilize the air currents coming from the wings of the geese in front to lift themselves (Taylor, Taylor, and Taylor-Ide, 2002). The lead bird, which tires easily, routinely drops behind in the formation to ride the draft, and the geese at the back sequentially move forward. If a goose moves out of formation, the increased drag on its wings encourages it to fall back into position. Further, geese honk loudly while flying to encourage others and to identify their respective positions in the V-formation. A tired, wounded, or sick goose is never left alone. Two or three geese descend with it to the ground to protect, nurture, and nourish it back to health, before joining another passing flock.

Snow Geese Flying in V Formation

Following are examples of how geese work together successfully to travel great distances during migration. Human organizations may have a great deal to learn from them in attempting to travel to their own goals.

FACT 1: As each goose flaps its wings, it creates an 'uplift' for the birds that follow. By flying in 'V formation, the whole flock adds 71 per cent greater flying range than if each bird flew alone.
Lesson: People who share a common goal direction and sense of community can get where they are going quicker and easier because they are traveling on the trust of one another.

FACT 2: When a goose falls out of formation it suddenly feels the drag and resistance of flying alone. It quickly moves back into formation to take advantage of the lifting power of the bird immediately in front to it.
Lesson: If we have as much sense as a goose, we stay in formation with those headed where we want to go. We are willing to accept their help and give our help to others.

FACT 3: When the lead goose tires, it rotates back into the formation and another goose flies to the point position.
Lesson: It pays to take turns doing the hard tasks and sharing leadership. As with geese, people are dependent on each other's skills, capabilities, unique gifts, talents, and resources.

FACT 4: The geese flying in formation honk to encourage those in front to keep up their speed.
Lesson: We need to make sure our honking is encouraging. In groups where there is encouragement the production is greater. The power of encouragement (to stand by one's heart or core values and encourage the heart and core of others) is the quality of honking we seek.

FACT 5: When a goose gets sick or is shot, two geese drop out of formation and follow it down to help or protect it. They stay with it until it dies or is able to fly again. Then they start out with another formation or catch up with the flock.
Lesson: If we are as loyal as geese we will stand by each other in difficult times as well as when we are strong.

A flock of geese in flight can illustrate the distinction between organization and organizing. An organization is composed of a group of individuals who engage in inter-dependent co-operative actions. Organizational members take inputs (materials, energy, and information) from the environment, process them, and return them to the environment as outputs (Farace, Monge, and Russell, 1977). So a flock of geese constitutes an organization (as does Harvard University, Dow Chemical, and the United Nations). However, the term organization is used in a static fixed sense without taking time into account. Organizing, on the other hand, refers to the process-oriented, time-varying nature of the behaviours of members in an organization (Farace, Monge, and Russell, 1977). So a flock of geese flying in a V-formation and regularly rotating its leadership is engaged in organizing. In essence, an organization results from the results of organizing.

Community Organizing Approaches

The word 'community' can mean different things to different people. Community can be used to refer to communities of association (*e.g.*, religious communities), gender, race, or geography. Cohen (1985) defines community as a system of norms, values, and moral codes that provide a sense of identity for members. Fellin (2001) describes a community as a group of people who form a social unit based on common location (*e.g.*, city or neighborhood), interest and identification (*e.g.*, ethnicity, culture, social class, occupation, or age) or some combination of these characteristics. In many community organizing approaches, geography is the determining factor for community, including "... people who live within a geographically defined area and who have social and psychological ties with each other and with the place where they live" (Mattessich, Monsey, and Roy, 1997, p. 6). This workbook uses a definition of community that emphasizes geography, including neighborhoods, and relationships, including social and psychological connections and networks. Scholars as far back as Alexis de Tocqueville (Stone and Mennell, 1980) have emphasized the engagement of the community as a focal point of a healthy democracy.

According to the Women's Health and Safe Motherhood Project-Partnerships Component (2000), community organizing is a social development approach that aims to transform the apathetic, individualistic and voiceless poor into dynamic, participatory and politically responsive community. Community Organizing (CO) is a deliberate process of raising awareness, building capabilities and mobilizing basic sectors, particularly, the marginalized to collectively identify their needs and address these needs. This process aims to build a strong organization of the basic sector who will sustain the efforts towards meeting their needs and improving their status. CO is the means towards attaining a desired state of empowerment and development by a marginalized sector in the society.

The two Approaches to Community Organizing are:

(i) *Process Approach*: People are organized to facilitate communication, education, hope, awareness, and a sense of community. By working together, the group learns how to address common problems and achieves specific objectives.

(ii) *Power Approach*: People are organized to acquire and demonstrate power. The threat or use of power helps to influence specific individuals to correct specific problems, create system changes, and resolve conflicts.

Basic Principles in Community Organizing

Community organizing as an approach has evolved over time with the changing social and political climate in the country. According to the Women's Health and Safe Motherhood Project-Partnerships Component (2000), the basic principles in community organizing include:

- *Start where the People are: Build on what they have and know.* This principle shows respect for existing and indigenous knowledge, skills and capabilities of people. Innovations, new ideas, approaches and technology will be more acceptable to people if these will be explained using language, concepts and practices that are familiar to them. Existing knowledge and practices will need to be appreciated and enhanced since this will build confidence in people that they have the innate abilities to help themselves. The 'wisdom of old knowledge and practices' can inform the process of transforming the current undesirable or deprived situation to the more acceptable or desired state.

- *Encourage Active Participation of the People at all Times*. This means providing opportunities and avenues for people in the community especially women to take part, share and contribute to decisions and courses of action that will improve their lives and well-being. Encouraging people to participate will build commitment on the part of people to support and sustain the collective efforts towards an improved status.
- *Walk your Talk*. The basic foundation for working effectively together towards collective well-being is trust and confidence. Trust is built once integrity is proven especially when what one says is seen as what one does, and vice versa. Honesty, transparency and integrity are values important in community organizing work so that sincerity and mutual trust are built overtime, and the people become confident that those helping them are sincere and do not have any hidden agenda or motives. This means saying, doing and living the principles of CO as well as avoiding raising people's expectations on things that cannot be delivered or provided.
- *Live and Work with the People*. Staying in the community and sharing their daily lives will not only facilitate the building of rapport and trust between the community organizer and the people but will provide opportunities for sharing knowledge, values and technologies affecting the people's lives and keeping them in their current situation. Exposure to community life and daily concerns will provide the context (social, cultural, economic, political) as well as the local opportunities needed to formulate more responsive and appropriate courses of action and options in the CO process.

- *Action-reflection-action*. The CO process is an iterative process of action-reflection-action where an analysis of the situation will necessarily lead to concrete actions and small victories, which then need a collective review to uncover the lessons brought about by the whole experience. The action-reflection principle is called 'praxis' in CO parlance and means 'theory in practice'. It is only by being faithful to this principle that the CO process will be successful in empowering the collective towards the attainment of a common vision, from small victories to more strategic actions addressing root causes and transforming disabling social, cultural, economic and political structures.

There a number of principles that might be associated with organizing or building people's organizations. Among these the most important is the 'Iron Rule' that emphasizes that an organizer or any professional that works with people must "never do for people anything that people can do for themselves and on their own." People must experience a sense of their own power, the ability to act and do things for themselves. Ishmael Mkhabela (2011) argues that we cannot emphasise enough that the focus of a people's organization is building people's power and increase their competence for addressing community affairs and ensuring that service and public as well as business organizations are responsive to their needs. In addition the following are principles that are worth observing by aspiring community organizers and community leaders:

- Broad-based community organizing will have to be a transparent and accountable process both within and external to the community organization.
- People's Power is predicated upon the thesis that combined members or community organizations and people's own organized money is the foundation of real power and influence.
- Organizing should mean building community organizations that are free from external ideological influence and political control.

- Organizing should recognise the basic values of the people and be values driven.
- Organizing should aim to win real and immediate improvements in the people's lives.
- Leaders, despite their different backgrounds, should mutually recognize each other.
- Organizing should recognize and embrace diversity and work to bridge the social and economic divides in the interest of community and organizing people's power.
- Organizing is about gaining public recognition and utilizing the organization as a springboard for development of other people's organizations throughout the nation.
- Meaningful change is impossible without confronting the entrenched power structure and associated interests.

Basic Values in Community Organizing

The Women's Health and Safe Motherhood Project-Partnerships Component (2000) has recorded the following basic values and aims in community organizing.

- *Human Rights:* Are universally held principles anchored mainly on the belief in the worth and dignity of people; it includes the right to life and to self-determination and development as persons and as a people.
- *Social Justice*: Means equitable access to opportunities for satisfying people's basic needs and dignity; it requires an equitable distribution of resources and power through people's participation in their own development.
- *Social Responsibility*: Is premised on the belief that people as social beings must not limit themselves to their own concerns but should reach out to and move jointly with others in meeting common needs and problems; society has the responsibility to ensure an environment for the fullest development of its members.

Aims of Community Organizing

The Women's Health and Safe Motherhood Project-Partnerships Component (2000) has also recorded the following aims of community organizing.

- *People's Empowerment*. Community organizing is aimed at achieving effective power for the people. Through the process of CO, people learn to overcome their powerlessness and develop their capacity to maximize their control over their situation and start to place the future in their own hands. It is their progressive realization of the power that they possess and the ability to influence the course of history that dramatically erodes the dehumanizing effects of powerlessness.
- *Building Relatively Permanent Structures and People's Organizations*. Community organizing aims to establish and sustain relatively permanent organizational structures which best serve the needs and aspirations of the people. These structures ensure people's maximum participation while, at the same time, they provide the venue through which the people's organizations can link up with other groups and sectors. It is also through these structures that alternative ways of doing things can be tested and a new system of values can be internalized so that localized experiences become the building blocks upon which the blueprint of a more desirable future is based.
- *Improved Quality of Life*. Community organizing also seeks to secure short-and long-term improvements in the quality of life of the people. Immediately, the process of mobilization can gain concessions for fulfilling basic needs for food, clothing, shelter, education and health. In the long-term, it should create a conducive environment for the development of human creativity and solidarity through equitable distribution of power and resources.

Social Organizers

Social Organizers are eyes and ears of a programme. The change agent is the community level field worker-Social Organizers. Usually, Social Organizers are the direct link between the community and some outside support from government, aid agencies or self-help groups. Social Organizers, according to Jan (2001), are:

- Those who start the process of critical awareness and generate people's action and initiate tile changes at different levels required to transform the present structure of society leading to integral human development.
- Primary social organizers initiate change and work at the local community level, whether they are members of that community and start working with the people or from other communities to bring about change.
- Intermediate social organizers, work in voluntary or extra governmental organizations at the district, provincial, or national levels and provide support to the field based social organizers and community organizations.

Some of Social Organizers come from within a community and such Social Organizers may know a lot about the people and problems in that community. Some of Social Organizers come from outside, and they may know a lot more about aid and other resources that can be sent to communities. Many others are local volunteers who mainly want to help in their communities. Where a community worker acts as an extension agent, he easily acts to supplement his/her role as a community organizer. Instead of trying to know what is happening to the community, the supervisor/management should try to find what the village worker is doing. Community worker is not only community organizer but is multi-purpose worker. He needs training in a large number of trades like agriculture, animal husbandry, health, sanitation, credit and banking, marketing etc. The advantage of a multi-purpose worker in backward areas are obvious from the fact that people of the backward areas are so backward an average worker can tackle the community on the spectrum of their needs. If the felt need approach is accepted as the cordial principle of rural development, there should be only one person to operate them (Jan, 2001).

Goal of Community Organizing

The importance of organizing local people for development work has been widely recognized. Both governmental and non-governmental agencies have implemented various projects that have needed and encouraged collective action by people. Often, however, such projects malfunction after the outside agencies retreat from the project site, suggesting that: 'making organizations' is not the same as 'making a system of making organizations'. The latter is essential to make rural organizations self-reliant and sustainable. Since what needs to be created is the system for making organizations rather than the organizations themselves, we should focus on societies in which the organizations for development purposes are formed.

The goal of community organizing is people's empowerment. Through Community organizing people learn to overcome their powerlessness and develop their capacity to maximise their control over their lives. They must be able to influence the course of history and erode the dehumanising effects of powerlessness. And through the process of confronting oppressive structures and institutions, people are transformed from dehumanised objects into human beings with dignity, who can assert their rights and can control their destiny. Consequently, Community organizing aims to establish relatively permanent structures of people's organizations, which will serve the needs and aspirations of the people and thereby ensure maximum people's participation. It is through these structures that people learn to internalise a new system of values so that localized experiences become the building blocks upon which the blueprint of a more desirable future is based.

Community empowerment is central to community development. The many definitions of community empowerment are broadly based on their interpretation as either interpersonal or contextual elements and as an outcome or as a process. However, it is as a process, progressing along a dynamic continuum: individual empowerment; small groups; community organization; partnerships; and political action, that community empowerment is most consistently viewed in the literature (Labonte, 1990; Rissel, 1994) and was developed in conjunction with the community development continuum by Jackson, Mitchell and Wright (1989).

The organizational aspects of community empowerment provide a link between the interpersonal elements such as individual control (Everson *et at.* 1997), social capital (Modra 1998) and community cohesiveness (Geyer 1997) and the contextual elements such as the political (Asthana 1994), socio-cultural (Gordon 1995) and economic (Taylor 1995) circumstances of a programme. They represent those aspects of the process of community empowerment that allow individuals and groups to organize and mobilise themselves toward social and political change. The organizational aspects in themselves may act as a proxy measure for the social aspects of community empowerment, for example, the existence of functional leadership, supported by established organizational structures with the participation of its members who have demonstrated the ability to mobilize resources, would indicate a community, which already has strong social support elements.

Laverack (1999) reviewed literature on the organizational aspects of community empowerment and categorized from a textual analysis of the literature and the validity of this data was cross-checked by two other researchers using a confusion matrix approach as discussed by Robson (1993, p. 222). The literature review identified the following organizational aspects within a programme context; participation, leadership, resource mobilization, problem assessment, links with others, organizational structures, asking why, the role of outside agents, and programme management. These were called the 'operational domains' (a 'domain' is a field or an area of influence) and we now provide an interpretation of each in relation to its influence on the process of community empowerment.

- *Participation*: The involvement of individual community members in small groups and in larger organizations must occur if this concept is to develop along a continuum. There is considerable overlap between the concepts of community participation and community empowerment and the two have been included as a part of a number of frameworks explaining grassroots participation. One of the most widely used continues to be Arnstein's (1969) ladder of participation. However, whilst individuals are able to influence the direction and implementation of a programme through their inputs and active participation, this alone does not constitute community empowerment. The difference between participatory and empowerment approaches reside in the agenda and purpose of the process. Empowerment and participatory approaches differ because the former has an explicit purpose to bring about social and political changes embodied in its sense of liberation and struggle.

- *Leadership*: Goodman *et al.* (1998) point out that both participation and leadership are closely connected. Leadership requires a strong participant base just as participation requires the direction and structure of strong leadership. Leaders play an important role in the development of small groups and community organizations, which are part of the continuum of community empowerment. Gruber and Trickett (1987) argue that participation without a formal leader who takes responsibility for getting things done, dealing with conflict and providing a direction for the group, often results in disorganization. In a programme context leaders are often introduced as external organizers because they are seen to have the necessary management skills and expertise. However, Rifkin (1990) points out that in most communities, leaders are historically and culturally determined and programmes which ignore this have little chance of success of being accepted or utilized by the primary stakeholders.

Constantino-David (1995) discusses the experiences of community development in the Philippines and the success of utilizing local leaders. Competent leaders were developed by NGOs amongst poor people who offered a more insightful understanding of the community problems and culture. However, it was found that a lack of skills training and previous management experience of these people created limitations in their role as leaders. Leadership style and skills can therefore influence the way in which groups and communities develop and in turn this can influence empowerment.

As a solution to the problem of selecting appropriate leadership, Goodman *et al.* (1998) argue that a pluralistic approach in the community, one where there is an interplay between the positional leaders, those who have been elected or appointed and the reputational leaders, those who informally serve the community, has a better chance of leading to community capacity, and likewise to community empowerment.

- *Organizational Structures*: Organizational structures in a community include small groups such as committees, church and youth groups. The existence of and the level at which these organizations function is crucial for the way in which people come together in order to socialize and to address their concerns and problems.

However, organizational structures are themselves insufficient to guarantee the organization and mobilization of a community. There must also be a sense of cohesion amongst its members, a concern for community issues, a sense of connection to the people and feelings of belonging manifested through customs, place, rituals and traditions (Goodman *et al.* 1998).

Wegelin-Schuringa (1992) found that community members in Pakistan, India and Cambodia who had a sense of community and who were able to inter-relate to their own situation and to that of others had a better chance of establishing organizational structures. The interpretation of organizational structures for community empowerment therefore has two distinct but inter-related dimensions: the organizational dimension of committees and community groups; and the social dimension of a sense of belonging, connectedness and personal relationships.

- *Problem Assessment*: Problem assessment is most empowering when the identification of problems, solutions to the problems and actions to resolve the problems are carried out by the community. In order to achieve this the community may have to acquire new skills and competencies. The importance of problem assessment toward community empowerment has been identified in a number of health programmes (Tonon, 1980; Pelletier and Jonsson, 1994; Plough and Olafson, 1994; Purdey *et al.* 1994; Roberts, 1997). However, Rifkin (1990) points out that whilst many programmes advocate for wider participation, community involvement is limited. These programmes lose the opportunity to involve the community in the decision-making process of defining wider problems which concern the stakeholders and have been shown not to achieve their purpose.

- *Resource Mobilization*: The ability of the community to mobilization resources both from within and the ability to negotiate resources from beyond itself is an indication of a high degree of skill and organization (Goodman *et al.* 1998). The experience of many programmes has identified the ability of community groups to mobilize or gain access to resources as an important factor toward empowerment (McCall, 1988; Barrig, 1990; Eisen, 1994; MacCallan and Narayan, 1994; Fawcett *et al.* 1995; Hildebrandt, 1996; Roberts, 1997). However, Rifkin (1990) points out that there is little evidence to suggest that resource mobilization alone will make the community groups more empowered. The community must also have a purpose and the skills and capacities necessary to achieve this purpose, as well as the required resources.
- *Asking 'why'*: Another important domain for empowerment is the ability of the community to be able to critically assess the social, political, economic and other contextual causes that contribute to their level of dis-empowerment. This process has been termed 'critical awareness', 'critical thinking' and 'critical consciousness'. It is a process of emancipation through learning or education and has been adopted as an approach in many programmes including non-formal education (Kindervatter 1979; health education (Minkler and Cox 1980; Werner 1988) and community development (Hope and Timmel 1988).

Empowerment education, as developed by the educationalist Paulo Freire, is one of the most widely used approaches for emancipation through learning. People become the subjects of their own learning through a process of critical reflection and analysis of the circumstances in their lives. Freire offers a three step methodology: listening to understand felt issues or themes; participatory dialogue using a problem posing approach; and actions identified by the community to resolve the issues identified during their dialogue in groups. This process has been successfully used in a, number of programmes toward empowerment (Wallerstein 1992; Wallerstein and Sanchez-Merki 1994).

- *Links with Other People and Organizations:* Links with other people and organizations include partnerships (Panet-Raymond 1992), coalitions (But – terfoss *et al.* 1996) and voluntary alliances (Korsching and Borich 1997) to address community problems. Fawcett *et al.* (1995) argue that partnerships serve as catalysts for community empowerment in which community members can take action to effect change in the policies and practices that influence their lives. Partnerships can be especially effective toward community empowerment because the individual partners share the same responsibilities, tasks and resources.
- *The Role of the Outside Agents.* In a programme context outside agents have been identified as playing an important role in facilitating action through infrastructural support (Constantino-David 1995), skills development (Minkler and Cox 1980), raising the level of critical awareness, technical expertise (Hildebrandt 1996), fostering the support of leaders (Vindhya and Kalpana 1988) and the provision of finances. The role of the agent is essentially to use their control over decisions and resources to allow others to discover their ability and competencies to manage their own lives.
- *Programme Management:* Rifkin (1990) argues that whilst most agents pay lip service to the ideas of sustainability and the management potential of the community, they find this very difficult to do in practice. Programme management

that empowers the community includes the control by the primary stakeholders over decisions on planning, implementation, evaluation, finances, administration, reporting and conflict resolution. The community must have a sense of ownership of the programme which in turn must address their concerns. Rifkin (1990) points out that the first step toward programme management by the community is to have clearly defined roles, responsibilities and line management of all the stakeholders. For empowerment to be influenced by programme management the outside agent must increasingly share their control over decisions and the access to resources with the community.

- *Implications for Community Development:* We have discussed so far the influences on the process of community empowerment, specifically the organizational aspects or 'operational domains'. It is these domains that can serve as a means by which the process of community empowerment can be made operational through assessment and planning in community development programmes by:
    - presenting a straightforward way to define and measure this construct as a process; and
    - acting as a proxy for the often more ambiguous and complex social elements of community empowerment.

We have raised several unanswered questions which must be considered as a part of the broader implications of empowerment research and practice:

- Are some domains more important than others for empowerment?
- Is it necessary for all the domains to be strengthened for the empowerment of communities?
- Can all the domains be equally supported by outside agents in a programme context?
- How are the operational domains inter-linked?

Each domain is inter-dependent and can individually influence the effectiveness and utilization of the process of community empowerment but it is not known if there is a hierarchy of importance or if a combination has more of an influence.

Community Questions: Organization, Readiness and Commitment

Before initiating the process of community mobilization, the community organizer must have the following assumptions about the targeted community:

- The community can organize itself to move forward.
- The community is ready to move forward.
- The community is committed to change once assets have been inventoried.

If the community mobilizer is not sure that the community meets these criteria, interested community members should ask and answer the following questions.

Community Questions

How is the Community Organized?

- Who are the organized groups/individuals in the community?
- Who is ready to move forward, revitalizing community strengths?
- Is the community ready for change?
- Will there be opposition to this effort? If so, can it be managed or overcome?
- Who will assume the leadership, as a support base, to make changes?
- When will the process begin?

By answering these questions, a community can determine if it is ready to commit and move forward.

Community Organizing: Methodological Characteristics

Community organizing has four distinguishing process or methodological characteristics. These are:

1. *A progressive cycle of action-reflection* begins with small, local and concrete issues identified by the people and the evaluation of and reflection on the action taken by them.

2. *Consciousness-raising through experimental learning* is central to the community organizing process because it places emphasis on the learning that emerges from concrete action and which enriches succeeding action. This dialectic relation between theory and practice progressively raises people's consciousness.
3. *Community organizing is participatory and mass-based.* Because it is primarily directed towards, and biased in favour of the poor, the powerless and the oppressed. Through a participatory process, the whole community (as much as possible) must be involved in the organizing experience.
4. *Community organizing is group-centred and not leader-orientated.* Leaders are identified, emerge and are tested through action rather than appointed or selected by some external force or entity. Thus Community organizing seeks democratic leadership where power resides in the people.

Steps in Community Organizing

The Women's Health and Safe Motherhood Project-Partnerships Component (2000) has recommended the following steps in community organizing.

Integration with the Community

A CO must be integrated in the community by being with the people, live with them and blend with its culture. S/he must be observant of how they live their daily routines and try living the same way. S/he should refrain from acting like a visitor or a tourist to be accepted by the people as member of their community. Trust is the key point here that begins with building rapport.

Joining the community activities such as follows can build rapport:

(a) *Economic Activities*

- planting and harvesting rice, vegetables and other crops;
- fishing, fish drying or other processing activities.
- weaving;

(b) Household Activities

- cooking;
- dish washing;
- cleaning the house and the yard;
- gardening;
- fetching water;

(c) Social/religious Activities

- feasts, canao;
- weddings;
- birthdays;
- funeral/wakes.
- religious rituals;

(d) House-to-house visits

Integration is the most critical stage of community organizing especially when the area is no longer 'virgin' or has already encountered several outside interventions in the past that did not make any significant positive change in their lives or at worst created more problems than solutions. The CO must be careful with the way they carry themselves because when integrity and trust are destroyed at this stage, the next steps will be difficult to take. The community's culture may clash with the CO's own values and preferences but they have to forget a part of themselves their own biases - to be able to understand, tolerate and accept the community's way of life and eventually integrate, be accepted and trusted by the people.

Core Group Formation

Core group formation is the process of bringing together the most advanced indigenous leaders among the leaders identified during the integration and social investigation stages. This step is important to ensure that the CO does not assume a community leadership role. At this stage, indigenous leaders must begin to assume a leadership role but the CO must continue training them in carrying out the tasks in a more systematic and organized fashion. While doing this, the CO must stay in the background and allow each member of the core group to facilitate and provide creative ideas and collective capabilities using their experience and expertise. Small tasks like facilitating a meeting could allow a member of the group to discover their potential.

Some of the leaders' ways of carrying out specific tasks and dealing with people and difficulties may not be as sophisticated as that of the CO's ways and ideas, but these small capabilities should be supported and recognized to build their confidence as well as enhance their leadership potential. At this stage, the CO must begin to train the core group in utilizing participatory leadership as well as other leadership skills. Training could be facilitated using the module on Leadership found in the succeeding pages.

The following criteria could help the CO in spotting the potential leader:

- Belongs to poor and marginalized sector.
- Well-respected in the community and has a relatively wide influence.
- Aware of the community issues and concerns.
- Desirous of change.
- Believes in the participation of as many people as possible in the process of community development.
- Values volunteerism.
- Can find time to perform the tasks of the core group.
- Must be able to communicate effectively and listen to community members.

Mobilization/Implementation

Mobilization is the actual community action undertaken to address and resolve the identified community issues and concerns. This refers to mobilizing people and material resources of the community to achieve concrete gains. This is where the people's confidence is strengthened and leads to realization of their collective strength and power as a people.

Evaluation

This is the process of looking back to "what has been accomplished, what was left out and what remains to be done" based on plans. Again, this requires the active participation of the people. The leader should again be technically rehearsed by the CO in anticipation of 'difficult' people who might have been disappointed with the outcome of the implementation of the plan. Further, the facilitator should be careful and focused to the objective of the session. Also, the facilitator must highlight the people's victory howsoever small it is to strengthen the people's self-confidence. Framework for evaluation must be prepared ahead of the actual evaluation.

Reflection-Action

Reflection means identifying and analyzing the lessons from the experience. Reflection must be processed in the cognitive as well as affective levels of the participants, and the individual must recognize her/his own strength and power and how the experience could help the persons grow as individuals and as a people. Reflection allows the person to realize their sense of worth as a member of a community, and at the same time realizes the power of being one with the others in the struggle to reach a goal. It is in this process when it is the best time to open the possibility of forming a formal organization with concrete direction and mission based on the identified problems, needs and aspirations of the community. This leads to designing concrete systematic collective action.

Community Organizing Models

Leah Lundquist *et al.*, of the University of Minnesota, in March 2012 summarised some of the important community organization models *e.g.*, Alinksy, Faith-Based Community Organizing, Pedagogy of the Oppressed, Civil Disobedience, Conciousness-Raising, Asset-Based Community Development, Social Entrepreneurship, etc. The salient features of these models are given below.

- *Alinsky Model of Community Organizing:* The community organizing model developed by Saul Alinsky owes its inspirations to the Communist theories of mass mobilization. Alinsky, on the lines of Marxist philosophy views the current capitalist economic and social systems problematic and the cause for all social issues such as: crime, unemployment, inequality, discrimination, declined morality and environmental degradation. Alinsky emphasizes working within the system to change the system. Just like Carl Marx, Saul Alinsky has little discussion of how a society should be structured and its function after the successful revolution overthrows an oppressive dominant system.

- *Faith-based Community Organizing (FBCO):* It is *Also known as: Congregation-Based Community Organizing (CBCO).* FBCO has its roots in the organizing of Saul Alinsky. In his organizing work in Chicago's working class neighborhoods in the 1930s and 1940s, Alinsky drew on the Jewish community for both human and financial capital. However, following Alinsky's 1972 death, Ernesto Cortés, Jr., a young organizer from San Antonio, began to explore the benefits of going beyond Alinsky's use of religious institutions as sources of people to a model of organizing that integrated faith traditions into the organizing itself. Through his efforts organizing among the lay leadership, mostly female, of Hispanic Catholic parishes in San Antonio, Cortés developed a unique model of organizing. This model – traditionally local in nature – has grown in prominence on the national level since 2008, building political power through new alliances and national organizing tactics (Swarts, 2010).
- *Pedagogy of the Oppressed:*

  The silenced are not just incidental to the curiosity of the researcher but are the masters of inquiry into the underlying causes of the events in their world. In this context research becomes a means of moving them beyond silence into a quest to proclaim the world." – ***Paulo Freire.***

Paulo Freire's model embeds community organizing in an education model, claiming that the purpose of education is to build an ethic of democracy through literacy and the development of critical consciousness. Freire has drawn upon, and woven together, a number of strands of thinking about educational practice and liberation. His social analysis is rooted in the branch of Marxist theory of 'diabolical materialism', and therefore sees the class struggle as relationships between two primary groups, 'the oppressors' and 'the oppressed'. Friere's analysis goes deeper to explore more complex relationships between these groups and how both of their class identities or self-images are derived from how the other class views them. Educationists and community organizers all over the world have drawn heavily from Paulo Freire's 'pedagogy of the oppressed.'

- *Civil Disobedience:* Civil disobedience was defined by political philosopher John Rawls (1971) as a "public, non-violent and conscientious breach of law undertaken with the aim of bringing about a change in laws or government policies" 16. Individuals are motivated to engage in civil disobedience by a range of values such as justice, transparency, security, stability, privacy, integrity and autonomy.
- *Consciousness-Raising:* Consciousness-raising (CR) as an organizing model originated in 1967 with the New York Radical Women's organization (NYRW) and became the predominate organizing model of the women's liberation movement of the 1960's and 1970's. Though it represented a unique theory for bringing about radical change, CR drew on the experiences of the earlier labor and civil rights movements. In fact, the term 'consciousness-raising' came from NYRW member Anne Forer recalling that labor movements had spoken of raising the consciousness of workers who did not know they were oppressed. She asked the other women to give her examples from their lives of how they had been oppressed, because she needed to 'raise her consciousness' (Sarachild, 1973). This model of a dozen or less women gathering to each discuss problems of collective oppression quickly spread from New York to Chicago and then across the United States. At the movement's peak in 1973, it is estimated that 100,000 women across the U.S., belonged to CR groups (Eller, 1995). As CR gained momentum in the feminist movement, gay rights activists also adopted the model.

- *Asset-Based Community Development (ABCD):* Asset based community development grew out of the earlier organizing models pioneered by Saul Alinsky and Jane Adams as well as the community development movement. While serving as Mayor of Chicago from 1983 to 1987, Harold Washington, was interested in experimenting with how a large municipality could effectively govern from the bottom up. John (Jody) Kretzmann, Neighborhood Planning Committee Chair and a policy consultant to the Mayor partnered with John McKnight, then Director of the Midwest Office of the U.S. Commission on Civil Rights, to explore this concept in other communities across the U.S. Their research style flipped typical urban social science on its head, not studying deficiency but finding natural leaders and collecting "hope stories" of community change. What they heard repeatedly was individuals saying, 'We started with what we've got'. The results of this research – described in their key publication *Building Communities from the Inside Out: A Path Toward Finding and Mobilizing a Community's Assets* – is what is known today as Asset-Based Community Development.
    - Through their research McKnight and Kretzmann outline six categories of assets every community possesses: *(i)* the gifts, talents, skills, and passions of individuals within that community; *(ii)* the associations in which individuals participate in with no expectation of compensation; *(iii)* the institutions individuals associate with as paid professionals; *(iv)* the physical assets; *(v)* the economic resources; and *(vi)* the community stories.
    - They describe three steps for harnessing these assets: *(i)* find them (They offer 'asset mapping' as a way to do this); *(ii)* connect them; *(iii)* harness them to a hopeful vision of the future.
- *Social Entrepreneurship:* Since the tech boom and rise of neo-conservatism in the early 1980's, a fundamental structural change occurred in society. Instead of looking to business

or government to solve societal issues, citizens began to 'innovate for social good' using the same entrepreneurial acumen driving new business ventures. Ashoka: Innovators for the Public, founded by Bill Drayton in 1980, was an early fosterer of this movement, funding and connecting social entrepreneurs from around the world. Ashoka has now grown to an association of over 2,000 Fellows in over 60 countries on the world's five main continents.25 Meg Wheatley and Deborah Frieze have recently merged this concept of social entrepreneurship with systems thinking in their 'Walk Out, Walk On' model, dubbing social entrepreneurs as 'Walk Outs' that refuse to work from negative dominant values or paradigms, 'walking on' to become social change pioneers.26 Similar to Ashoka, *Walk Out, Walk On* seeks to organize individual entrepreneurs for collective impact.

4 Catalysing Community Mobilisation

"You have to first change yourself, to be able to change the community."

The Koran

INTRODUCTION

Community mobilisation is not a spontaneous process. Community mobilisation does not happen by itself. It must be stimulated and encouraged. The poor need to be stimulated and sensitively assisted to initiate such processes. A critical analysis of today's social reality and the various modes of interacting with that reality demonstrate the need to empower poor and oppressed peoples nurturing in them a positive self-image and confidence to allow them to act on their own behalf. People's belief in themselves is a necessary precondition for them to act with others to build a more just society. But how does one act about accomplishing this task?

Community mobilisation need to be catalysed by an external facilitator and/or an internal animator. Articulate, committed and confident local leaders/animators have to emerge or be trained/sensitised to manage the process. External facilitators also have a role. They connect these local leaders/animators and the poor with the mainstream organizations. They also bring in new knowledge for the participants, where necessary.

The community mobilization perspective enables the organizations of the poor to embark on a learning path. Social animation is essentially an organized or a collective participatory process of interaction among members of a social group/community/area (sharing a certain degree of homogeneity of interests and concerns) which facilitates both charging and release of the creative energies of the poor towards understanding and solution of obstacles to their own development.

Animation - A Life - giving Process

Animation is acknowledged as a process of non-formal education of the poor by which they acquire an ability to analyse their situation, become aware of the forces acting on them and mobilize themselves to appropriately react to those forces. It is a process of assisting the poor to develop intellectual capacity to investigate the reality of their life-situations, analyze relevant issues, understand the factors creating poverty and deprivation and through such understanding to perceive self-possibilities for change. The process of animation helps in breaking mental barriers and showing possibilities for change. Wignaraja and Sirivardana (1995) contend that "animation is the outcome of a specific mode of interaction between the outsiders and the poor" resulting in conscientization. They further argue that the participatory approach seeks to achieve an interaction between the two knowledge systems (the knowledge base of the poor rooted in experience and knowledge derived from formal education) creating a mutual learning process.

Animation means, literally, to breathe life into some thing. Animation is a process of stimulating people to become aware and conscious of the problems and deprivation they suffer from while they regard themselves as principal actors in their lives and not mere objects. Animation is also described as a process of assisting people to develop their own intellectual capacities, that is, to stimulate their critical awareness; this critical awareness enables rural people to examine and explain issues in their own words and, as a result, to realise what they can do to bring about change.

Animation is that stimulus to the mental, physical, and emotional life of people in a given area which moves them to undertake a wider range of experiences through which they find a higher degree of self-realization, self-expression, and awareness of belonging to a community which they can influence (quoted by Simpson 1989: 54).

In more self-consciously 'radical' terms, (and with a nod to Freire), animation is described by one Italian commentator as: a form of social practice oriented towards the conscientisation [presa di conscienza] and the development of the repressed, deprived or latent potential of individuals, small groups and communities (Contessa quoted in Maurizio 1991).

Animation, according to Ambrose (1992), is a life-giving process. The situation can be compared, for example, to a seed in which the potential of life lies dormant until it is planted in the soil. With appropriate care it soon begins to sprout and grow. Animation is the process which energizes and activates the inner potential of a person to blossom and grow. Through animation, a person becomes alive and vibrant to create and transform the situation and his or her environment. It is a conscious effort to keep alive the flame of hope by one who is enlivened with hope. It is initiated by a person, according to Ambrose (1992), who is concerned about the plight of the poor.

What triggers off this life-giving process in the animator? The triggering mechanism is the vision that the animator is imbued with and committed to. It is the vision of a new society founded on the values of love, equality, justice and peace. Their experience in working with the poor revealed to them an untapped reservoir of potential in the poor. Such persons consider the poor as resources and want to make the poor the best instrument to transform the society. The animator therefore focuses much of his or her energy at mobilizing this hidden potential. It is this approach that Ambrose (1992) calls as the animation process.

It generally happens that in the work of animation, there is first a person who is imbued with and committed to the vision of a new society, and he or she attracts others committed to the same vision. In other words, the vision and the commitment to this vision of a just society, make a person, an animator who interacts with people to infuse in them a new life and spirit. In the animation process, one of the vital components is the interaction between the animator and the animated.

Through the process of animation, the animator arouses and fans the flame of a new spirit among the poor to make this vision a reality. What was latent in the poor now begins to manifest itself in a strong desire to move towards the envisaged future. The animator's presence in the midst of the poor creates confidence in them. They realize that they can trust this person. This trust soon multiplies and leads to mutual trust among the members in the community.

The impact of animation can be seen by the liberative actions taken by the people. They enter into a forward movement. They begin to act as subjects who have control over what will happen to them. Their destiny is no longer decided by others: they themselves decide. This is the qualitative difference that occurs in their lives. Their situation may not dramatically change in quantitative terms, but a process of irreversible change has nonetheless set in. It triggers changes in others by a contagious process. When the poor act in this manner, it surprises the rich and vexes the vested interest groups. It is at a cost to themselves that the poor move ahead in action. This process is fundamentally rooted in an inward awakening. It is an awakening of the spirit within to move forward, to be creative, and to activate one's potentialities to build a new society.

Animation therefore is a process of giving and infusing life or spirit in someone. This process occurs not only in individuals but also in the entire community both at the national as well as the global levels. It is futuristic in orientation. Fr. Frederick D'Souza (2012) argues that animation is an awakening and action-oriented process aimed at social transformation affecting, at general level, all people and at specific level, the poor. It initiates a dynamics in a person and in the community to struggle for empowerment to bring about change among themselves and in their situation of poverty and marginalisation and to affirm their dignity as persons to create a more just society.

Animation among the Poor: Humanity is endowed with the unique gift to create and recreate society in order to protect and promote life in its fullness. This is neither an automatic nor an unseen process but the deliberate choice of a community.

The poor and the marginalised are relegated to live in dehumanized conditions. The harsh conditions of life have pushed them to the brink of death, allowing them to remain merely at the bare survival level with great risk. Yet the poor dream of a life that would be better and more human one day. The process of animation is aimed at triggering this desire for a better life among the poor and translating it into action. This does not happen spontaneously. It is a process that is initiated and sustained by the animator in a group who helps the poor to become aware of their situation, its root causes, the forces interacting as well as their strengths and weaknesses.

The Brazilian educationalist and one of the pioneers of building awareness among the poor, Paulo Freire (2007), gives a powerful illustration in this regard. In a conversation with a group of peasants, Freire reveals how the initial stage of awareness is evoked.

At a certain point, some of the peasants told him "Doctor Freire, you are such a learned man. Let us not waste time in talking to you. You please talk to us and we shall listen to you. That would help us.' Freire, realizing the mood of the peasants, did not resist their proposal and took the occasion to initiate a process of building critical consciousness.

'What you say is true,' he replied. "I do accept your statement for the moment. But will you permit me to ask you a few questions?" They answered 'Surely, please do so.' Freire asked them; "How is it that I alone am capable of saying something good for you to listen and that you feel that your job is only to listen?" The peasants replied, "It is evident, Sir, because you are a university-educated person. You know several things that we, illiterate peasants, cannot know. Hence we can only listen to you." Freire said: "It is true that I am university educated and that you are illiterate. But how is it that I happen to be so and you remain illiterate?"

"Of course, your parents were having the means to educate you and send you to the university while our parents did not have the means to do so and hence we remain illiterate," came the quick reply from the peasants. 'Permit me to ask you one more question' Freire asked, "How is it that my parents had the means to educate me while your parents did not have the means?" The peasants retorted: 'It is very simple. It is God's will.'

Then Freire told them: "Please listen to a small story I am going to tell you. A farmer had three children. The first was a boy. When he was born, the father said to himself, 'I shall make this boy a great scholar and intellectual. He will get all university degrees and excel in learning." He saw to it that the boy would get the best education and become a - great intellectual in the country. The second one also was a boy. The father said to himself, 'I shall make him a beggar in the street. Let him beg and earn his life by begging, whether he starves' or dies of disease I shall not bother about him'. He executed in practice what he thought and made him such a beggar. The third one was a beautiful girl. The father said to himself, 'I am not interested in this child. 1 shall make her a prostitute. Let her earn her livelihood by being a prostitute.' He took efforts to see that she becomes a prostitute in life.'

After narrating this story, Freire asked them "what do you think of this farmer? Shall we call him a good and loving father because this is the normal way a loving father behaves towards his children?" The peasants in their normal way rose up in one voice with full emotion and condemned the father in the narrated story. They retorted, "he is a cruel and mad man. He cannot be called a father at all. We peasants will never treat our children like this. We do not at all determine the future of our children like that. We give the best we can and offer all the means at our disposal to help our children to come up. It depends on each child. We never predetermine like that."

After this, Freire asked them, 'How do you address God?' They said, 'He is our loving Father who does good to us.' Freire then asked, "If, as a human father you will not predetermine the future of your children and condemn them to something degrading, how can God, whom you call a loving Father, predetermine that I should be university educated and that you should be illiterate. Is it really God's will? Is it God who wants discrimination in society and keeps you like this or are there some other forces?"

The peasants had a moment of silence. Then a few voices sounded, "It cannot be God's will if God is our loving Father. We believe that God is our loving Father. It must be some other human forces that create all these social discriminations and maintain them."

'If it is so,' replied Freire, "can you find out which are those forces? How are you kept under those forces? How do they maintain their control over this situation? What is it you can and should do to tackle them to live as full human beings with dignity, equality, justice and peace?" The peasants unanimously voiced "we do understand the situation now. We must think deeper and find out all these and we shall know ourselves better so that our lives will improve".

Awareness is a moment of awakening. In their silence the peasants realized that they had to change. Although conscious of their situation of poverty, they were unable to move forward. Paulo Freire draws out the answers from the people themselves. What then accounts for this internal change in people which lead them to perceive their reality in a new way? What is the process which takes hold once a poor person's perception of 'why they are poor' changes?

The Role of External Organizations

The process of social mobilisation may be initiated, facilitated and co-ordinated by one or more persons, often belonging to some organization, which is usually non-governmental. Common designations of these persons are social mobilisers, community mobilisers, community workers, catalysts, change agents, facilitators and animators.

A recurring theme in the literature and practice of community mobilisation is the proper role of external organizations. In some cases, community mobilisation is both prompted and carried out exclusively by community members. More often, however, mobilisation is a collaboration between the community and one or more external organizations, which may be local, national, or international and either private or governmental. In many cases, an outside organization is the impetus for or catalyst behind a mobilisation effort. External organizations often bring important elements to the table, such as technical expertise, broad experience, financial resources, or simply an outside perspective that may be lacking in the community. External organizations play an important role by helping community members raise awareness about these problems and build momentum in the community towards the development of sustainable solutions.

Community mobilisation efforts are no less authentic when they involve outside players – and are often more effective – but all those involved must be careful to ensure that the role external organizations play does not undermine one of the key goals of mobilisation: building community capacity. In general, as long as the role of outside players is confined to advising, facilitating, and supporting the work of community members, participation by outsiders can be very beneficial. It is only when external actors begin to direct or manipulate the effort that the building of community capacity is potentially compromised and sustainability is undermined. External players need to keep in mind a simple rule of thumb: community mobilisation is not just something done *to* the community but something done by the community.

The stimulation of people so as to undertake self-reliant initiatives requires two essential steps:

- The development of an expanded awareness of the reality in which they live - the space/time dimension.
- Based on such critical awareness, increased confidence in being able to get organized so as to make a difference.

The overall process involves a movement away from the classic manipulation and dominance mode towards a more humanistic animation and facilitation mode.

Humanistic Animation and Facilitation Mode	Rather than	Classic Manipulation and Dominance Mode
Start from where people are - their experiences, knowledge, perceptions and rhythm of work and thought		from a preconceived political agenda or an externally conceived set of assumptions
Stimulate the people (animation) to undertake self-analysis of their life situations (a self-inquiry into the economic, social cultural environment in which they live) and help them derive from such self-inquiry facts, figures and conclusions to serve as an intellectual base for initiating changes		the use of a closed framework of analysis or a social analysis carried out by outside intellectuals
Assist the people to organize themselves and to create their own organizations		organizing people into externally determined structures to serve goals set up by outsiders
Facilitate the actions for change decided by the People's Organizations (POs), and in particular assist them to deal with logistical and practical problems with which they may not initially be fully equipped to cope		implementation of externally conceived projects/programmes
Stimulate and assist the POs to carry out self-reviews of their their activities, including any failures, and to plan future actions		monitoring and evaluation carried out be by outsiders
Conscious measures taken by the external agent to make his/her role progressively redundant in order to pave the way for and thus ensure self-reliant capacity build up of the Pos		attempting to provide continued leader-ship and patronage or to project one's own image
Such a phasing out would necessarily require assistance in developing local cadres who could eventually replace the external agents		the use of a large number of external agents, which is costly and usually requires access to foreign funds

Elements of Animation

The process of animation leading to social transformation, argues Ambrose (1992), has the following components: vision, awareness, motivation and liberative action. In addition, the animation process itself carries with it a certain dynamics. What is this dynamics? Through all these, there is an underlying element that weaves them together - faith. One is required to dwell at length on all these elements. But in this chapter, I shall discuss each of these elements.

- *Vision:* Persons working with the poor experience the present reality of injustice and exploitation in society vis-a-vis the poor. This creates a tremendous dissatisfaction and makes one think and dream of a society where such evils would not be present. It is this concept of a new, future society that one longs for which we call 'vision'. It is this vision which makes a person an animator instilling in the poor a commitment to act to build a better society. Vision gives meaning to one's life and action embodying in it a value system that is transformative. The vision carries with it a particular world view, a way of perceiving and analyzing how society is organized. The animator serves as a catalyst transforming the animated to create a new future.

The animator also perceives this process as a divine task done in partnership with God who embodies a just society. Therefore, God's continuing presence provides support to and a focus for the group. This realization creates a new attitude in the animator that, irrespective of success or failure, it is his task to continue to work with people and motivate them. This is a personal decision and a dedication born out of an irresistible urge to bring about a just social order.

- *Dynamics:* Animation entails a series of actions that sets several processes in motion. Dissatisfaction with existing conditions makes a person visualise a new future which we have termed vision. It is this vision that converts a person into an animator. An animator will be irrelevant if the person does not have individuals or groups to be animated. The vision makes the animator seek out a group of people who are poor and oppressed to start the animation process. After selecting the group, the animator finds creative means to transmit the vision.

Communicating the vision effectively entails a process of gaining the attention and confidence of the group. This is accomplished largely through the credibility an animator establishes with the group. This credibility is based on the understanding by the group that this person is someone genuinely interested in their lives and is prepared to stand with them even at the cost of his or her own life.

Communicating the vision credibly also entails a process of awareness building that helps the poor understand the wider forces and mechanisms operating to exploit them. Once awakened to this reality, the poor begin to question this injustice. A self-confidence and positive self-image begins to take hold. As this occurs, the: animator also motivates them to mobilise themselves for collective action.

Once an action programme is undertaken collectively, this dynamics starts the process of bringing about a 'We' feeling in the group. Soon they realize that as individuals they are powerless and ineffective. Only when they unite to work together are they able to change the situation. They also realise that it is not enough to act as a single group. They must gather more groups together from different areas and to build momentum in their actions questioning and challenging the status quo.

Setting short-and long-term goals is another aspect of the dynamics of the animation process. Critical reflection on their situation enables the group to decipher the limited possibilities available to them in their environment. It also allows the group to assess their circumstances and take appropriate decisions. Some of these decisions may be short-term while others are long-term oriented. As people's self-image improves leaders emerge from within the community itself who become the medium to express the resourcefulness of the group and hence are service able to the group. These leaders imbibe the vision fully and march in union with the group towards the set goal.

All that we have described above can be called the dynamics of the animation process. When such a dynamics is introduced into the community, it induces change not only in the individual but also in the community itself. The poor who are awakened enter this process and set in motion a series of actions which can result in making the poor a powerful force to transform society.

- *Awareness:* Awareness is another essential element of animation. To be aware means to be conscious of what happens in one's surroundings. It is not mere knowledge of the situation but a knowledge that probes into the root causes of problems and understands the mechanisms that maintain the status quo.

The first moment of awareness awakens the poor's self-esteem helping them to see that they are children of God who desires their well-being. It is this sense of dignity and self-respect which Pcnable a person to look beyond the immediate problems of survival. This was the experience of Freire's peasants and of the women who came to Mallika's assistance.

When we are aware, we have the possibility to arrest another person's control over us. How does this happen? The poor are often told that they are poor because of the sins of their past, because of their own laziness or because of God's will that they be poor. The poor have heard this so often that they accept it without questioning. Awareness breaks through this complacency allowing the poor to analyse the situation uncovering the root causes of the problem. Realizing that the injustice they suffer is not their fate, the poor take up actions to transform their community. This realization impels the poor to take action because inaction means allowing oppression to continue. Therefore, awareness in the animation process is intimately linked to specific actions.

Another important dimension of awareness is the strong group identity that results creating in people the capacity to initiate as well as sustain the involvement of its members. This necessitates that the group seriously assesses their relative strengths and weaknesses. This enables them to foresee difficulties and move forward only when the poor fully get involved. Awareness is an important step towards empowering the poor liberating them from the shackles of their superstitious beliefs.

- *Motivation:* Motivation is an inner urge to attain a desired goal. A well motivated person can succeed not only in turning his or her problems into opportunities but also in realizing the goals she or he has set in life. Motivation springs from within. A committed person can inspire another to attain the same goal. Thus the contagious nature of commitment is itself a motivating factor. The poor are normally motivated only to secure basic needs. But, the animation process enables the poor to move from their normal behaviour to a higher level of longing for social transformation. It sets the direction and in turn becomes a motivating factor.

Motivation induces courage to accept challenges and face the future without fear. It raises the person to constantly transcend self in order that the entire community may rise up together. Paulo Freire's peasants understood their self-dignity as children of God which motivated them to claim their common identity in order to tackle the root causes of the problem. This self-transcendence is possible only by the faith of the community in God expressed in its stand for communitarian values.

- *Liberative Action:* Liberative action is the acid test of animation. It is this action that sets the community on the road to true freedom and liberation, a goal to be attained in the future. The change induced among the poor is not merely for economic or material benefits. It is primarily a cultural change. It is a change in the thinking pattern of the poor to opt for a better quality of life.

Liberation must be understood at two levels personal and social. The individual members must go through the painful process of shedding personal interests bringing about a change in their individualistic ways of thinking and their attitudes and acquire a position to act on behalf of the community.

- *Faith Element:* Faith is the driving force in the entire process of animation. It is faith that searches for deeper awareness of the situation and it is faith that motivates the person to get involved in action. Even if failures come on the way, nothing stops the person from pursuing his goal. Every failure is counted as a stepping stone to move forward. It enhances further search in the direction of the goal.

One basic realization that the group attains is that God is present in their midst. They see their actions as being undertaken by God through them. God is the author and supporter of this movement. Thus animation is a goal-oriented process aiming at making God's rule come about in society, so that all people will do God's will respecting and recognizing one another as brothers and sisters and thus live in happiness, peace and harmony.

Our concern with animation is to raise awareness and critical consciousness in the marginalised and oppressed people and to channel their energies towards building a new future instead of employing them for mere survival. The poor are the primary agents in this task and their resourcefulness is maximised in their collective efforts.

The community gains a deeper understanding of the present reality, absorbs the vision and analysis imparted by the animator and identifies the role of each one of them in building up the new society. Gradually the community gains confidence to act together in the performance of this task. It is this solidarity that motivates the community to take action. It brings an experience of freedom and liberation to the people which further strengthens their confidence to get involved in collective actions. Every action moves the community forward towards its goal when it is well guided by constant reflection. Thus, action becomes liberative allowing the growth of the entire community instead of the gain of a few individuals. The awareness of the community of its strength to achieve the possible and at times even the impossible, reflects the dimension of faith of the community. Thus, the process of animation has an inbuilt dynamics to evoke a sustained commitment from the people. The following sections deal with the various elements of animation to reveal this hidden treasure.

Internal and External Facilitators

Groups need meetings that make progress, and good facilitation can make this possible. A skilled facilitator, or process manager, designs an effective process and guides the discussion so that it gets results. Facilitators can be either internal to your group, or external. Both types have advantages and disadvantages. While the trained external facilitator intervenes through praxis and an action reflection process in the lives of the poor to release their creativity, the internal facilitators emerge from within the process. The external facilitator does not go to the poor with inputs. The Bare Hands approach gives the facilitator immediate identity that distinguishes him/her from other deliverers of welfare, who come with services. Internal cadres are those who are responsible individuals and can give time to the community. Initially there is skepticism about the external facilitator who comes with Bare Hands. A facilitator after entering the village, starts interacting with the poor, acquires identity with them poor and begins the dialogue process. A facilitator does not tell the people what to do or hurriedly organize them as in PRA or RRA to receive inputs. They first investigate their reality, and then starts saving and then organize themselves for action.

Animator and Facilitator

The role of outsiders may be conceived as consisting of two main elements, namely: *Animation* and *Facilitation*. Animation, according to Wignaraja and Sirivardana (2000:242), is a process of assisting the poor to develop intellectual capacity to investigate the reality of their life-situations, analyze relevant issues, understand the factors creating poverty and deprivation and through such understanding to perceive self-possibilities for change. The process of animation helps in breaking mental barriers and showing possibilities for change. They are animated when they understand the reality and perceive possibilities for changing that reality. The outcome of animation is conscientisation and awareness creation. Animation is the outcome of a specific mode of interaction between the outsiders and the poor. These persons are called catalysts or animators.

They can be outsiders to the particular location or persons thrown up from within the local process. The essence of this interaction mode is the evolution of a subject-to-subject relation between the two parties (replacing the conventional subject-to-object relation). The poor have a knowledge-base rooted in experience, practice and living with nature and society. This knowledge has its own validity and rationality. On the other hand, outsiders bring with them knowledge derived from formal education. These are two different knowledge streams each having its own scientific basis. The delivery approach to development seeks to transfer formal knowledge to the poor and disregards the poor's own knowledge as unscientific or irrelevant. It is a subject to object relation. On the other hand, a participatory approach seeks to achieve an interaction between the two knowledge streams creating a mutual learning process. It is an interaction between the two worlds, capable of systematizing the knowledge of the poor, creating new knowledge and generating seeds of change. Animation seeks to break the dichotomy between subject and object and to evolve, as far as possible, a relation between two equals.

Such an interaction mode, argue Wignaraja and Sirivardana (2000:243), requires the adoption of a dialogical approach and even these steps cannot be taught or applied mechanically. Teaching, instruction and transfer of skills will be replaced by discussion, dialogue, stimulation of self-reflection and analysis, and sharing of experience and knowledge. The starting point for this purpose should be an attempt to initiate a dialogue with the people on the reality of their life-situations. The reality that people face (poverty, underdevelopment and deprivation) should be posed to the people as a problem for their investigation, as a challenge for them to respond. By raising key questions such as: why do we have low incomes? why is our production low? Why do we buy our needs at high prices and sell our produce cheap? Can we not find new kinds of work in the informal sector? What access do we have to different kinds of resources? why do we eat certain kinds of food? The catalyst/animator has to stimulate/provoke the people to come out with ideas, issues and factors and that they perceive as barriers in improving their livelihood. Dialogue with the people must lead to a re-evaluation of poor people's own basic perceptions of issues pertaining to their life-situations.

Dialogues enable the poor to systematise their own experiences. This is also an investigation into their reality and research. Besides, the interaction with the animator enables them to improve their knowledge-base by absorbing the relevant formal knowledge brought in by the animator. The outcome is a synthesis of their own and formal knowledge. From such problematisation, analysis and the knowledge creation that follows, they will begin to perceive self-possibilities for change which form the basis for their actions to change the reality. Hence, actions are rooted in the investigations and analysis carried out by the people themselves assisted by the animator. This approach may be contrasted to the normal run of development projects where the underlying social analysis for projects is carried out by outside professionals and the poor are at best involved in the implementation phase of the projects.

Wignaraja and Sirivardana (2000:243) further argue that animation is a necessary but not necessarily a sufficient condition to enable the poor to undertake and manage development actions to transform their realities. There are a host of factors which operate to keep the poor passive rather than active. Given their behaviour patterns (often non-innovative and non-experimental in nature) and lack of experience in undertaking self-initiatives for change, it will take time before they begin to develop the confidence in their abilities to bring about changes. Hence, an external input in the form of facilitation is often required to assist the poor to initiate actions for changing their conditions. Animation by breaking mental barriers begins to show possibilities for change. Facilitation is an attempt at assisting the poor to overcome practical barriers to action.

Facilitation is a service role which assists people to undertake specific actions designed to strengthen their participation; these actions can include the acquiring of particular technical skills, gaining access to available resources or translating their own ideas into feasible projects. The catalyst/animator with his/her formal education, wider knowledge of socio-economic contexts, and links with the governmental machinery and service delivery personnel should be able to assist the people to cope with their practical problems. Such facilitation can take several forms such as:

- Assisting them to acquire basic management and, where necessary, technical skills, building on their own knowledge Assisting them to develop contacts with formal service agencies, institutions and bureaucracies relevant to their action prograrnmes, and to develop skills and knowledge required to deal and negotiate with them.
- Assisting them to improve their access to material resources, such as: credit available within the socio-economic system.
- Assisting them to translate their developmental ideas into concrete activities and programmes and to work out the implementation plans (a kind of consultancy role).
- Facilitation can also result in the reorientation and sensitisation of the support system, as a result of the ensuing dialogue, apart from the more formal re-training of the support system staff.

A facilitator is expected to perform the following functions:

- Offer support in the strengthening of local diagnostic skills (identifying problems or bottlenecks) whether or not the problems are technical.
- Where useful and possible, help with the analysis of how desired change may be facilitated by technology.
- Be prepared to support the community in tackling issues of power and vested interests where these are factors in the changes that are needed.

What are Facilitation Skills?

Facilitation skills are essential for anyone seeking to guide a group of people through a process of learning or change in a way that encourages all members of the group to participate. Each person has a unique viewpoint and valuable knowledge to share. Without their contribution, the group's ability to understand or respond to a situation is reduced. The facilitator's role is to draw out knowledge and ideas from different members of a group. They can help them learn from each other and think and act together. Facilitation is about empowering others. It involves letting go of control over the outcome of a process and giving that responsibility to the group.

The Purpose of Facilitation

The Brazilian educator, Paolo Freire, believed that education should be liberating. Rather than giving learners answers, education should aim to increase the learner's awareness so that they are able to identify problems and their causes, and find solutions to them. A facilitator's role is to help a group through this process by asking questions that encourage new ways of thinking about and analysing their situation. The facilitator does not know all the answers. Their role is to help the group think critically about their own needs and interests, and to make decisions for themselves. There should be a balance between offering ideas to guide the group and patiently listening and questioning.

The facilitator's role is also to encourage each member of the group to contribute to the best of their ability. Everyone has valuable knowledge and a valuable contribution to make. But people can be reluctant to share their knowledge. They may lack the confidence or may not consider what they know to be important. Sometimes people do not want to share their knowledge because it gives them a certain amount of power and advantage over others. However, when we do share our knowledge, everyone benefits. The person sharing it does not lose it after giving it away, and the person receiving it has received something new which they in turn can pass on to others. The facilitator's role is to build trust and respect between the members of the group and to encourage dialogue and learning, from which the whole group will benefit.

What Makes A Good Facilitator?

A good facilitator has certain personal characteristics and skills that encourage group members to participate in a discussion or activity.

Characteristics of a Good Facilitator

A Good Facilitator should be:

- Humble.
- Generous.
- Patient.
- Understanding.
- Accepting.
- Inclusive.
- An encourager.
- An enabler.
- Affirming of everyone's knowledge.
- Sensitive to the needs of others.
- Willing to learn from mistakes.
- Dynamic, a motivator.
- A good listener.
- Good at summarising others' ideas.
- Confident.
- A good communicator.

Facilitation is about getting a balance between these different characteristics – for example, between being a good listener and a good communicator, between being patient and dynamic. Although certain skills and techniques can be learnt and applied, the most important thing is the facilitator's ability to relate to individual group members in a way that makes them feel valued and encouraged. This will affect the way the whole group works together and what it will achieve.

Skills of a Good Facilitator

A Good Facilitator should:

- Be well prepared whilst remaining flexible.
- Think and act creatively.
- Deal with sensitive issues and manage people's feelings.
- Encourage humour and respect.
- Negotiate with and influence others.
- Keep to time without being driven by it.

'Facilitation is the art, not of putting ideas into people's heads, but of drawing ideas out.

ANON

'A facilitator is best when people barely know that he or she exists... A good facilitator is one who talks little. When the work is done, the aim fulfilled, they will all say, 'We did this ourselves.'

LAO TZU 500 BC

Good facilitation is not easy. It is like conducting a music band. Though the music is written down already, it is the conductor's job to build the right atmosphere, to help each individual to be their most creative and to blend everyone together to form an exciting and productive team. A facilitator is like a conductor. Great music emerges when everyone is communicating together. Good communication, just like good music, is more about listening than talking. If everyone plays all the time, there is nothing but an unpleasant noise. It is the conductor's job to help each player to listen to others, to keep quiet until it is the right time for them to play.

A good facilitator is interested not only in whether an objective is achieved but how. The process is just as important as the product. The process of building local knowledge and skills is vital if the group is to gain the confidence and ability to initiate and sustain positive change.

It is very important for a facilitator to understand contradictions. The poor in South Asia are not only divided among themselves but are also dependent on others who are often rich and powerful. This is a disempowering process as this dependence results in passivity and also dependent on others who are often rich and powerful. This is a disempowering process as this dependence results in passivity and feeling that their situation is unchangeable. There are two levels of dependency, one created by the system and the other by the poor themselves. The poor are dependent and there are contradictions there. Most conventional poverty strategies work on a harmony model. But a political approach requires recognizing of the poor who can work together in groups (SAPNA 2001).

Facilitator Roles for Intervention

Group Dynamics Adviser	*e.g.*, bringing to the groups attention an important issue *e.g.*, a disruptive group member; when they are conspiring to suppress; so that the problem can be faced and handled.
Consultant	about management processes, organizational structure.
Process Facilitator	*e.g.*, suggesting ways of getting a difficult decision unblocked.
Learning Facilitator	*e.g.*, to insist on more time being spent on process review rather than task.
Coach/Tutor	*e.g.*, giving advice on a selection of a management technique; getting people to keep 'learning logs'.
Co-ordinator/ Convener	*e.g.*, arranging meetings or other events on behalf of a task group.
Scribe	*e.g.*, using a flipchart to help a group with its work.
Observer/Note taker	Keeping notes in two columns - task and process - for use in reviews.
Discussion Leader	*e.g.*, temporary take-over of the group process to get them back on track.
Exemplar/ Demonstrator	*e.g.*, showing a learning group how to review its process.
Catalyst/Assumption Challenger	*e.g.*, a creative intervention that lifts a group out of its rut of tramelled thinking.
Norm Establisher	*e.g.*, create a climate in which it is OK to give and receive personal feedback.
Resource Investigator	*e.g.*, helping to satisfy a group's need for information not immediately available.
Pace-maker	*e.g.*, if a group does not manage its time well, then chivying it to complete the task.
Reminder	*e.g.*, drawing attention to the group's remit, if this seems forgotten.
Dynamiser	*e.g.*, after the event, stimulating people to implement any plans they have agreed.
Task Facilitator	*e.g.*, helping a group analyse the problem.

Social mobilisation is primarily a mechanism of empowerment, although certain activities may not be directly empowering. It involves a broad range of measures for sensitising disadvantaged people about problems which they are faced with and the societal context of these problems; it commonly promotes organization of the disadvantaged for increased strength and influence; and it usually involves practical advice and training for combating problems and improving the quality of life.

For effective empowerment, the social mobiliser should conscientiously try to abide by the following principles of work:

- Facilitate process of learning through soft while persistent mediation, avoiding directives from above.
- Actively promote, even insist on, genuine discussion and consultation before decisions with implication for more than an individual are arrived at.
- Promote engagement in concrete development activities which people can readily see the purpose of.
- Act as a liaison person between weak local groups and outside institutions, while promoting the ability of the former to manage such relations on their own over the longer-term.
- Commonly, seek to promote suitable local persons for the role of future change agents in the communities.

In pursuance of these principles, the mobiliser should work in conformity with additional underlying principles of participatory development. Most essentially, the facilitator should approach each situation with humility, have a deep sense of respect for every participant, genuinely recognise local knowledge, and develop a capability to relate to complexity and uncertainty in a relaxed while purpose-conscious manner.

Although the emphasis should normally be on promoting people's own analysis and action, much social mobilisation incorporates elements of advocacy. That is, the mobiliser and the organization which he or she represents want to promote some social values or development ideal.

Work among disadvantaged people to help them improve their lot – being very common in social mobilisation – is usually grounded on an ideal of greater social equality, and the advocacy element may become particularly strong when this involves organization and other measures against oppression by other people.

Other examples of advocacy may be to promote adherence to some religious tenets, create greater sensitivity to and respect for ecological principles, and promote people's understanding of democratic principles of governance.

Development organizations and social mobilisers need to be highly conscious about the mix of advocacy and self-analysis in their mobilisation efforts, and they should clergy their attitude and approach in open discourse, both within their organization and in their interaction with people who are or are intended to be beneficiaries of the organization's work.

How to be a Good Facilitator

Be an Active Listener

Good facilitators show interest in what people have to say. They listen closely enough to summarise or paraphrase what is said, to pick up on the direction of discussions and to detect underlying attitudes or judgements. Active listening is key to all facilitation skills.

Be Observant

Good facilitators notice group dynamics, including who is speaking and who is not, and how various groups of people interact, *e.g.*, women and men or different ethnic groups. They use observation to understand how and when different methods must be used to ensure that everyone has the opportunity to participate.

Ask Questions

Good facilitators use questions to start, focus and deepen the learning of the participants. A simple 'Why?' is often enough to move a discussion to a deeper level. Who? What? When? Where? and How? are all good questions for bringing out details.

Be Flexible

Good facilitators respond to the needs of the participants and are willing to adapt or change methods, tools and questions in order to do so.

Be Organized

Good facilitators are well organized. All necessary materials and logistics are prepared so that people do not lose time and become frustrated. The facilitator keeps the overall development objectives in mind throughout the entire process.

Be Knowledgeable but Clear

Good facilitators are knowledgeable about development, but they are also able to communicate in simple statements and to ask focused questions. Good facilitators speak in plain language and do not use fancy words or jargon.

Be Assertive but not Controlling

Good facilitators know when to intervene during discussions and when to stay quiet. Facilitators focus on mobilising the knowledge of the participants and provide guidance when the tasks are unclear or when the discussions start to lose focus.

Community Mobilisers as Facilitators

There is no 'ideal' community mobiliser. People from all kinds of backgrounds can be effective community mobilisers. Attitudes, behaviours and skills are more important than who the person is or what qualifications they may have. Community mobilisers need to be able to motivate and establish strong and trusting relationships with different kinds of people. They need to be committed to the community mobilisation process and to be willing and able to participate in the community at times and in places that are convenient to community members. Different community mobilisers will face different opportunities and challenges. Building a team of community mobilisers provides an important opportunity to combine different skills and experiences.

Community members are likely to feel more relaxed with mobilisers who share important characteristics with them, such as: gender and age. Community members acting as mobilisers will have a strong understanding of their community and the relationships within it, which will facilitate acceptance by the community. Mobilisers who are from the locality will find their local knowledge useful and may already have good contacts with the community. So wherever possible mobilisers should be members of, or peers with, the community group they will be working with (*e.g.*, young men working with other young men). It is very helpful if community mobilisers can be not only from the same group or community but also positive role models.

Mobilisers from outside the community may find it easier to ask questions about social or cultural issues that challenge assumptions and stimulate discussion. They may bring new ideas and experience from mobilising with different communities. Language is an important issue in community mobilisation. Community mobilisers should speak the language normally used by community members. Expecting community members to communicate in a second language, or a language that is spoken by only certain community members, will seriously affect community participation and trust. There are no literacy or educational requirements for being a community mobiliser.

We should promote young development professionals as community mobilisers. They work with local communities and service providers and facilitate the project cycle. They are competent to dialogue with communities and to apply the relevant tools for good communication and co-operation.

What Skills do Community Mobilisers Need?

Community mobilisers need to combine a range of knowledge, attitudes and skills in order to be effective.

Attitudes include

- A willingness to examine and challenge their own assumptions, opinions and beliefs.
- A genuine respect for all community members.
- A non-judgemental and accepting approach.
- An understanding that different people have different views and perspectives.
- A belief in community capacity to take effective action.

Skills include

- Good communication skills, especially listening.
- Good facilitation skills to enable communities to conduct their own analysis of their lives and situations.
- Awareness of political, gender and cultural issues and relationships.
- An ability to challenge assumptions sensitively (*e.g.*, about the role of women).

Knowledge includes

- The community mobilisation process.
- The principles of community mobilisation.
- Knowledge of development programmes.
- Understanding of the ethical issues related to community mobilisation.

Other skills and knowledge that may be needed at different stages in the community mobilisation process include:

- An ability to help communities form organizations.
- An ability to identify capacity-building needs among communities (*e.g.*, leadership skills, networking and partnership-building skills).
- An ability to help communities mobilise resources.
- Advocacy skills.
- Project planning and management skills.
    - ❖ *Provide Capacity Building to Community Mobilisers:* Finding all these skills in one person is almost impossible! Community mobilisers will have different strengths and weaknesses. For example, a person may have very strong facilitation skills but limited knowledge of development programmes. Where possible, provide training or capacity building for community mobilisers to address important weaknesses, but remember that some skills take considerable time to develop. People often find it easier to learn new skills and knowledge than to change attitudes and beliefs. Providing intensive support from the start to inexperienced community

mobilisers from within the community may benefit the community more than devoting resources to training external people.

- *Balancing a Team:* Of community mobilisers by including people with different strengths and weaknesses will help address those weaknesses and enable community mobilisers to learn from each other.
- *Learn from Others:* People and organizations starting community mobilisation for the first time need to assess their capacity carefully. Identify key weaknesses before starting together with communities and plan how these will be addressed. Visiting communities that are already mobilising successfully, or organizations with experience in community mobilisation, can help identify skills and knowledge that need strengthening. Building partnerships with people or organizations that can provide ongoing capacity building is helpful.

Role of Community Mobilisers

- To facilitate dialogue, establish contacts and working relationships, encourage contributions.
- To initiate, encourage, advise, but leave the main responsibility to the local implementing partners.
- To contribute to bridge the gap between service providers and local communities.
- To strengthen the self-confidence and capacity of people to voice their interests.
- To encourage local entrepreneurs and leaders to invest into business and employment.

The community mobilisers role is to balance outputs and processes in the project cycle. They need to find an appropriate balance between facilitation and management or between capacity building and physical project progress. On the one hand, capacity building, encouraging people to contribute, establishing working relationships between local implementing partners and service providers take time and might result in slow progress. On the other hand, people will expect that at the end of the day, the project is completed and is of good quality.

Community Mobilisers have to Reflect on their own Perceptions and Attitudes

- *Roles and Responsibilities:* Community mobilisers are not 'heroes on the ground' who manage everything for 'their community'. Instead, they clarify which tasks are those of the local implementing partner, which those of the service provider and finally which are the ones for them-selves. Teaching and training others to take individual responsibility is the key task of community mobilisation.
- *Negotiating Space for Local Action:* Villages are no peaceful entities with everybody supporting each other. Village communities are diverse societies with different social classes, caste and gender. Different spaces have to be found for different social classes, *e.g.*, public meetings, informal gatherings, private 'chatting'. Vulnerable groups have to be brought into communication with the village elite.
- *Self-reflection:* Community mobilisers have to reflect on them-selves and their values: "Do we have and show respect for the poor? Do we empathise with the poor? Are we prepared to develop a close relationship with them?"
- *Relationship:* Space and time are critical factors in building relationships with people. Open and warm relations have to be cultivated. For instance, one may play with children, establish communication with them and then reach out to their parents more easily.
- *Joint Learning:* Learning is an ongoing process, and it is a collective action. Joint learning takes place when community mobilisers, villagers and officers exchange ideas and discuss. Community mobilisers learn and improve their skills by sharing their field experiences.
- *Do's and don'ts':* There could be a long list of do's and don'ts' in community mobilisation. Key principles are:
    - Avoid being a preacher and advisor, but listen in the first in- stance to what people have to tell.
    - Create a culture wherein people unreservedly express their ideas, fears, needs and aspirations.
    - Do not impose your advice and solution on people, but seek to jointly develop a way forward.

Personal Characteristics of Social Mobilisers

The term social mobilisers are sometimes also referred to as: community agents, community assistants, community workers, local catalysts, change agents, social workers, animators or facilitators. They must have integrity, passion, and commitment to people. In addition to these qualities they also must have the ability to:

- Recognise that everyone has a role to play and to create the space for people to fulfill that role.
- Accept that contradictions are part of leadership.
- Work skillfully and with modesty.
- Know where to get the facts.
- Match theory with practice.
- Be accountable and work in a transparent way.
- Be clear about one's strengths and weaknesses.
- Keep learning.
- Know when to follow.
- Listen deeply.
- Have a sense of humour.

Community Animator: One who Inspires, gives Life to, Invigorates

The role of an animator is rarely given a formal title within a group. However within most successful groups there will be at least one animator. These are people who bring new ideas, enthusiasm and a vision for making change possible. They rarely push themselves forward but have a real concern for the well-being and progress of the group. They don't just talk about new ideas, they make them happen practically. Animators believe in the potential of people in their communities and help provide the energy that is needed for change. The roles and responsibilities, and qualities of animators include are given below:

- An animator may be employed (or contracted) by an organization or by a local community to stimulate debate, discussion and action on issues or relevance to the community.

- The animator needs to be seen as non-partisan in this respect, with a broad remit to raise awareness, stimulate thought and involve the local community in identifying issues of importance to them.
- The animator will have leadership qualities in this context, in that she will act as a motivating element within communities, encouraging broad local involvement and participation.
- She will need to have excellent skills with people, an ability to listen and to speak, to draw out local issues, to co-ordinate group sessions and events.
- She will need a good, broad knowledge of community development and of the organizational map in order to advise and inform communities and agencies of activities elsewhere and to fit the unstructured aspirations of communities into an appropriate context, and promote partnership approaches.
- The animator will support community initiatives in obtaining appropriate support for the development of their ideas.
- Community Facilitator: One who Expedites, makes easy.
- A community facilitator will assist the community in the achievement of its aims, bringing skills and knowledge to whatever process the community is involved in to support the achievement of specific aims.
- A facilitator will act as a support person who enables the community to meet its aims.
- A facilitator will identify training needs in the context of the community's aims and support the appropriate individuals to gain those skills.
- Facilitators will have management and people skills which may be applied to specific projects or to community involvement techniques such as community conferences.
- Facilitation will usually be the follow on stage to animation.

What does a Social Animator do?
(Activities Undertaken)

1. Transfers knowledge.

2. Organizes the group.
   - supervises activities;
   - establishes priorities;
   - listens, speaks;
   - moderates;
   - manages conflicts;
   - motivates;
3. Builds trust.
4. Establishes co-operation with other groups; organizes meetings.
5. Seeks out leaders.
6. Supports, helps, activates social groups.
7. Builds coalitions.
8. Injects ideas.
9. Withdraws.
10. Does not impose.
11. Suggests - inspires, does not impose.
12. Co-operates, teaches, acts as a model.

How is Social Animation Work done? (Methodological Principles)

1. By using activation methods.
2. By providing personal example and examples from life experience.
3. By using the project method.
4. By initiating self-help.
5. By diagnosing through action.
6. By stimulating mutual engagement on behalf of the local community.
7. By making a contract with the group.
8. By seeking people to join in the work.
9. By creating a space for co-operation (integration).
10. By making it easier to understand problems and needs.
11. By animating people (seeking leaders).
12. By preparing the search for good solutions.

13. By organizing meetings.
14. By suggesting by not intruding.

Why? (Inherent Values)

1. To transfer knowledge, values.
2. It is a vocation.
3. To share one's own knowledge.
4. To form attitudes: moral, social, civic.
5. For self-fulfilment.
6. For satisfaction, pleasure, self-worth.
7. Has a debt of gratitude, wants to pay it.
8. Is tied to the community (need to serve).
9. Identifies with the community.
10. 'I don't have the disposition for normal work'.
11. Creative work, creativity.
12. Perceives problems that are important.
13. To improve the quality of life.
14. Because s/he is an animator.
15. Believes in the truth, beauty, good.
16. Has a vision of development.
17. Has such a need.
18. Wants to do something, unconventional, new.
19. To test him/herself in action.

For what Purpose? (What will be Achieved?)

1. To transfer knowledge.
2. To point out the road to people.
3. To facilitate the development of talents.
4. To teach certain attitudes (co-operation, accountability, responsibility...).
5. To implement programmes, projects.
6. To meet community, group needs.
7. To initiate community development.
8. To help people believe in their abilities.

The Profile of a Social Animator

Mission

In the belief that people are able to help themselves - we activate them as social animators through education, inspiration, support and motivation for the purpose of resolving local problems and for community development, based on the principles of respect for differences, partnership and tolerance. The role of an animator is rarely given a formal title within a group. However within most successful groups there will be at least one animator. These are people who bring new ideas, enthusiasm and a vision for making change possible. They rarely push themselves forward but have a real concern for the well-being and progress of the group. They don't just talk about new ideas, they make them happen practically. Animators believe in the potential of people in their communities and help provide the energy that is needed for change.

Functions

The accepted profile of the social animator is a representation of his functions (eight are specified) presented as a 'cluster' of abilities (knowledge, skills, attitudes, resources). Whereas 'knowledge' and 'skills' are apparent, 'attitudes' and 'resources' require additional explanation. By separating out 'attitudes' the significance of one's own example and the emotional aspect of animation is emphasised. The attitude of the animator must be consistent with the knowledge that is transferred. This is an ethical requirement, but also conditions the effectiveness of his work - an animator works primarily by changing social relationships. Each false impression resulting from an inconsistency between knowledge and attitude destroys trust, and thus the very foundation of animation work. The concept of 'resources' relates to the need to build them. Knowledge, skills and attitude should result in the creation of certain specific resources, which are the animator's 'storehouse' in fulfilling his various functions. One's own desk and chair are not the most important thing for an animator, but without these very resources, the animator will not be able to carry out the functions. In other words, if an animator is not able to transform knowledge, skills and attitudes into resources, certain abilities will be lacking to enable effective action.

The Functions of an Animator

Facilitator Facilitating Community Co-operation

- *Goals:* The goals of an animator's work encompass several levels simultaneously: the group, the chosen community, and the entire local community:
  - ❖ to develop a local network of co-operation and social communication;
  - ❖ to promote 'synergy' among the many actors of the local social scene working together.

Area	The Animator as a 'Reflective' Practitioner
Knowledge	• The animator has experience in group and community 'co-operation' and understands its strength and meaning. • He knows how to facilitate ('enable leading') in various situations and social activities to increase strength, creativity and influence; he educates himself in this area.
Skills	• Thanks to training and his own experience, he has the 'skills of facilitation' at his disposal (tools and techniques of running meetings and group work) used to enable groups, communities and local society to work together effectively. • He is able to encourage others to make new contacts in the community.
Attitude	• He is aware of the meaning and strength of synergistic relationships and social co-operation in groups and communities (based on observation and his own experience). He does not lead, but enables the emergence of accepted leadership. He knows how to make contacts in the community. • He is open to creating various forms of co-operation that include various partners. He is characterised by a partnership approach. • He is consciously aware of his own mission, which is to facilitate the co-operation of various social actors and powers. He accepts himself as a liaison and catalyst in community relations.
Resources	• He is able to identify potential community partners, co-operates with many people. • He has broad partnership contacts in the community.

The accent within the framework of this function is placed on co-operation, which is the basic mechanism used by an animator. It is worth emphasising the need for a certain 'delicateness' in using this mechanism, evidenced in an avoidance of such concepts as: leading, organizing, co-ordinating the establishment of mutual contacts among participants of community activities. We refer more to communicating and facilitating, to result in a situation where the residents and institutional partners enter into a new type of relationship. The 'facilitative' way an animator works should cause (at times force through the lack of directing) the participants of, say, a meeting on providing meals to children, not only organize something quickly (passing on the responsibility to the co-ordinator), but to better understand the causes and conditions of the problem, and above all to have everyone become personally involved (emotionally and actually doing the work) in the solution.

This approach of co-operation is based on creating new solutions and preparing the community to cope with other types of problems. But in order for this to happen, the animator must know how to avoid the temptation to manage and lead, which would certainly lead to effective action, but would not address its quality or future perspective.

Supporter

Strengthening and Equalising Social Opportunities

- *Goals*: The goals of an animator's work encompass several levels simultaneously: the group, the chosen community, and the entire community:
    - to combat marginalisation and the exclusion of various groups and communities;
    - to develop social and civic participation;
    - to infuse marginalised communities with faith, conviction and social skills;
    - to work towards inclusion and social cohesion;
    - to encourage the participation of disadvantaged groups in social and public activities.

Area	The Animator as a 'Reflective' Practitioner
Knowledge	• The animator is experienced in contacting and working with disadvantaged groups. • She has practical knowledge about the causes and results of social marginalisation and exclusion. • She understands the need to pay particular attention to communities that are threatened with marginalisation.
Skills	• She is able to initiate and guide self-help, support and learning groups. • She knows how to mobilise and motivate disadvantaged groups to undertake self-help, social and educational activities. • She knows how to organize and support local informational and educational systems for individuals and groups at risk of becoming socially excluded.
Attitude	• Sensitivity to social inequalities. • Tolerant of differences. • Actively works to combat social inequalities.
Resources	• She understands the situation of disadvantaged groups, knows people skilled in working in these types of communities. • She has information and contacts that enable her to work in communities threatened with social exclusion.

A basic challenge in initiating co-operation in local communities is addressing the differences among particular groups in the community, especially those that are marginalised. It is difficult, then, to talk about and introduce the principles of partnership and co-responsibility when a portion of the people affected do not have the power to participate. 'Preparing the actors for the game' is an essential function of the animator. How does one go about strengthening a group of the long-term unemployed so that they will be able to overcome their dominating personal problem (lack of work and its consequences for the family) and join in local activities on behalf of educating and providing new opportunities for youth? The role of the animator will not be that of resolving the problem of joblessness, but she will point out a new way of dealing with the problem (meeting other unemployed persons with positive experiences, self-help groups). The animator enables the organization of a given group (getting to know each other, choosing a leader) in such a way so that they not only see the problem, but also their own power which will help them cope better with their difficulties and also have a voice in other issues important to themselves and the community.

Educator

Moderating the Learning Situation in the Local Community

- *Goals*: The goals of an animator's work encompass several levels simultaneously: the group, the chosen community, and the entire community:
  - ❖ to develop the community education system;
  - ❖ to intentionally create opportunities for learning;
  - ❖ to learn from events and social actions;
  - ❖ to promote the sharing of experiences and knowledge.

Area	The Animator as a 'Reflective' Practitioner
Knowledge	• The animator understands that education and development is a lifelong learning process and does not have an exclusively formal character (courses, workshops). • He is experienced in using non-school learning methods. • He recognises the potential knowledge of ordinary people. • He understands the educational role of everyday social situations, as well as the need to plan various forms of learning for specific groups and communities.
Skills	• The animator is able to organize meetings or workshops that enable active learning based on the experiences and knowledge of the participants. He is able to use everyday social situations as learning experiences and, as a result, broaden the community's educational impact. • He is able to define the learning needs of individuals, groups and communities and then propose educational support (training, work shops).

	• He is able to lead workshops or self-learning meetings.
Attitude	• The animator is open to the social and educational condition of the community. • He is convinced that social and civic activities and situations have educational and developmental value. • He is engaged in creating and developing lifelong learning based on local community resources.
Resources	• The animator has identified people and organizations that are involved in formal and informal education. • He is able to identify people, groups and communities that can share their knowledge with others. He, or others in his team, is personally prepared to conduct active learning activities for the group and community.

Next to facilitating co-operation, the educational function is the very essence of preparing a community for development. Education, understood broadly as the development of abilities for active participation in social life, should pervade every activity of the animator. For this to happen, one cannot think of education solely as an activity connected to the formal educational system identified with a school. The animator must gain skills in the area of non-formal education and so-called, incidental or informal education. And again his role is not primarily to organize courses, workshops and other forms of training, but to recognise educational deficiencies and needs blocking the opportunity for community work (excluding and weakening specific groups).

Only then, based on this recognition, can an animator attempt to 'invite' or 'draw in' people to an educational activity. He consequently proposes that 'we do something together,' but in such a way as to also say 'let's prepare' and 'let's learn.' Moderating a learning situation is then based on foreseeing and provoking situations that are conducive to sharing knowledge and practical experiences during the implementation of a project (such as: building a play area for children, a water system, a local holiday), and, when necessary, securing the help of experts. In this understanding of education, usefulness and reflection on the connection between learning and action is more important than certificates and diplomas (although they may also be needed at times). Therefore, the animator's involvement in education touches primarily on the informal learning that takes place in everyday life that is not perceived as being taught something, but more as play, free time activity or work.

Specialists question whether and to what degree informal education can be directed. In the approach presented here, it is presumed that the animator perceives various forms of informal educational opportunities, uses them, attempts to moderate and link them (strengthens, ensures continuation and development) with forms of non-formal education (workshops, training programmes) as well as with the offerings of schools (especially those directed to the local community). By utilising various educational forms, the animator becomes a moderator of local community education.

Motivator - Engaging and Mobilising Society

- *Goals*: The goals of an animator's work encompass several levels simultaneously: the group, the chosen community, and the entire community:
    - to awaken individual and group action;
    - to develop social and civic participation;
    - to promote volunteerism, self-organization and social self-help;
    - to encourage participation in social and public activities;
    - to motivate residents to organize activities for the purpose of introducing specific and goal-oriented changes in the community.

Area	The Animator as a 'Reflective' Practitioner
Knowledge	• The animator is experienced in leading groups, in working with volunteers, non-governmental organizations and in civic campaigns. She has experience in motivating and organizing people to work together in the community. • She understands and knows the mechanisms of social self-help and self-organization. • She knows of practical examples of organizing and mobilising society. • She knows the characteristics and meaning of the functioning of 'small groups' and non-governmental organizations for social purposes. She also has knowledge of the formal and legal framework that governs social activities.
Skills	• The animator is able to work in small civic groups, taking advantage of their potential and dynamic. • She is skilled in the abilities of organizing activities as well as in activating and directing the social process. • She knows how to lead meetings and group activities related to addressing social needs, which she is able to identify. • She knows the principles of directing and leading groups and non-governmental organizations. • She is able to find and support developmental opportunities and motivate group and group leaders. • She is able to inspire the establishment of new civic groups and motivate them to independent action and co-operation among themselves. • She is able to organize broad campaigns to address local problems. She knows how to see the links between community action and local community development.
Attitude	• By her own example, the animator encourages others to become socially involved. • She is able to mobilise people to action in a planned way.
Resources	• The animator knows the main problems and needs of various communities. • She has information about existing civic and self-help groups in the community, she knows the community leaders. • She knows the needs and resources of the community as a result of conducting an assessment and preparing a map of local resources and needs.

'Imagination is more important than knowledge,' said Albert Einstein. And creativity is imagination with the reins let loose... The art of inspiring - indispensable in the animator's arsenal of skills - relies on creating such a community where the residents will be able, to the greatest extent possible, to meet their own needs as a result of their personal efforts. Many community members expect that something will rather be done 'for them' than 'by helping them do it themselves.'

Mobilising relies on using the skills of interpersonal relations (awakening, convincing, group work) to help others undertake and implement activities. By mobilising, the animator may cause a situation where things, issues or situations become possible, practical and easy for those who were not previously able to tackle them on their own. The concept of mobilisation includes: *encouraging, exerting influence, inspiring, stimulating people to act, causing people to want to act and to do so with pleasure,* in other words, it is *a power that pushes people to act in a specific direction. When a given activity is completed, motivation may disappear.*

Mobilisation is seen at many group stages and relations, and can be manifested primarily by:

- Granting trust.
- Identifying with the implemented or completed activity.
- Entrusting with responsibility.
- Allowing people to act on their own, the opportunity for self-control, responsibility for the final effect.
- Expressing satisfaction.

The systematic and mutual use of these practices prepares the group and community to mobilize at the moment it is tested, that is, when specific activities must be conducted in the community.

Thus in this context, it is rather a longer process than a set of techniques to use for the quick mobilisation of strengths.

Integrator - Developing Community Bonds and Communication

- *Goals*: The goals of an animator's work encompass several levels simultaneously: the group, the chosen community, and the entire community:

- to integrate and build the community's self-identity;
- to create flexible relationships between the various actors of the local scene;
- to create a platform for co-operation in the community;
- to develop the local community network.

Area	The Animator as a 'Reflective' Practitioner
Knowledge	• Based on experience, the animator recognises the meaning of interpersonal and inter-group relationships and bonds in the community. • He takes advantage of the various forms of workshop learning/improvement. • He is aware of the character, meaning and steps of the process of creating group and community bonds. He understands the meaning of cultural and social capital in creating an integrated local community.
Skills	• Group and community bonds are developed using intuition and planning. People will want to work in groups and with other groups as a result of his activities. He is able to delegate authority and tasks. • He is able to use in practice the basic techniques and tools of developing co-operation in a conscious and planned way (mediation, negotiation, moderating meetings). • He knows how to use the mechanisms of the network structure of community relationships. • He develops the group's mission.
Attitude	• He is aware of the significance of existing social relationships in groups and the community and of creating them. • He is open, tolerant and friendly. • He works on creating the climate/atmosphere of the group. • He consciously builds and reacts to relationships in the group and community.
Resources	• He is able to identify, gather and assemble data, bases, experts, etc. • He systematically broadens knowledge about the resources required to work as an animator. • He has contacts, partners in institutions, and knows how to call on them.

While the facilitator's function of community co-operation has a dynamic character, with an expectant effect in the form of a mutual effort for the purpose of doing 'something' effectively together, the function concentrating on community bonds and communication is more 'nurturing' in character. Within its framework, we come to know the community (map of the local community), identify specific groups and communities (as well as their problems), observe relationships and the patterns of communication. The essence of this examination is to make an estimate of the social capital, that is, the level of trust, self-organization and social solidarity.

With this knowledge about the degree of community integration, the animator works to address the identified factors blocking the functioning of the local community (for example, residents and newcomers, young-old, housing estate A and housing estate B) by starting with mutual communication.

These efforts are not undertaken with a specific, quick effect in mind. They are rather a strategy to get people representing various communities to meet, in its broadest meaning, and get to know each other (traditions, histories, ideas, prejudices, views, and misconceptions). Local events, especially the holidays of a given locality, are an evident sign of a community's level of integration. The way they are organized (from the top down by local authorities or by the cooperation of partners, commercial-recreational or civic-integrating) shows what has been achieved thus far (a form of motivation), and also uncovers the weak areas of a given community.

At such a time we see who becomes involved in community life, and who stands at the side. The time between such 'holidays' can then be devoted to various activities whose purpose is to bring specific groups of residents together in such a way as to enable them to do something together. Within this function, the animator refers not only to activating, but also, and perhaps primarily, to the community's emotions. In order to integrate a community, rooted stereotypes and prejudices must be overcome. Above all, we must reach for the positive emotions connected with a given place (history, the spirit of a place) and its people (historical figures, leaders), which is often referred to as the concept of 'small fatherland.'

Developer - Specialist in the Development of Local Communities

- *Goals*: The goals of an animator's work encompass several levels simultaneously: the group, the chosen community, and the entire community:
  - ❖ to develop programmes that organize and develop the local community;
  - ❖ to take full advantage of the resources and strengths of the local community;
  - ❖ to base local development on social and civic participation.

Area	The Animator as a 'Reflective' Practitioner
Knowledge	• The animator has practical knowledge about activating groups, communities and local society as a result of his own experience in systematically broadening her knowledge in the fields of organizing and local community development. • She has knowledge of the issue and community development methods.
Skills	• Project implementation is directed towards increasing the opportunities of groups, communities and local society. Projects of a social and educational intervention character are prepared based on a community diagnosis and identification of its developmental profile.
Attitude	• She feels the need to increase opportunities for the development of groups, communities and the entire local society. • She is interested in and wants to increase her knowledge about local community development.
Resources	• She is aware of the community's needs and resources, is familiar with the basic documentation regarding local development. • She has educational and programmatic materials on local community development mechanisms.

The 'developer' function consolidates various animation efforts by joining them into a specific overall strategy described as activating and developing the local community - or local community development.

The social animator must know how to relate and place her activities (at times disparate, focused on a small community or single problem) in the broader perspective of local community development. Work with a community of skin head youth is focused on an actual problem affecting a specific group, but it also relates more broadly to the entire local community. The animator should be able to orient herself and move within both these dimensions. Her work with a group affected by a problem (skinhead youth, the unemployed, physically challenged) should enable co-operation to occur so that the problem can be addressed by mutual efforts (first by defining it anew and understanding its causes), and next, connect this work to the life of the entire local community.

To do so, an animator needs knowledge and skills in community development, for this allows her to maintain her strategic direction during the many daily, small animation activities underway. While riding the wave of various people's needs and energies, one must keep in mind that these particular waves have to join in a broader perspective. When it is seen, it can also be shown to others so that it becomes an essential perspective and value for many. A mutually shared vision has great influential power, playing a mobilising and unifying role in the development of a given community.

Co-ordinator of the Social Project

- *Goals*: The goals of an animator's work encompass several levels simultaneously: the group, the chosen community, and the entire community:
  - ❖ to address social problems based on implementing projects;
  - ❖ to plan and introduce social innovations in the community;
  - ❖ to direct social projects.

The functions of the animator discussed thus far can be described as 'soft' abilities, referring to the complicated and delicate realm of interpersonal relations. The function of development project co-ordinator has a 'hard' character. With this function, various activities undertaken by the animator form a certain whole within a specifically determined framework - they become a project. When the term 'project'

Area	The Animator as a 'Reflective' Practitioner
Knowledge	• The animator has practical experience in implementing community projects. He understands the process of planning: from problem to vision and planning changes, from implementation to evaluation. • He has knowledge and knows how to use the principles of planning and designing social innovations. • He understands the steps and process of introducing change in the community.
Skills	• He is able to diagnose problems and plan social and educational projects (goals, methods, tasks, outputs and results). • He knows how to prepare grant applications with a team. • He bases his work on the animation project system. He sets measurable goals for innovative projects. He is able to co-ordinate and manage projects (team management, securing resources and funds, monitoring implementation and the change process).
Attitude	• He 'thinks and acts' using the project method. • The process is participatory - many partners engage in planning and implementing the project.
Resources	• He has knowledge about the group and community resources and problems. He knows about external sources of support for local community development projects.

is used, it refers to a social phenomenon in the form of an ordered process, where: the time of implementation, methods, partners, tasks, time schedule, budget and indicators of implementation are planned. In planning, the animator introduces factors ordering and co-ordinating his work. He perceives and reflects on the series of single activities he is engaged in (contacts, meetings, workshops) and places them in a logical sequence. Thus, the purpose of undertaking animation activities is not solely to engender activity (social change) regardless of its character, but to order it in such a way that it takes on a developmental dimension, that is, it better responds to human needs. The way to organize this process is the project, and specifically in the extended and long-term perspective, a programme of development (several projects).

Evaluator - Evaluating Social Change

- *Goals*: The goals of an animator's work encompass several levels simultaneously: the group, the chosen community, and the entire community:
  - to evaluate the effectiveness, efficiency and impact of implemented animation projects;
  - to correct projects that are underway;
  - to prepare future animation projects based on the evaluation of solutions used thus far.

Area	The Animator as a 'Reflective' Practitioner
Knowledge	• The animator knows the evaluation principles of his own social practice, as well as the principles and methods of monitoring and evaluating social and educational community projects.
Skills	• The animator is able to develop basic indicators for the project for evaluation and monitoring. • She creates and implements social projects and programmes utilising the principles of systematic evaluation. She changes her own and the team's animation practice based on the results of evaluation.
Attitude	• The animator accepts the need to assess project implementation and her own animation practice. • She recognises the necessity to systematically reflect on her work (through evaluation).
Resources	• The animator works together with people who are able to fulfil a monitoring and evaluative role. • She has contact with external evaluators.

As it befits a 'reflective' practitioner, one of the animator's functions is reflection - evaluation of her own work. Monitoring, and making changes based on its results in one's work, should not be an occasional procedure when accounting for donations, but one of the basic functions of an animator. This is even more important when considering that an animator's work deals with the delicate nature of interpersonal relations where it is easy to lose objectivity. There is a threat that emotions will reign, and though they are needed and indispensable, when evaluation is lacking, they can become so absorbing that there will be no room left for working together. This is why both self-evaluation as well as evaluation conducted by external observers is important. An animator should be psychologically prepared for this (willingness to undergo assessment) and have the required skills. In order for self-evaluation to be effective and provide real knowledge, clear and well-thought out procedures must be prepared, so that it isn't limited to just 'reflective musings,' though this is also useful. Contact should be established with external experts interested in animation work so that they can join the team as ongoing evaluators.

5 Facilitating Community Mobilisation

INTRODUCTION

There are two ways the word facilitation is used in community empowering. One is a facilitation method of training and organizing participants which is more effective than lecturing or preaching. The other is to set up an enabling environment of facilitating self-help, where the laws, the administrative regulations, procedures and practices, and the attitudes of leaders, technical experts and administrators support increased responsibility and self-reliance of low-income communities.

Almost all development programmes today have turned increasingly to participatory approaches to get work done better and faster. With this change toward greater use of community groups and committees, has come an increased demand for skilled *social organizers*. One approach to facilitation involves the social organizer in a very limited role – serving as the community organization's timekeeper, 'traffic cop' when discussions heat up, and recorder of the community decisions. The active facilitation approach sees the role of the social organizer somewhat differently, that is, as a temporary community or team leader. This leadership role has a very significant impact on community organization's effectiveness, despite the fact that the social organizer does not get involved in the content of the community organization's work. The social organizer employing the active facilitation approach enables the community members to focus their work on the task at hand knowing an unbiased professional is providing the structure, processes, and the push – this is probably the most distinguishing characteristic of the approach – to help the community organization get where it is trying to go.

Facilitation and community mobilisation needs may differ from subproject to subproject, and also from community to community. For example, a community requiring funds to build a simple trench may require much less facilitation than a water supply project. In the same way, some sectoral projects (*e.g.*, rural water supply and sanitation) prefer to select communities up front and provide intensive facilitation before subproject implementation. For other types of projects, such as education/health, mobilization of the community is done once a community has identified a priority, submitted an application, and received initial funding. Yet in others, particularly when trying to target very poor communities with little capacity, up front facilitation may be provided to help the community identify priorities and prepare a proposal. The information obtained at this stage feeds into the capacity assessment, taking into account their needs for technical assistance from preparation to implementation stages.

One of the main objectives of the facilitation process is to ensure that all community members, including women and marginalized groups, have been consulted. Facilitators use a variety of participatory techniques to mobilize the community, help them identify and prioritize needs, and develop a comprehensive plan for mitigating identified problems. Facilitators can comprise a range of actors, including NGOs that work closely with the community, staff or consultants working for central or local government, and/or community leaders who have been trained by the project.

Depending on the context, the process can last anywhere from one week to several months and may result in a community development agenda. During this process, communities –

together with community leaders and facilitators – provide concrete suggestions as to how the problems in their community can be overcome and how much financial and non-financial support they will require. The participatory process ensures that dissenting voices are heard and that consensus is built around the plan. This chapter highlights the areas and tools that would help the field workers make the process of community mobilisation more easy and effective.

Social Organizers as Active Facilitators

The social organizer in the active facilitation approach to group mobilisation has a strong attachment to the community organization, its members and its task. Unlike conventional Social Mobilisation approaches, in this approach, the social organizer shares responsibility with the community organization for getting their task accomplished or its failure and drop out. Marshall Ganz (2005) has described and elaborated the following characteristics of the social organizers:

- Organizers identify, recruit, and develop leadership; build community around leadership; and build power out of community.
- Organizers challenge people to act on behalf of shared values and interests. They develop the relationships, understanding, and action that enable people to gain new understanding of their interests, new resources, and new capacity to use these resources on behalf of their interests. Organizers work through 'dialogues' in relationships, understanding and action carried out as campaigns.
- Organizers interweave relationships, understanding and action so that each contributes to the other. One result is new networks of relationship wide and deep enough to provide a foundation for a new community in action. Another result is a new story about who this community is, where it has been, where it is going – and how it will get there. A third result is action as the community mobilizes and deploys its resources on behalf of its interests – as services or as advocacy.

- Organizers develop new relationships out of old ones – sometimes by linking one person to another and sometimes by linking whole networks of people together. Organizers work with people to interpret why they should act to change their world – motivation, and how they can act to change it – strategy.
- Organizers motivate action by deepening people's understanding of who they are, what they want, and why. Mobilizing feelings of anger, courage, hopefulness, self-worth, community and urgency, they challenge feelings of fear, despair, self-doubt, isolation, and apathy that inhibit action. They help people articulate their values as a shared story of challenges they face, why they must face them, and why others should help – rooted in who they are, where they've been, where they want to go.
- Organizers deepen understanding of how to act by creating deliberative opportunities for people to strategize how to turn resources they have into what they need in order to take advantage of opportunities to get what they want.
- Organizers focus on the taking of responsibility to act. Empowerment for a person begins with taking responsibility. Empowerment for an organization begins with commitment: responsibility its members take for it. Responsibility begins with choosing to act. Organizers challenge people not only to understand, but also to take responsibility, to choose, to make commitment, to act.
- Organizers work through campaigns. Campaigns are highly energized, intensely focused, concentrated streams of activity with specific goals and deadlines. People are recruited, programmes launched, battles fought and organizations built through campaigns. Campaigns polarize by bringing out those ordinarily sub-merged conflicts contrary to the interests of the constituency. One dilemma is how to depolarize in order to negotiate resolution of these conflicts. Another dilemma is how to balance campaign work with the ongoing work of organizational growth and development.

- Organizers build community by developing leadership. They develop leaders by enhancing their skills, values and commitments. They build strong communities through which people can gain new understanding of their interests as well as power to act on them – communities which are bounded yet inclusive, communal yet diverse, solidaristic yet tolerant. They work to develop relationships between a constituency and its leaders based on mutual responsibility and accountability.

Abid Ullah Jan (2001) in his book 'Developing Meso-Level Institutions' has argued that "the social organizer in the active facilitation approach to group mobilisation has a strong attachment to the community organization, its members and its task. Unlike conventional Social Mobilisation approaches, in this approach, the social organizer shares responsibility with the community organization for getting their task accomplished or its failure and drop out". The roles and responsibilities of the social organizer (SO), according to Abid Ullah Jan, can be summarized as:

- *Neutral Servant of the Community Organization*: As in all community organization facilitation, the social organizer in the active facilitation approach has an unbiased service role. He or she is bound to be neutral, that is, to treat all participants and all ideas in the community organization with the same respect. The social organizer has no interest in what decision is made, but has a strong interest in a decision being made; no preference for one outcome over another, but a strong preference that an outcome be reached; no preference that one community organization member or another being heard, but a clear interest in all participants having a chance to be heard.
- *Process Advocate*: The social organizer proposes processes for helping the community organization get its work done, invites ideas for process alternatives from community organization members, and ensures that the agreed-upon process is used so long as it is working. The responsibility of the social organizer is not to advocate one particular

process, but to advocate whatever process the community organization has agreed to use. In this way, the social organizer helps the community organization stay on a productive course.

- *Progress Advocate:* The social organizer is responsible for helping the community organization establish and maintain forward movement. It is this push factor that frequently earns the social organizer using the active facilitation approach the undying appreciation of community members. As progress advocate, the social organizer is continually assessing the community organization's progress toward its objectives and considering and proposing not only: Community organization processes, for example, ways to manage VO members interactions or optional decision-making methods, but also Task processes, for example, breaking the community organization into different sub-committees to get several tasks done concurrently, proposing a planning step be inserted before the community organization launches into a discussion of an issue, or eliciting commitments to follow up assignments by individual members of the community organization.

Abid Ullah Jan (2001) in his book 'Developing Meso-Level Institutions' has given in great details the various methods for facilitating social mobilisation which are given below.

How does an So Facilitate Mobilisation?

Compared to conventional community mobilisation methods, the social organizer in the active facilitation approach has a more extensive role in planning for, facilitating, and following up on a community's progress. What the social organizer does includes:

Before the Community Meeting

- *Purpose and Objectives for the Meeting:* The social organizer meets with the office bearers of the VO before hand to find out what the meeting is expected to accomplish and thoroughly plans as to what does he want to achieve from this meeting.

- *Develop an Understanding of the Agenda Points:* Through such means as review of related materials or advanced surveys or interviews of the VO members, the social organizer becomes knowledgeable about issues affecting the community organization and the meeting.
- *Design the Meeting:* Ideally the office bearer/activist should be involved in a meeting from the initial planning so that he or she can design the whole meeting.
- *Preparation and Circulation of the Agenda:* To make it a habit and part of the new organizations system, the social organizer ensures that the agenda contains key information and is circulated before the meeting to all VO members.

During the Meeting

- *Facilitate the Community Members:* To make sure that the community learns the proper way to conduct its meetings, the SOs have to conduct the initial meetings as demonstrations. The broad category of activities that an SO needs to keep in his mind at such meetings includes:
- Manage the agenda and progress of the community organization:
  - ❖ adjust time, tasks, and processes;
  - ❖ give the community organization feedback on progress;
  - ❖ encourage the community members;
  - ❖ keep the meeting objectives before the community organization.
- Ensure that all VO members and ideas have a chance to be heard.
- Help the community organization reach consensus and make-decisions in other ways.
- Help the community organization resolve differences.
- Track ancillary issues (issues raised at a time when the community organization can't productively deal with them).
- Track follow up or action items.

- *Help the Community Organization Plan for follow up:* Ensure that next steps, who's responsible for doing what, and due dates for follow up are clearly established before the meeting ends.
- *Help the Community Organization Evaluate the Meeting:* Offer evaluation questions for the VO members to answer, covering both task and process aspects of the meeting.

After the Meeting

Ensure that meeting registers are properly maintained – Often the Secretary or President of the community is the best person to take responsibility for quick preparation of the meeting minutes in the meetings register, including at a minimum: Date; Objectives; VO members; Decisions or outcomes; and Follow up assignments. The ways in which the active facilitation approach is carried out and techniques for social organizers to use are described in the sections that follow.

Designing a Meeting

Social organizers work very closely with the office bearers of the VOs throughout the process of designing a meeting. The amount of time and effort that goes into meeting design varies according to the duration, complexity, and size of the meeting. For meetings to be most effective, VO members need to have:

- A clear understanding of the objectives and intended outcome.
- A clear understanding of the process(es) to be used and confidence in the social organizer who will manage the process(es).
- A clear understanding of the role of everyone in the room (including themselves).
- Confidence in the utility of the meeting; belief the goal is reachable.
- The opportunity to participate substantively.
- The opportunity to have input to process changes.
- Confidence that follow up will occur and be managed.

- *Learn VO Members' Objective:* The SO must know about the objectives and expectations of the community members from a specific meeting and needs to address those concerns during the meeting to avoid any grievances or discouragements.
- *Gathering Basic Information:* Find out, or help the office bearers decide: how many people are expected to attend the meeting, how much time is available for the meeting, and when and where the meeting will be held. Also, the SO should convey this information to the persons who will accompany the SO to such a meeting.
- *Learn about Issues Impacting the Meeting:* Again, in meetings with the initiating communities, the office bearers/ activists, some or all of the VO members, or from other sources, the SO should focus on such issues as:
  - the history of the issue and/or the community organization;
  - relationships within the community organization or between the community organization and others;
  - feelings within the community organization about the task or the community organization.
- *Consider the Complexity of the Meeting:* Although most of the community meetings are not that complex and the SOs take them for granted. But this becomes their habit and they start taking some serious meetings for granted as well. Determining the complexity of the meeting and its facilitation requirements involves analysis of the following considerations:
  - length of the meeting – The longer a meeting is, the more complex the facilitation challenge;
  - nature of relationships among the VO members – If, for example, VO members have a history with one another that is characterized by personality differences or difficulty reaching agreement, the facilitation requirements for a meeting of the community organization are greater;

- ❖ difficulty of the subject matter and the task – Clearly, a meeting to propose a redesign of the agency by a consensus of the VO members is more complex than meetings to exchange information on the status of State consolidation efforts.

- *Reviewing Meeting Materials:* It is important that you be familiar with any materials that will be presented or discussed at the meeting particularly when there are guests invited, who are not regular members of such meetings, such as programme officers or a chief guest etc.
- *Developing a Draft Agenda:* The SO must learn and try to impart the same to the community activists and office bearers how to include not only topics and times, but also processes to be employed in the meeting. The SOs must be guided by a number of design considerations as they develop the agenda of any important meeting, whether that be with the community or the programme planning.
- *Review Draft Agenda with Community:* It should be the community to draft and share the agenda with the Social Organizer, but in the initial stages, or some extremely important meetings in which outsiders are involved, depending on the circumstances, the SOs should review the draft agenda with the meeting planners from the community, and, if time is available, circulate it to VO members for comment.

Opening a Meeting

Meetings often open with welcoming and other introductory comments by the convener or other significant player in the organization initiating the meeting. The main objective of opening a meeting is to begin the process of creating an environment in which VO members:

- Know what to expect and what is expected of them.
- Believe the meeting is a good investment of their time and energy.
- Develop trust in the social organizer and the other VO members.

- Have confidence that a product will result from the meeting.

How to Lead Community Organization Discussions

Discussions can be a creative and productive way to develop a shared understanding of a subject within a community organization and to explore a subject in some depth. Discussions are a critical precursor to a community organization developing a consensus decision where that is a goal. The reasons for having community organization discussions in a meeting are several:

- Help VO members get interested and involved in a subject.
- Enable VO members to fill in information gaps and to clear up misunderstandings.
- Enable VO members to review and analyze subject matter that has been presented to the community organization verbally or in writing.
- Identify areas of agreement and disagreement in the community organization so that differences can be understood and resolved.

Understanding Team Formation

Social organizers need a sound understanding of community organization dynamics in order to be of real help when working for their team building. Like all good teams, the community organizations have an especially challenging task in the early stages of their development. Five stages of development have been identified:

Stage 1: Forming

In which the members of the VO meet one another and begin exploring their roles in the team, their relationship with one another as team members, and ideas about how the team will operate.

Stage 2: Storming

In which members of the VO begin to understand their differences, encounter divergent ideas about their task, their roles, and the processes by which they will do their work.

Stage 3: Norming

In which the members of the VO begin to recognize a common interest in the team and its task, develop common goals for the team, clarify roles of individuals within the team, and develop strategies for working together smoothly.

Stage 4: Performing

In which the members of the VO work productively to achieve their goals and carry out their work.

Stage 5: Adjourning

This is the real testing time in which members of temporarily established VOs, having completed their task, prepare to disband. This stage is generally characterized by reluctance to part.

How to Help a VO Through the Forming Stage

The social organizer can help a team during the Forming stage by:

- *Ensuring VO Members Really get to know one Another:* The SOs shall provide a process for in-depth introductions if VO members don't know one another's behaviour. If they do know each other, but have not worked in the team situation before, the SO shall offer a process by which they can begin sharing their values about the work at hand, for example:

"As you introduce yourselves, please explain the reason or reasons why you signed up as a team member for this organization."

"As you introduce yourselves, please describe what you would like to see come out of working as team member of this community organization."

"After you have introduced yourselves, please develop a joint statement – a few sentences – about what you will be able to accomplish as a team that might not have been accomplished or accomplished as well if you were doing this work as individuals.

- *Establishing Ground Rules:* When the SOs first begin working with a new VO, for example, they have to facilitate the VO members as a team through development of a series of ground rules.

Operational ground rules, for example, to:

- Meet once a week.
- Hold meetings to one hour unless all VO members agree to extend the time and can stay.
- Rotate recorder and timekeeper roles among VO members.
- Have one person (rotating) collect agenda items from VO members and circulate agenda by two days before meeting.
- Have recorder write down meeting minutes on the spot or at the most circulate record of decisions made to VO members within one week of meeting.

Process Ground Rules, for Example, to:

- Make decisions by consensus.
- Write consensus proposals on flip chart before polling for consensus.
- Where consensus cannot be reached timely, assign a sub-team to develop a proposal (working outside of the whole team).
- Take consensus poll by a showing of: thumbs up for agree with, thumbs to the side for can live with, thumbs down for cannot live with.

Behavioural ground rules, for example, to:

- Listen to and respect others' experiences, ideas, concerns, insights.
- Be candid – put real issues on the table, including areas of disagreement.
- Actively seek consensus – look for common ground, be open to compromise, offer consensus proposals.
- Deal with issues affecting the team in the team – don't complain about the team outside of the team.
- Speak one at a time; raise your hand to be called on if discussion gets heated.
- Creating feelings of inclusion – The SOs and the community leaders shall use non-judgmental, supportive language and behaviour, for example, they shall: *Acknowledge* and reinforce different thinking, and working

styles in a positive way *vs.* expecting all team members to adopt a particular, narrow set of beliefs, or practices; *Respond* to challenges in a receptive, non-defensive manner, establishing an open dialogue with all members of the team *vs.* demeaning or closing off discussion of concerns expressed by some members; *Support* each person in the team, especially when outlying views are expressed or special needs or problems emerge *vs.* allowing any individuals to become isolated in the team.

How to Help a VO through the Storming Stage

As a social organizer you can help a VO to work as a team during the Storming stage by:

- *Dealing with Differences Openly:* Bring differences out into the open; use the ground rules to encourage different points of view being expressed, listened to, and respected.
- *Handling Issues Affecting the VO, in the Team:* Help the VO members explore differences in team members' background, so differences in point of view can be understood in context. Involve all VO members in resolving issues, for example, when issues about the team's work are raised by one or a few people, encourage the whole team to help define, analyze, and resolve the issues. Encourage the VO members to work out their issues together, and not to bring up complaints or disagreements outside the team.
- *Having Team Members Work Together in Mixed and Changing Sub-community Organizations:* Provide opportunities for team members to work with each other in various combinations, for example regroup them for different activities. This will give everyone a chance to get to know and trust all other members of the team.

How to Help a VO through the Norming Stage

The SOs can expedite the VO's progress toward and through the Norming stage with these approaches:

- *Get the Team to Agree Explicitly on what it is Trying to Achieve:* The SOs must facilitate in way to have the community members develop a consensus statement of the organization's vision, mission, or common purpose early on in their work together. Social organizers must instill the habit of having team members discuss what the objectives are for that specific situation at the start of each meeting or each new task.

- *Help the VO Develop Common Values*: For example, the activists should lead a discussion on the importance of the project at hand, possible positive outgrowths of their efforts, or what would make this project or effort the biggest possible success. The VO may also benefit from a discussion of what is a team, so that they can establish common values about themselves as a team.
- *Create Opportunities for Shared Experiences*: The SOs should provide chances for community members to *(a)* develop their understanding of issues together, for example, making exposure visits, or attending expert presentations, etc., *(b)* perform tasks together, make assignments to sub-community organizations rather than individuals, or *(c)* evaluate team progress together.
- *Offer Opportunities to take Risks Together:* For example, if the VO is to make a presentation to higher management about the community's work, the SOs shall encourage them to do it together. Or if a particularly difficult project has to be undertaken, the SOs should have them do it, or at least plan it, together.

6 MOBILISING YOUR COMMUNITY
METHODS AND MODELS

INTRODUCTION

Community mobilisation is a proven development strategy that has helped people around the world identify and address issues related to sustainable development of rural poor. Community mobilisation not only helps people improve their living conditions, but by its very nature strengthens and enhances the ability of the community to work together for any goal that is important to its members. The end result of a successful community mobilisation effort, in other words, is not only a 'problem-solved' but the increased capacity to successfully address other community needs and desires as well. Among other benefits, community mobilisation efforts can:

- Increase community, individual, and group capacity to identify and satisfy.
- Their needs.
- Improve programme design.
- Improve programme quality.
- Improve programme results.
- Improve programme evaluation.
- Be a cost-effective way to achieve sustainable results.
- Increase community ownership of a programme.

Like any development approach, community mobilisation is not a panacea; it is not the answer to every development issue nor the right approach for every community. And even within the same community, it may be the right approach for certain developmental issues but not for others. In the right circumstances, however, it has been proven to be a powerful tool for unleashing the potential of individuals and communities around the world.

Community mobilisation is a capacity-building process through which community individuals, groups, or organizations plan, carry out, and evaluate activities on a participatory and sustained basis to improve their living conditions and other needs, either on their own initiative or stimulated by others.

Community mobilisation is a deliberate process of involving local institutions, local leaders, community groups, and members of the community in taking action on a particular issue. It is potentially an effective strategy for creating change in the community because community mobilisation can:

1. Improve the probability of the initiative to reach a broad audience by involving people who have a variety of roles within a community.
2. Minimize the risk of introducing unacceptable ideas or messages that could appear foreign to the community and/ or target audience.
3. Contribute to sustained behavioural change (Many efforts suffer a drop in behaviour change after the programme is over.)
4. Encourage local capacity building and promote investment in objectives.

Who can do Community Mobilisation?

Communities mobilise themselves! However, they may need support from the outside. Supporting the process from the outside requires a range of skills, experience and understanding. Organizations that reflect the principles and values of community mobilisation will provide more effective support to community mobilisers. People and organizations considering involvement in community mobilisation need to make sure that they have sufficient capacity, commitment and resources to support a community to achieve sustained change.

Leadership for Community Mobilisation

Communities most able to mobilise effectively have leadership characterised by the ability to:

(i) Include both formal and informal leaders.

(ii) Provide direction and structure for participants.

(iii) Encourage participation from a diverse network of community participants.

(iv) Implement procedures for ensuring participation from all during group meetings and events.

(v) Facilitate the sharing of information and resources by participants and organizations.

(vi) Shape and cultivate the development of new leaders.

(vii) Cultivate a responsive and accessible style.

*(viii)*Focus on both task and process details.

(ix) Be receptive to innovation and risk-taking.

(x) Be connected to other leaders.

Source: Adapted from Goodman *et al.* (1998)

Prerequisites for Community Mobilisation

Some important prerequisites for achieving god community mobilisation are:

- An agency philosophy in which local authorities and communities are viewed as equal partners deserving of respect and transparency; a commitment to a significant long time scale of involvement; a commitment to the concept of community ownership.
- Agency staff has a long term commitment to the project and shares the agency vision stated above.
- Donors who are sympathetic to the approach of community participation and ownership and are willing to provide adequate flexibility for a responsive project.

Community Mobilisation in Practice

Before embarking on community mobilisation, it is essential to be familiar with basic information about the community: stakeholder analysis. Identifying individuals who can explain the dynamics of the situation can be very difficult.

Once such persons have been identified and are willing to be interlocutors as well, their help is invaluable. Initial information about the relevant history of the community, its important governance structures, various interest groups and stakeholders, and problems and issues can be collected. At the same time information about the project/programme objectives, strategies, resources available, and time frame can be shared.

Social change is a complex process. Many factors work behind it. We can develop an overall social awareness by influencing these factors to disseminate common message to the general people. Through social mobilisation a kind of pressure can be exerted on the individual, family or society to ameliorate their living conditions.

Poor people remain busy with his day-to-day works. Due to the curse of poverty they do not dare to go beyond their traditional thinking. They cannot go beyond what they do daily. To bring them out of this orbit there should be a greater awareness in the society. Social mobilisation cannot be developed suddenly. It is organized through a set of steps.

Mobilising the Community

The goal of the mobilization plan is to raise public consciousness about the issue, garner citizen support, and create a critical mass of active programme participation. Its early focus should be on assessing attitudes, determining expectations, providing problem-impact information, and developing and using information as a catalyst for community action and involvement.

Basic needs must be met before more advanced needs can successfully be addressed. Stakeholders are no longer interested in a basic need after it is met. A group, an organization, or an individual will remain open to challenge as long as there is a sense of security about basic needs being met.

Some programmes define themselves as 'community mobilization programmes' in their title, goals, objectives, activities, and indicators. Many others make use of mobilization methodologies in order to accomplish programme objectives in a more participatory and empowering manner. Whether implementing a targeted community mobilization programme, or applying community mobilization methods to a programme with different overall goals, there are tools and approaches that are common and proven. However, there is a great deal of room for creativity in adapting mobilization activities or combining tools in order to meet the specific needs of a programme or community. What will work best in the context is determined by many factors and takes curiosity to discover. A few questions to consider:

1. What really motivates this community?
2. What are the main interests among community members at this particular time?
3. What are their hopes for the future?
4. What cultural practices are positive for the community that the mobilization process can reinforce?
5. What resources, heritage or local knowledge do community members value most?
6. Whose voices are missing from decision-making in the community?
7. Are there external influences that are helpful or harmful for the community that projects should take into consideration?

But remember, there is no one way to 'do' community mobilization. Different organizations/agencies have developed different models for mobilizing the community to accomplish different goals. In what follows, attempt has been made to present in brief the salient features and characteristics of different models of community mobilisation which the practitioner of community mobilization can adapt to suit the requirements of their clientele. More details on these models can be obtained from the web-links given.

(i) Joshi and Moore Model.

(ii) CIRDAP model.

(iii) All Together: Community mobilisation for HIV/AIDS, International HIV/AIDS Alliance Model.

(iv) Tanzania Advocacy Partnership Programme (TAPP).

(v) Southern African AIDS Trust (SAT) Model.

(vi) HRD Centre Sarhad Rural Support Corporation (CSRSC) Model, Peshawar, Pakistan.

(vii) IFSP Model, Sri Lanka.

(viii) SNVL Model, Nepal.

(ix) PILLARS Guide.

(x) ICSSA – Independent centre for strategic studies and analysis (ICSSA) Model Health Communication Partnership (HCP), USAID.

(xi) Wignaraja And Sirivardana Model.

(xii) Future Generations' SEED-SCALE Process for Community Change Model.

(xiii) W.K. Kellogg Foundation and The Healthcare Forum Model.

(xiv) Mercy Corps' Community Mobilization Approach.

(xv) Social Mobilization as a Strategy for Poverty Alleviation – Experiences From UNDP-Supported South Asia Poverty Alleviation Programme in India.

JOSHI AND MOORE MODEL

Joshi and Moore (2004) argue that in principle, one can distinguish four different mechanisms or strategies that external agencies can use to encourage the mobilisation of the poor. Two or more may be combined in practice, but they are best treated separately for purposes of exposition.

(i) *Provocation:* In reality, the most widespread mechanism by which governments in particular succeed in mobilising the poor may be by angering them by treating them badly: failing to truck in emergency drinking water supplies during drought; forcibly displacing people to build highways, dams or shopping malls; compulsorily acquiring food grains from producers at low prices, etc. Provocation is potentially a powerful instrument, but one that rarely can be wielded with finesse or precision and which anyway involves first hurting the poor. It does not merit further discussion.

(ii) *Conscientisation:* This is the practice of despatching 'social mobilisers' to empower the poor by encouraging them to examine their situation (usually collectively) and, hopefully, to decide collectively to do something to change it. This technique is most commonly adopted by non-state organizations - political parties, religious organizations, and other NGOs of various kinds. Agencies that employ social mobilisers to work with the poor in relation to agency programmes – and there are plenty of such cases in the development field, including government agencies – are vulnerable to two kinds of moral hazard. First, they have every incentive to control the process and discourage mobilisation once it becomes uncomfortable for them. Second, as we illustrate in the next section, the agencies and their field staff easily slip into the role of salespersons, using conscientisation techniques to 'market' to their clients (the poor) the products that the agency has available, even if they are inappropriate. Casual evidence and logic suggest that where both the conscientisation process and programme management are in the same hands, authentic mobilisation is unlikely. Conscientisation is far more likely to be effective if employed by one external agency to mobilise the poor in relation to the activities of other agencies. It can be a powerful strategy, but is intrinsically oppositional. It is properly part of the armoury of non-state actors, not of governments. When used by government agencies, it is unlikely to generate effective mobilisation.

(iii) *Organizational Preference:* Government agencies, in particular, are well placed to mobilise the poor by giving preferential treatment to grassroots organizations that claim to represent the poor. This preference can have two main components: recognition and licensing of certain categories of organizations (and not others); and channelling resources to the poor through those organizations, in order to strengthen the organization and encourage the poor to become involved. These kinds of arrangements are generally labelled 'corporatist'. But corporatism has a bad reputation. In Anglophone culture in particular, corporatism is associated with statism and not with democracy or an autonomous civil society. Are we not just opening the door to co-optation: institutional arrangements through which the state mobilises and organizes socio-economic groups in its own interests and in ways that closely circumscribe the autonomy of the organizations involved and their capacity genuinely to represent the interests of the poor Co-optation is a potential threat whenever a grassroots organization enters into any relationship with a powerful external agency, but this is especially so within corporatist structures.

However, co-optation and demobilisation of grassroots organization are not the only potentially 'unbalanced' outcomes of corporatism. There is a tradition of political analysis that focuses on the opposite process: the gradual assertion of independence by organizations initially established or shaped by and in the interests of state agencies. At the extreme, this can lead to the 'capture' of state agencies by the societal interests that they are attempting to organize. True, the poor have limited resources to help them struggle for autonomy. But they often have room to manoeuvre in relation to external agencies. Even while they are being used or exploited, grassroots organizations may exploit the relationship for their own purposes. In particular, they can enjoy leverage and bargaining power if the external agencies *(a)* are disunited, with elements within them seeking support and allies from other sources *(b)* focus their attention and energies elsewhere, leaving grassroots organizations with considerable local autonomy by default; or *(c)* are dependent in some way on a level of performance from grassroots organizations that can only be achieved through permitting them autonomy and initiative. Even explicitly corporatist systems can generate organizations that bring to the poor both resources and some degree of – often heavily contested – organizational autonomy. For grassroots political entrepreneurs have incentives to move into these organizations and to try to expand their scope and autonomy. For example, the corporatist rural workers unions that were established in rural Brazil by military regimes in the 1960s provided both 'cover' behind which local politicians, trades unionists and social activists could operate and legitimacy for parallel organizing activities conducted by the Catholic Church. They helped to lay the basis for the rich network of social movements for the rural poor that are found in present day Brazil (Houtzager 1998). The very existence of privileged corporatist unions encouraged opposition trades unionists to enter them and compete for power. In some cases this has generated levels of union activism and responsiveness to members well in excess of the standard expectations for corporatist arrangements (Pinhanez 1997). Similarly, the corporatism practised by Mexico's long-term ruling party (the PRI) has provided the means for the development of partly-autonomous local movements of the poor by opening up competition for control of public resources at local level. For example, locally-organized food councils were given control of food stores, supplies of subsidised basic foods and means of transport. Not all food councils were dominated by the local elites or by the local representatives of the PRI. There was continual struggle around these programmes, that partly reflected divisions within the PRI itself. Jonathan Fox views the struggles as an important part of the story of the gradual widening of the scope for autonomous associational activity in Mexico (Fox, 1994).

Depending very much on the political context, corporatist arrangements for giving organizational preference can encourage the poor to organize on their own behalf. We should not dismiss them as irrelevant to our concerns. They are however less than ideal. There are four significant characteristic problems:

1. Any degree of local organizational autonomy that is achieved is constandy under threat, and has to be continually reasserted.
2. Insofar as the organizations receive and redistribute public money, they may become a major charge on the government budget, with much of the benefit going to the non-poor – as happened in the Mexican case cited above.
3. The fact of organizational preference may result in local organizational monopoly, and then in lack of

accountability and misuse of resources and power. This was often the case, for example, with the corporatist rural workers unions in Brazil, with their guaranteed income from the state and monopoly control over pension funds (Houtzager 1998).

4. Corporatist sponsorship of poor people's organizations is potentially a useful if limited means through which 'friends of the poor' within state agencies can help empower them.

(iv) *Creating an Enabling Institutional Environment:* The *conscientisation* and *organizational preference* strategies are activist: they involve external agencies directly doing things on behalf of the poor - and that activism itself leads to moral hazard. The main argument of this paper is that there are considerable opportunities to stimulate the effective, autonomous organization of the poor by adopting a more *parametric* strategy: establishing and maintaining a framework that would encourage poor people themselves to take a more active role. This is now orthodoxy in the context of government policy towards the private sector: do less directly and concentrate more on creating an enabling environment. A similar argument applies to public action and the political organization of the poor. The environment in which poor people and external organizations interact is frequently inimical to collective action by the poor. It is characterised by so much uncertainty and arbitrariness that investment in collective action is not worthwhile. External agencies should focus more on creating incentives to collective action, above all by removing the obstacles that they themselves create. Four dimensions of the performance or behaviour of external agencies are of special interest to us:

- *Tolerance:* We take it as given that collective action on the part of the poor is more likely where the political environment is not hostile and punitive. The fact that little more is said by us on this reflects our belief that the point is obvious, not that it is unimportant.

- *Predictability:* This refers to the extent to which external programmes are stable over time in content, form, and procedural requirements. The more predictable a programme, the more it is worthwhile for politicians and social activists to invest in learning about it and in trying to mobilise around it.
- *Credibility:* This is essentially a behavioural concept: the extent to which, in their relations with the poor, public officials can be relied on to behave like good partners in an enterprise, *i.e.,* to do their job correctly and reliably.
- *Right:* The extent to which *(a)* the benefits received under external programmes are recognised as moral or – better – legal entitlements, and *(b)* there are recognised (preferably legal) mechanisms that the beneficiaries can access to ensure that these entitlements are actually realised.

This looks like a wish list. The key point, illustrated by the case studies, is that it is not a list of the necessary conditions for the creation of an enabling institutional environment. A relationship can be highly enabling in one or two of these dimensions even when the general environment appears quite bleak. External agencies do not have to perform well on every dimension in order to generate positive results. Context is very important. The relationship between poor people and external agents can be enabling both when, it appears generally concordant (*i.e.,* co-operative and harmonious), and when, it is discordant (characterised by tension, conflict and distrust).

CENTRE FOR INTEGRATED RURAL DEVELOPMENT IN ASIA AND PACIFIC (CIRDAP) MODEL

The Centre on Integrated Rural Development for Asia and the Pacific (CIRDAP) is a regional, intergovernmental and autonomous organization. It was established on 6 July 1979 at the initiative of the countries of the Asia-Pacific region and the Food and Agriculture Organization (FAO) of the United Nations with support from several other UN bodies and donors.

In the CIRDAP model it is argued that social mobilization is not a ready-made product available in a super-market. It is a participatory process where people are educated, organized, motivated and enabled to undertake social enquiry and analysis for understanding their life situation and taking decisions and actions to change it for their well-being. Such a complex process cannot be achieved in onetime transaction. The following stages have been documented in some projects involving social mobilization process.

- *Reconnaissance Phase:* This phase is basically meant to explore or survey the area focusing on initial planning and operational aspects. As part of social mobilization, the project team tries to understand the situation, diagnose the contextual dimensions, and build up rapport with the villagers for further collaboration.
- *Awareness Building:* As part of the project, an intensive effort will be made to generate awareness on various programmes planned in the project area and educate the intended beneficiaries on the roles and responsibilities of various agents involved in the project. Having studied project area and the living conditions of the poor in the project area, the project team would finalize, in consultation with the villagers, the type of interventions to be undertaken.
- *Sensitization Phase:* This phase in social mobilization involves sensitizing the senior personnel, project management team and other department officials connected with the poverty alleviation efforts. The project personnel undertake extensive tours to the project areas to explain the social mobilization strategy to the people. This period is also used to identifying, study the functioning of NGOs and other development partners working in the around the project area and seek their support for possible collaboration.
- *Institution Building Phase:* The project will use social counselling as a means to enable people to realize the adage 'united they stand, divided they fall.' In this phase, the institutional framework will be firmed up. Any alliance building with NGOs and development partners

will also be formalized during this phase. The project would also organize some exposure visits for the beneficiaries so that peer-group learning can be hastened and attitudinal changes could be achieved. The frame work on thrift and credit would be developed. The village level workers could be trained in technical skills to help the women self-help groups. It is also aimed to increase the quantity and quality of social animators and catalysts well versed in planning, mediation, managerial and implementation skills.

- *Consolidation Phase:* Social mobilization is a slow process. Organizing the poor would take some time. Usually, the help of NGOs is sought to facilitate the social mobilization process. The quality, size, resources, expertise, credibility and spread of the NGO are a critical factor in achieving this. But the basic principle is that whatever output is achieved under social mobilization must be consolidated through better facilitation, supervision and monitoring of the activities of the beneficiaries under the project interventions.

INTERNATIONAL HIV/AIDS ALLIANCE, 2006, MODEL

Source: http://www.ovcsupport.net/libsys/Admin/d/Document Handler.ashx?id=909

The International HIV/AIDS Alliance (the Alliance) is the European Union's largest HIV-focused development organization. It was established in 1993 as an international non-governmental organization to support community action on HIV/AIDS. In its toolkit on "*Community mobilisation for HIV/AIDS*, the alliance describes the process of community mobilisation. It has been argued in the toolkit that community mobilization is a capacity-building process through which individuals, groups or organizations plan, carry out and evaluate activities on a participatory and sustained basis to improve their health and other needs, either on their own initiative or stimulated by others.

How to Mobilise Communities

The process of community mobilisation is flexible, responding to the different circumstances and needs of various communities. There is no fixed model for community mobilisation and the time scale will vary from community to community. However, there are usually six stages in community mobilisation:

Stage 1: Starting together – identifying and involving different stakeholders and getting organized.

Stage 2: Assessing together – learning more about the community and the problems different people face, and identifying possible solutions.

Stage 3: Planning together – prioritising problems and deciding how to solve them.

Stage 4: Acting together – taking action and implementing activities to address the identified problems.

Stage 5: Monitoring and evaluating together – considering the results and impact of activities, and using monitoring information to adjust plans, including monitoring and evaluating the community mobilization capacity-building process, as well as activities specifically to address the identified problem.

Stage 6: Scaling up together – learning how to do more activities or expand existing ones.

Stage 1: Starting together

Starting together means deciding with the community where we should start mobilising, as well as with whom, when and how. It introduces the community to us and us to the community. It involves getting the commitment of the community to the process and beginning to learn about the development situation in the community. The overall aim of starting together is to build trust with the community. It is perhaps the most critical stage of the community mobilisation process, as how we start often sets the tone for how we will continue.

Starting together helps to:

- Engage community members in responding to problem solving efforts right from the start.
- Agree broad objectives of the mobilisation process with the community.

- Build trust between the community and your organization.
- Develop a model of participation on which to build community mobilisation.
- Build self-esteem and confidence among community members.
- Identify or develop co-ordination mechanisms with community members and stakeholders.
- Avoid repetition of existing activities and identify unmet needs and gaps in services.
- Avoid conflict; for example, due to people feeling left out of the process.
- Encourage community ownership of future initiatives right from the start.

Where, when and with whom do we mobilise?

In order to mobilise communities successfully, we need to consider carefully where, when and with whom we mobilise. Our own priorities about which communities to mobilise with will influence our decision about how to mobilise. Governments and donors may also influence our decision. The community is key in deciding when, where and with whom to start mobilising. There are a number of practical issues to consider.

❖ *What information about needs already exists?* Start by gathering as much information as possible about different areas. We can use sources such as research reports, government departments and people with knowledge of the area. Information about different areas and the communities living there is likely to be incomplete at this stage, and we need to use our judgement about gaps and people's opinions about different areas. Exploratory visits to different areas and a rapid assessment may be helpful.

❖ *Different people's priorities:* Be aware that government and donor priorities about where and when we mobilise may be influenced by political or other concerns. Their ideas also may be based on incomplete information about communities and needs in different areas.

- *What activities are already taking place?* We need to consider the activities other communities and organizations may be already carrying out in different areas and any activities they may have planned. Your mobilisation process might be able to complement or scale up existing processes. However, we also want to minimize overlap and duplication of effort. Two similar community mobilisation processes in the same community can lead to confusion and even conflict.
- *Consider the logistics of mobilising in different areas:* For example, are there particular concerns such as security? If so, how will this affect community mobilization efforts? Are we able to access an area and co-ordinate our activities in an area easily? In a further example, community mobilisers should stay where community members are, or as close as possible. This helps mobilisers to develop a deeper understanding of life in the community and demonstrates their commitment to the community. It also makes it easier for mobilisers to be available at times and places convenient to the community, and reduces logistical and transport difficulties.
- *Where is the greatest need?* We need to work with communities in greatest need.
- *Some communities can be very hard to reach*. They may be invisible to outsiders and their existence not generally acknowledged. For example, in some places the existence of men who have sex with men is not recognised by the wider community. But these hard-to-reach communities are often the most in need. Starting together, involving many stakeholders and using participatory tools such as mapping tools will help us learn more about the existence and identities of different communities.
- *The motivation of the community*. Where possible, we start community mobilization when a community has also expressed interest in the development process and in development issues.

- *Are people able to participate freely?* Where barriers to participation are very high (*e.g.*, when community members cannot meet freely) we may need to establish relationships with gatekeepers or other stakeholders before we can decide when to mobilise. People whose basic needs are not met (*e.g.*, for food and shelter) are likely to find meaningful participation in community mobilisation activities difficult. People involved in illegal activities such as drug use or migrant workers without permits may be unable to participate in meetings or discussions for fear of harassment or arrest. Communities with the greatest needs are often among the hardest to reach, and it is important not to dismiss the possibility of mobilizing successfully because there are many obvious difficulties. Be aware that in some situations there may be significant risks to community members who start to mobilize.
- *When we have the capacity to start:* Before we mobilise, we need to assess our capacity. Do we have the skills and resources necessary to mobilise effectively? Do we need to address any weaknesses before we start? How can we do this? We start community mobilisation when we are confident that we have the commitment and resources to work with the community for long enough to achieve sustainable results.

Stage 2: Assessing together

Assessing together means building the capacity of the community to carry out a detailed exploration of the development issues existing within it. The assessment focuses on broad areas of concern identified by the community during Stage 1. We use a series of participatory tools to enable community members to identify and analyse issues, share knowledge and ideas, enhance their knowledge of the situation and begin to identify the way forward. The knowledge, skills and understanding we develop by assessing together helps mobilise a community-led response to development.

Assessing together helps to:

- Provide detailed information about development issues in the community for planning together *(see Stage 3).*

- Increase general community awareness, knowledge and understanding of development-related issues.
- Enable specific community groups to share knowledge and ideas, so helping to develop appropriate and effective interventions.
- Build relationships with and between stakeholders.
- Build understanding of the perspectives of different community members.
- Build community ownership of the process, increasing effectiveness and sustainability of mobilisation.
- Build skills and capacity of community members in the assessment team.
- Build self-esteem and confidence among community members.
- Contribute to the impetus for community action.
- Build trust between all stakeholders.

Stage 3: Planning together

Planning together means deciding how we and the community will respond together to address the different problems and issues identified during the assessment. Together, we review the current situation by analysing the assessment findings. We then prioritise the most urgent problems and needs. We choose strategies to address these issues depending on their feasibility, impact and sustainability. Planning together also involves deciding how these strategies will be put into action. We need to agree the practical details of who will do what and when. We also need to decide how we will monitor progress towards our shared vision of the future.

Planning together helps to:

- Develop a shared vision and sense of purpose in the community of how they can cope with development issues.
- Use the experience and knowledge of many people to select the most appropriate strategies to respond to problems raised during the participatory assessment.
- Inform and interest community members and stake-holders in the intervention.

- Co-ordinate the involvement of all stakeholders.
- Make sure that the activity plans are appropriate for the community and the groups within it.
- Build community ownership and control of the plan.
- Clarify expectations within the community regarding the plan.
- Assist effective and efficient use of resources.
- Provide a community framework for action and monitoring progress.

Stage 4: Acting together

Acting together means:

- Doing what the community planned with their active participation.
- Solving difficulties in carrying out activities.
- Co-ordinating our activities with other stakeholders.
- Staying motivated and managing our expectations.
- Monitoring, developing and adapting our plans.

Acting together helps to:

- Co-ordinate the efforts of different stakeholders in order to improve the effectiveness and efficiency of the mobilisation.
- Solve day-to-day problems.
- Build the skills and capacity of community members to mobilise.
- Develop community ownership of the mobilisation.
- Build relationships between different stakeholders.
- Use learning to improve the quality and effectiveness of strategies and activities.

Stage 5: Monitoring and evaluating together

Monitoring and evaluating together helps us to assess the progress we are making towards our aims and objectives. It enables us to answer important questions, such as:

- How well are we doing?
- How far are we from meeting the aims and objectives we have set ourselves?

- Are we doing the right things?
- What difference are we making?
- What do we need to change about what we are doing or how we are doing it?

Monitoring and evaluating often overlap: they answer the same questions, they are talked about together and we can use the same tools for monitoring and for evaluating. However, it is also useful to think about how monitoring and evaluating are different from each other. Monitoring is a routine process. We use it to adjust and improve our plans and activities on a frequent basis. Evaluation is a more in-depth assessment of what we have done, what we have achieved and what impact there has been on poor people.

Stage 6: Scaling up together

Scaling up together means doing more activities in order to increase our impact on poverty situation. We can scale up together in several ways. We may work with more vulnerable groups or communities; for example, starting together in new locations or with new communities. We may add new activities to address needs within a community that complement those we carried out in our original mobilisation process. We may also add in new types of activities, such as advocacy, networking or resource mobilisation. It is important to plan scale-up carefully and to be realistic about what we can achieve. Scaling up often involves learning new skills and working with other people and organizations. It means that we evaluate our experience, capacity and resources, and decide how to expand our activities, while maintaining the quality and effectiveness of what we do.

Scaling up together helps to:

- Increase the impact of our activities by reaching and involving more people living in poverty situation.
- Increase our range of activities, meeting different needs in the community.
- Enable learning and skills-sharing across communities.
- Increase our influence on poverty alleviation policy and decision-makers by combining many voices.

- Strengthen sustainability of activities by building links to external resources.

TANZANIA ADVOCACY PARTNERSHIP PROGRAMME (TAPP) MODEL OF COMMUNITY MOBILISATION

Source: http://www.impactalliance.org

From January 2002 to September 2005, Pact Tanzania implemented the Tanzania Advocacy Partnership Programme (TAPP). In its 'community mobilisation manual;, the TAPP argues that community participation does not happen by itself. It must be stimulated, encouraged and facilitated. This manual is aimed at those who are seeking tools, ideas and approaches to facilitate the mobilisation of communities around a cause.

In this 'how-to' book, intended for community mobilisers who want to stimulate social change in a community to work towards poverty eradication, good governance, increased transparency – in short community empowerment. This manual identifies key steps in the community mobilisation process; it stresses the role and responsibility of the community leader or co-ordinator of an activity, community networks and other Civil Society groups, including local citizens.

A community mobilisation programme ideally consists of a locally organized and planned community intervention, where the individual stakeholders and other development workers collaborate on a range of complementary interventions. A number of research studies have shown that community mobilisation can change attitudes, norms, practices and individual behaviours. This can facilitate structural change within the community, which in turn works to empower communities and bring about positive change. The mobilization process usually does not occur spontaneously. Effective organizers and leaders must guide it. The process depends on co-operation among a variety of agencies, groups, and individuals, cutting through denial and apathy, as well as managing inter-organizational suspicion and conflict, so that the process leads to changes in awareness, understanding, and improved response to the problem.

Key Steps in the Community Mobilisation Process

1. ***Getting Started***
   - Getting Prepared,
   - Knowing your Goals,
   - Know your Target,
   - Get Skills,
   - Raise Awareness.
2. ***Problem Recognition***
   - Articulating the Problem,
   - Leadership,
   - Tapping the Influence Structure,
   - Organizing Concern.
3. ***Problem Assessment***
   - Purpose,
   - Elements,
   - Participants and Capacity building Process,
   - Specific Assessment Arrangements,
   - Summary.
4. ***Obtaining Support***
   - Developing a Community Coalitional Structure,
   - Summary.

1. *Getting Started*

"If you do not know where you are going, then any road will do"

Citizens need to be prepared before they mobilize. They need:

- Clarity and agreement about the issue they are addressing and why?
- Knowledge of how the political system can help address their issue.
- Strategies and skills to articulate demands and alternative solutions.
- Organization to give them a base of collective power from which to speak.
- A sense of identity with a broader campaign, and an understanding of how their actions link with other advocacy strategies.

- An understanding of the power dynamic in which they operate and the risks they may face.
- A clear, tested message to communicate to the public and decision-makers.

Criteria for designing mobilizing actions

Mobilising actions should:

- Present opportunities to learn new skills-such as planning, defining clear demands, public speaking, going door-to door to get other involved, running a meeting etc.
- Offer practice in leadership-encourage new leaders to emerge, and build their leadership skills.
- Demystify politics and power-by exposing people to how public decision making works through direct contacts with decision makers, research about how decisions are made etc.
- Have a concrete and feasible aim – constituents must be able to see their victories and assess their losses
- Boost morale and give constituents a sense of their collective possibilities.
- Encourage people to try new things if they have never spoken publicly before, they should be encouraged and helped to do so.
- Actions should also:
- Be thoroughly planned-careful planning increases confidence.
- Be fun-people's lives are full of demands and duties, so advocacy has to be more than just exhausting.
- Take account of the political environment to ensure that your constituents do not take unnecessary risks.

2. *Problem Recognition*

Articulating the Problem

Concerned individuals – a group of local citizens, a coalition of CSO representatives, or some combinations of them - should express the problem in such a way that it is recognized and others are influenced. The problem or the situation must symbolize a terrible social or human problem (actual or impending) that requires understanding and a strong, effective response.

The problem must be identified in clear and forceful terms for example.

- The threats to the community's well-being as child headed households continue to flourish must be stressed in clear and no uncertain terms.
- The need for a coalition or a whole community rather than a particular CSO group response must be emphasized.
- Only a rudimentary outline of an approach to the problem, however, is appropriate at this early stage of the mobilization process.

Leadership

Some community individual(s) or organizational representative(s) must be concerned about the presence of the problem or issue in the community. At times, this may be a public official – *e.g.*, counselor, Member of Parliament, or District Commissioner – a community, religious, professional, or academic group leader(s).

The authority and power of a concerned community, individual(s), or CSO leader creates the impetus for the development of community mobilization process.

Concern, anger, and indignation must exist in at least one person over the presence or increase of the problem such as increased number of orphans in the community, increased child headed households increased number of babies undergoing female genital mutilation. The problem must be seen as a major threat to community's future and the leadership must express deep feelings and impress upon others that a problem exists and that something needs to be done about it. The CSO group should create the impetus for addressing the problem.

Tapping the Influence Structure

At this stage, it is important to conduct stakeholders' analysis and classification before you engage any influential people or group. The analysis will enable you to understand who is doing what and where? As well as help you understand who influence decisions in a community.

Contact must be made with influential leaders in the community. The initial local leaders or particular agency persons are aware that their agencies or local groups alone cannot change the situation or the conditions that create it. They must propose that the problem can be reduced through combined efforts of local citizens and key institutions in the immediate and larger community. Accordingly, they will need to contact and influence key policy-makers and other local administrators. The major institutional leaders to be influenced include the district commissioner, Member of Parliament, the police, social welfare, teachers, health workers, religious leaders, or a business leader.

They should emphasize the need to come to grips with the problem in some coalition or collective community-oriented manner. A strategy for influencing major leaders should be developed.

They need to assess the political or organizational costs and benefits of action or inaction for each of the major influential and their organizations contacted.

They should communicate clearly that benefits would be maximized if these major leaders plan immediately and act appropriately, or else costs will increase if they delay.

Organizing Concern

An efficient approach to commencing the mobilization process is necessary. The initial moral or organizational leaders, once they have taken steps to articulate the problem and influence significant others to do likewise, must consider the means for efficiently organizing community wide efforts:

- The leader(s) will need to obtain or allocate some available resources for administrative or staff assistance in the implementation of these early mobilization steps. Fundraising may be required from some local public, private, or a foundation source.
- The leader(s) should arrange for an assistant or community organizer to per form a variety of support tasks such as personal contacts, letter writing, and telephoning.
- At this stage, the concerned leader(s) must take upon him/her and his/her organization public responsibility for continuing to identify and label the problem.

- The leader(s) must spread the word far and wide that the problem exists and indicate in no uncertain terms and through specific examples some of its destructive aspects.

3. *Problem Assessment*

Purpose

The purpose of the assessment, from the perspective of community mobilization, is to establish a common definition of the problem in the particular area and to begin the process of shared community/agency responsibility for understanding and developing resources to address it. Most important are the creation of initial relationships and a process of mutual respect in sharing views.

Technical planning questions must be answered as part of the mobilization and community design effort.

Techniques for identifying needs:

(a) Surveys.

(b) Observations.

(c) Questionnaires.

(d) Listening to people.

(e) Participation in meetings and community organizations.

(f) Interviews-structured and unstructured.

(g) Request from the community, petitions.

(h) Brainstorming sessions on problem situations.

(i) Records, reports and studies.

(j) Recommendations of members of Parliament or local legislature.

Elements

The assessment for organizing purposes, however, must be technical as well as process-oriented. The techniques and answers developed to obtain answers should comprise the basis for meaningful data systems and ongoing planning. The leader, organizer, or other staff person responsible for conducting the community mobilization should answer the following types of planning and programme Development questions related to mobilization issues:

(a) What are the nature, extent, and seriousness of the problem?

- ❖ What is the scope of the problem, *i.e.*, how many? Where and when does the problem manifest itself?
- ❖ What are the key characteristics, *e.g.*, age, gender, school, employment status
- ❖ What is the nature of the problem or issue
- ❖ Is this an emerging (reemerging) or chronic problem?

(b) What are the causes of the problem?

- ❖ The immediate and basic causes of the problem should be identified.
- ❖ What are the immediate or precipitating reasons for problem to occur?
- ❖ What are the longer-term causes, *e.g.*, HIV/AIDS, poverty or inadequate schools?

(c) What resources and programmes are presently available within and outside of the community to address the problem?

- ❖ What agencies are presently providing special activities and programmes relevant to the problem?
- ❖ Resources available to deal with the problem.
- ❖ If they exist, are such programmes reaching community members at risk?
- ❖ What are local community or grassroots groups doing with respect to the problem?
- ❖ What existing taskforces, community councils, or co-ordinating groups available which can be used as a basis for dealing with the problem?
- ❖ What public, voluntary, and foundation resources could possibly be made able to deal with the problem?

The key elements of the assessment, from a community mobilization perspective, however, need to emphasize how these particular planning questions or components can be related to community decision-making and citizen participation.

The leader(s) or community organizer must be able to determine:

- Who will be influential in reducing the problem.

- In what way these influential people should participate in the problem reduction process.
- How local citizen groups can be involved.
- How the mobilization process is to be structured, *i.e.*, how best to build agency and community organization capacity in a co-ordinated way for long-term effect.

4. *Obtaining Support*

Political and economic support must be obtained for the planning process and action programme to follow. Further more, the organizing agency, community leader, or preliminary group that has initiated and/or developed the assessment stage must plan and develop an action programme on the basis that political, moral, and economic resources are likely to be invested. Support must now be assured from the community's power structure or key decision makers, as well as groups or organizations representing citizens directly affected by the problem.

The organizer and community leaders must:

- Continue to see the problem as sufficiently serious to warrant ongoing attention and policy development.
- Have evidence that the problem is at least partially solvable.
- The organizer or community leader must understand the value or threat of the problem politically to the public official at a given time and place.
- Persuade officials that the approach that seems to be emerging will provide governmental leaders with additional political support or success at minimal or limited cost.
- Persuade officials that failure to deal with the problem appropriately will endanger community support and threaten the official's political assets.
- Demonstrate that specific policy and administrative leadership is available to develop an appropriate communitywide structure and approach.
- Establish a basis for continued grassroots involvement and support.

- Provide evidence that new money needed for the proposed structure and programmes can be made available.

The organizer will need, through a series of formal and informal meetings among CSO and community influential people and officials to:

- Develop a plan acceptable to political and government leadership.
- Employ politically meaningful knowledge and tactics to influence key public officials.
- Encourage groups and organizations to begin to plan and move ahead with initial programmes and actions in some co-ordinated way.
- Follow up on decisions and agreements made in order to ensure that they are implemented in a manner consistent with an approach that is suitable not only for dealing with the problem in rational way but also political-interest terms.
- Use the media to maintain political/governmental intentions to implement agreements.
- Attack a government or public agency, if necessary, not in an 'all-out' manner, but with opportunities for compromise and reconciliation.

Developing a Community Coalitional Structure

Different structures may be required in different kinds of problem communities. Consideration should be given to the structure and processes necessary to implement a problem-solving approach in a particular community. Of special interest are the distinctive arrangements required in emerging and chronic problem area, with due regard to differences interests and characteristics of the problem and community response to it.

The organizer in the emerging problem jurisdiction should:

- Involve MPs, religious groups, activists, schools, youth agencies, or police as key actors in the development of an appropriate coalitional structure, supported by grassroots organizations, business and industries.
- Focus on in emerging problem area.

- Stress that key programmes should be centered in problem areas and on prevention and early intervention.
- Encourage community groups to reach out to people in support of remedial programmes directed at special organizing emphasis in the emerging problem area.
- Approach coalition-building among the key organizations through formal and informal means including contacts at social gatherings.
- Facilitate the development of a common approach to the problem among agencies and local groups with emphasis on better utilization of existing resources on behalf of targeted community.
- A wide range of approaches is required in the chronic problem area.
- Facilitate the development of special mechanisms and activities by agencies to address the problem;
- Encourage the development of advocacy committees comprising a variety of different organizations and community group representatives with respect to the problem
- Develop special advisory or operational committees that have special information-sharing concerns about the problem.
- More formal mechanisms and resources are also necessary.
- Focus on a variety of formal mechanisms to integrate or co-ordinate efforts across agencies and community groups at both policy and operational levels, on regional, or district bases.
- Assist this special body (or bodies) to focus on prevention as well as intervention and suppression approaches.
- Assist in the planning of programmes in close connection with other actors. Persuasion and pressure may be necessary to achieve collaborative effort.
- Advocate, along with grassroots organizations, for increased resources and the development of crisis as well as long-term programmes which addresses the issue.

- Establishing Appropriate Agency/Community Group Interactions and Programmes.

The organizer must be especially alert to those conditions and factors which tend to subvert collaborative or coalitional efforts. He should persuade and pressure certain groups and organizations and develop appropriate techniques to facilitate a co-ordinated community approach. Consortium funding and monitoring arrangements must be established.

The organizer needs to:

- Be aware of those key organizations and their representatives who prefer not to join the community wide organization and its programmes.
- Quickly diagnose such situations and develop appropriate means to overcome resistance, or at least mitigate the effect of the particular organization's absence in the community wide effort.

Many considerations and techniques are required to overcome organizational resistance to a community approach.

- Overcome obstacles, if necessary, through a 'carrot and a stick approach', including various social action measures, *e.g.*, marches, petitions, use of media, legal processes, and conflict resolution tactics.
- Co-opt organizations and community groups, to the extent possible, through the provision of resources contingent on cooperation or collaboration in selected community programmes.
- Use influence or pressure from political figures or leading members of the community to persuade organizations or community groups to participate with organizations of different (or antagonistic) approaches. In most of these cases, approaches can be reconciled and reciprocal roles developed that are essential to the creation of a consistent gang suppression and intervention strategies.
- Be aware that a community co-ordinating structure can often become a token or ceremonial arrangement where no real interagency programming or significant community group co-operation takes place.

- Assist the interagency council to develop graduated collaborative programmes requiring simple co-ordinative mechanisms at first.
- Understand that the problem must be addressed with sustained effort over a substantial period of time, usually several years.
- Seek additional resources for various programmes, only on a coalitional basis.
- Understanding and sensitivity to groups with conflicting values and interests, and the development of long-term commitment to dealing with the problem are required.
- Be sensitive to community interests and conflicts.
- Be sure to involve minority groups leaders closest to the problem such as women, people with disabilities youth in critical decision making and programme implementation;
- Maintain media involvement.
- Establish outside advisory monitoring and evaluation groups to keep the participant organizations and groups honest and on track.
- Creating Meaningful and Shared Goals, Objectives, Strategies, and Procedures.
- Specific goals and objectives for the reduction and prevention of the problem and issue should be based both on the elaboration of specific organization strategies of suppression, social intervention, and opportunities provision and also on a general strategy of community mobilization, consensus and co-operation within and across agency and community group programmes.
- Goals, objectives, and priorities must be carefully addressed.
- Goals are more general and determine the overall direction(s) of the community coalition's problem-solving efforts. Objectives are more specific, accompanied preferably by timelines. Long-range objectives should stem from goals and short- range objectives should assist in the achievement of long-range objectives.

- Operational goals should be realistically related to the particular nature and scope of the problem, to express community concerns, and to existing political interests. Objectives should target the needs of specific types of groups.
- Priority short – and long-range objectives to deal with different aspects of the problem must be explicitly detailed not only for particular agencies and community groups but for the community as a whole.

The organizer should:

- Emphasize the development of reciprocal roles and activities by the various actors, community-based groups, and grassroots organizations.
- Detailed procedures of staff collaboration across different actors and community groups are required.
- Encourage the use of explicit agency and community group agreements, regular as well as crisis meetings, especially areas mostly affected by the problem, to discuss how they will co-operate.
- Develop accountability mechanisms so that each programme, including patterns of relationships within as well as across agency and community group programmes, is periodically reviewed.

Summary

The community mobilization process moves ahead when key community organizations, and political and grassroots leaders agree that a special structure is required to deal with the problem. Not only political but economic resources must be invested in the mobilization process. The structure that develops must consider community interest, key characteristics of the problem, and the existing response to it. A broad range of CSO staff and community representatives must be involved.

The organizer must be especially alert to those conditions and factors that tend to subvert coalitional or collaborative efforts. Specific goals and objectives must be established that attempt to reduce and prevent the problem based on a general strategy of community mobilization, consensus, and co-operation. Short – and long-range objectives must be established not only for particular agencies and community groups but for the service delivery and community system as a whole.

SOUTHERN AFRICAN AIDS TRUST (SAT) MODEL

Source: http://www.jsieurope.org/docs/cmeiacst_training_manual.pdf

Southern African AIDS Trust Supporting Community Responses to HIV and AIDS in Southern Africa in September, 2004 published Training Manual on Community Mobilisation and Empowerment for Improved Access to Care, Support and Treatment for people living with HIV and AIDS. The aim of this training manual is not to create perfect model communities, but to mobilise communities to identify what they have that can be put to better use, and to make linkages and partnerships to expand the knowledge, skills and resources available to them.

The SAT model of community mobilization and empowerment includes the following steps:

- Recognition of the need to mobilise.
- Creating community ownership of the issue.
- Identification of internal community resources, knowledge and skills to address the issue.
- Identification of priority needs.
- Community planning and action.
- Increasing the capacity of the community.

A Community mobilisation and empowerment action cycle

Community mobilisation and empowerment strategies

- Participatory baseline surveys.
- Participatory planning.
- Holding community meetings and giving feedback through regular reviews.
- Forming community committees and/or organizing community groups.
- Networking with other stakeholders.
- Raising community awareness (advocacy).
- Educating the community.
- Gaining commitment from NGO forums.
- Local resource mobilisation.
- Identifying entry points (*e.g.*, gate keepers, influential community leaders).

Benefits

- Builds community capacity.
- Motivates community participation and vice *vs.* – community involvement is motivational.
- Increases resource utilization.
- Attracts support from other stakeholders.
- Promotes sustainability (programmatic, financial, etc.)
- Allows for re-planning.
- Enhances community ownership.
- Easier to achieve goals and objectives because of common vision and unity.

Challenges/barriers

- Inadequate supportive environment.
- Poor access to services.
- High level of stigma, denial and discrimination.
- Impoverishment.
- Inadequate information, skills and training.
- Weak networks, poor co-ordination and lack of consistency (*e.g.*, in messages).
- Cultural and traditional barriers.

- Lack of understanding the community and environment.
- Lack of appropriate representation by community groups.
- Competition and duplication of efforts.
- Poor governance.

Strategies for sustaining relationships

- Information sharing/reports.
- Establishment of strong networks.
- Regular reviews and feedbacks.
- Joint plans.
- Make use of locally available resources.
- Ensure close and participatory monitoring process.
- Accountability and transparency of implementers to beneficiaries, government, etc.
- Involve the community from the beginning.
- Be honest and realistic with the community about what may be achieved.

CENTRE SARHAD RURAL SUPPORT CORPORATION MODEL, PESHAWAR, PAKISTAN

Source: http://commdev.ca/CommOrg/CommTrgPpt.pdf

Abid Ullah Jan (2000) published the Community Organizing: Community Change Participant's Manual for the Sarhad Rural Support Corporation, Peshawar, Pakistan. In this manual, Jan has identified the following seven stages of community organizing.

Stage 1. Getting Started.

Stage 2. Targeting Issues and Setting Priorities.

Stage 3. Targeting Supporters and Opponents.

Stage 4. Planning for Action.

Stage 5. Organizing a Power/Process Structure.

Stage 6. Mobilizing the Group to Achieve Small Victories.

Stage 7. Continuing the Process.

Stage 1: Getting Started

The organizer must:

- Be invited by the community, by its leadership.
- Help to highlight frustrations and raise issues.

- Cultivate hope for a better way.
- Instill a desire for change.
- Be seen as a winner.
- Demonstrate stick-to-itiveness.
- Help the community see why this effort is important from its perspective.
- Help people feel that they have the power to make the necessary changes.
- Help develop a core group of concerned citizens – informal and formal community leaders.

Stage 2: Targeting Issues and Setting Priorities

The term 'targeting' as used in this and other stages relates to the need for organizers and community-change organizations to identify and select specific issues and individuals that they desire to affect by an action or development. With the assistance of the organizer and a core group of community members, the host community must:

- Identify important issues and commonly held problems.
- Define desired changes.
- Rank problems and set priorities.
- Develop a shared vision for problem resolution.
- Understand that controversy is a part of creating change – without controversy people may not be energized enough to act. A controversial issue is a redundancy.

Stage 3: Targeting Supporters and Opponents

At this stage, the organizer and a core group of community members must focus on the priority issue and begin to:

- Identify people – supporters – who are concerned about these issues, who are willing to work toward the desired change, and who have the ability to create the change.
- Identify people – opponents – who will stand in the way of the desired change and who have the ability to make or prevent the desired change.

Stage 4: Planning for Action

The organizer and a core group of community members must:

- Develop a plan of action to effectively address the presenting issue/problem.
- Assess the current power structures and other factors that create or maintain the problem.
- Analyze the environment – examine the external and internal obstacles, external and internal opportunities, and resources.
- Define the targets – those who are most affected by the problem, those who can help create the desired change, and those who will stand in the way of the desired change.
- Develop strategies for organizing the supporters into a group/organization to address the issue and the opponents.
- Design strategies for mobilizing the organized group to create the desired change.

Stage 5: Organizing a Power/Process Structure

Change comes from a group of people with a shared vision and shared concerns, who are willing to combine their resources to work together on a specific set of issues. It comes from organizing people into a group/organization that uses process and power to create change.

The organizer and community members must:

- Educate and energize the public on the targeted issue.
- Cultivate relationships with supporters.
- Design structural and communication links for addressing the identified problems, bringing the supporters together, and implementing the action strategies that will create the desired change.
- Bring the supporters together to form a group that will work together to create the desired change.
- Develop leaders to support the agenda and implement the action plan.

Stage 6: Mobilizing the Group to Achieve Small Victories

At this stage, the organized group of supporters executes the tactics to create the desired change.

The organizer must help the group to:

- Select the appropriate tactics.

- Keep the actions simple and fun.
- Own the actions.
- Use tactics that will achieve small victories to advance the desired change.

Stage 7: Continuing the Process

The organizer must work with the organized group to:

- Make sure it receives feedback.
- Monitors actions.
- Evaluates effectiveness of strategy on overall goal.
- Redefines actions.
- Identifies new problems, priorities, and strategies.
- Implements revised action plan.

Examples of community issue

Lack of Drinking Water

A few angry citizens in a remote village met a few weekends ago to discuss what they could do to get rid of troubles they are going through due to lack of drinking water supply in the village. Women in particular spend long hours to go and fetch water a few miles down the dangerous track. Your Community Partnership wants to get involved with this issue.

The Link Road

Your village has three community organizations. The small track that links your village to the main road is not jeepable. All of your transportation is done with the help of donkey and mules. It becomes even harder when someone gets sick and moving him up to the main road to take him to the hospital becomes an uphill task. The whole community is in need of a wider link road to the main high way. Your Partnership wants to get involved.

Targeting Supporters

Supporters:

- Assess who is most affected by this issue.
- Assess who has the potential to help you create the desired change.

Targeting Issues

Issues:

- Convert private troubles into public issues.
- Select an issue that people can get excited about.
- Define what change you want to see occur.
- Select an issue that is winnable.

Targeting Opponents

Opponents:

- Assess who has the power to stop or hinder the desired change.

Types of Mobilization Tactics

- Persuasion.
- Negotiation.
- Direct Action.

INTEGRATED FOOD SECURITY PROGRAMME (IFSP) MODEL, TRINCOMALEE, SRI LANKA

Source: http://www.ifsp-srilanka.org/wp-28-soc-mob-concept.pdf

To improve the living conditions of the rural population and to promote reconstruction and redevelopment the Sri Lankan government proposed a support programme for food and nutrition security for Trincomalee and Ampara districts in 1996. This proposal was appraised in September 1997 and the Integrated Food Security Programme Trincomalee (IFSP) was agreed for a first phase starting from August 1998 to May 2001. The IFSP has been implementing a large number of small scale projects. Systematic planning and mobilisation of target groups (people from all three communities who are affected by the ongoing conflict and are at food risk) as well as services providers (government institutions and non government organizations) is a precondition for sustainability.

Social mobilisation within IFSP does not follow a blueprint approach. It has some elements in common with other approaches in Sri Lanka such as empowerment of poor groups through awareness creation, as well as self-organization to encourage people to make use of their own potential and resources.

Social Mobilisation within the Project Cycle

How does social mobilisation fit into the Project cycle? Social mobilisation is the entry point for a people centred development process. The social mobiliser is expected to associate himself/herself with the project area through he whole project cycle. The cycle starts with the selection of villages and ends with the evaluation of projects. The mobilisation tasks are defined at each of the seven steps of the cycle as well as for the four mobilisation phases in between the steps.

Step 1: Village Selection

The social mobilisation co-ordinator assists in:

- Evaluating the village data sheets.
- Selecting villages.
- Allocating villages to the social mobilisers.
- The Social mobilisers study and consider all available information, in particular from the village data sheets before entering the village.

Community Mobilisation Phase

The social mobiliser takes a leading role in:

- Building up mutual confidence with entire village community.
- Motivating the people to become involved in a learning and action oriented development process to improve their livelihoods.
- Stimulating reflections on different issues, sensitise for the negative and positive development factors and the cause/effect relationships of poverty and to jointly learn about potentials and constraints for development.
- Identifying different interest groups in the village and creating space for the less powerful and poorer groups to express their needs.
- Getting an overview on the functioning of existing community based organization (CBOs).
- Preparing villagers for Participatory Needs Assessment (PNA).

In this first phase of community mobilisation, the social mobiliser has to contact the village frequently (*e.g.* 1-2 times a week). The frequency of visits depends on the size of the village and its ethnic composition. First the village leaders should be contacted.

A village workshop is to be held to introduce the social mobiliser to the villagers and to motivate the different groups to participate and to create an atmosphere conducive for a communal learning and action process. In the following, the social mobiliser contacts different families through household visits, to identify the different social groups and their specific living conditions and problems. The second workshop is meant to sensitise for the negative and positive development factors through an analysis of cause/effect relationships of poverty. The last activity in this phase is to prepare the villagers for the following PNA workshop and its aim.

Step 2: Participatory Needs Assessment (PNA)

The social mobiliser is responsible to support the preparation of logistics (arranging time and location for meetings, accommodation, food) for the Preliminary Investigation Visit (PIV) and PNA to follow.

The social mobiliser is a member of the PNA team with a particular role. Due to his/her background knowledge about the socio-economic situation in the village he/she supports the PNA team with additional information, however, has to refrain from interfering in the process. His/her role is a passive one and can be described as:

- Facilitator for logistical preparation and for establishing a good rapport with the village.
- Back-stopper for additional information, during PNA as well as during report writing.
- Observer of the process, during PNA.

Group mobilisation phase I

Strengthening of selected CBOs (for implementation of community projects) and action groups (for implementation of poverty projects)

The social mobiliser should take a leading role in:

- Introducing the potentials of collective action.

- Discussing the role of the identified organization in the community, their strengths and weaknesses.
- Assisting the groups in finding a common vision and in determine what they want to achieve.
- Identifying one contact person per group, and where necessary select other office-bearers, like a treasurer
- Building up the capacities of the contact persons that they can act as a link person between the different stakeholders and assist the social mobiliser in mobilising the group members.

During this phase the social mobiliser is supposed to visit the village one or two times a week. At the beginning of this phase, the social mobiliser organizes a joint meeting of all groups identified during PNA. He/she explains the benefits of collective action. Afterwards, in separate group meetings the social mobiliser analyses together with the respective groups their strengths and weaknesses. The next step is to assist the groups in selecting their representatives (wherever necessary) and to organize themselves. Strengthening of the selected CBOs should be done in close co-operation with the respective departments or NGOs, which originally formed the groups, as they are responsible for the further guidance of these local groups.

Step 3: Screening of Project Proposals and Discussing them with the Divisional Secretaries

The social mobilisers facilitate

- The Technical Project Committee (TPC) with additional information about the socio-economic situation in the village.
- The Divisional Development Committee meeting (DOC) with specific local information.

Group mobilisation phase II

Strengthening of selected CBOs (for implementation of community projects) and action groups (for implementation of poverty projects)

The social mobiliser is responsible for:

- Training of groups in general group management, *e.g.*, self-organization, leadership, clarification of responsibilities, etc.

- Training of groups in financial management, that the groups are able to calculate family income and expenditure, as well as costs and benefits of the envisaged projects.
- Supporting the feeling of ownership for project implementation and project maintenance through clarification of responsibilities of the groups (contribution, maintenance).

The social mobiliser contacts the villages one or two times a week. In this phase she/he works intensively with the selected groups (CBOs and action groups). Training is given to the groups on general group management, like self-organization, leadership, clarification of responsibilities etc. Furthermore the groups have to be trained in financial management, that they are able to calculate family income and expenditure as well as costs and benefits of the envisaged projects themselves. The social mobiliser should intensify efforts to build up the capacity of the contact persons.

Step 4: Elaboration of Project Plans

The social mobiliser facilitates

- Service providers to elaborate project plans in a participatory, sound and pragmatic way.

Step 5: Final approval of projects

The social mobiliser informs:

- The target groups about the project approval.

Step 6: Project Implementation

The social mobiliser is responsible for:

- Mobilising and facilitating the service provision . motivating poorer groups to participate.
- Encouraging the villagers to demand service provision.
- Monitoring the project process and train the groups in self-monitoring.

Additional resource mobilisation phase:

Facilitation of access to financial service and credit institutions

The social mobiliser is involved in:

- Motivating group members to join existing saving programmes, and/or assist creating own saving groups.

- Informing the groups about existing credit possibilities and their conditions and to link interested groups with representatives of these institutions.
- Arrange meetings with other experienced groups to learn from their experiences.
- Encouragement of villagers to start additional income generating activities and small enterprises.

The social mobiliser is also involved in:

- Analysing previous experiences with income generating activities and drawing conclusions from failures for future activities.
- Creating awareness for own opportunities and limitations.
- Organizing meetings with resource persons or experienced groups.
- Linking target groups with service providers active in this field.

In this phase the social mobiliser prepares the groups to take the development process in their own hands. The main task is to provide information on saving and credit as well as alternative income generating activities. Linking the groups with competent resource persons and service providers is seen as an adequate alternative for starting an own saving and credit programme within an IFSP.

Step 7: Project Evaluation

The social mobiliser is supporting:

- Evaluation of project implementation and impact by the local groups themselves the TPC which is responsible for the evaluation.

With the evaluation of projects the project cycle comes to a preliminary end. It has to be assessed what villagers have learned during the project cycle and in how far dependency from outside assistance has been reduced. To some extent, additional support from project management side might be still needed, before the social mobiliser can be withdrawn from the village.

Evaluation is a necessary step to learn from experiences in the past and to draw conclusions for improving social mobilisation in other villagers. In addition to that, it will be necessary to do continuously monitoring to be able to make adjustments, wherever necessary at earlier stages.

Process and Impact Monitoring

The social mobiliser joins and may take the lead to:

- Monitor the process of the project implementation.
- Monitor the group development.
- Observe unplanned negative impacts. To avoid negative impacts the social mobiliser has to be an impartial, neutral person (especially in uncleared areas it will be important to keep in contact with both sides).
- Identify common subjects and interests.
- Facilitate discussions within groups and dialogue with other groups.

Process and impact monitoring is an ongoing activity throughout all phases. It combines the monitoring of group development, of project implementation and of possible unplanned, negative side effects. At the beginning of social mobilisation it would be the task of the social mobilisers. At later stages she/he needs to train the groups in self-monitoring. Self-monitoring consists of joint learning by sharing ideas and experiences, and by reflecting on the successes and failures of the past.

SNV/NEPAL MODEL

Source: http://books.icimod.org/index.php/search/publication/51

In the book 'Developing Sustainable Communities: *A Toolkit for Development Practitioners*' Published by the International Centre for Integrated Mountain Development in the year 2004, Kathmandu, Nepal, for SNV/Nepal, the social mobilisation is presented in seven stages: Appraisal and Rapport Building, Social Analysis, Social Capital and Group Formation, Social Action, Alliance Building, Advocacy, and Social Reflection.

It has been argued in the SNVP-Nepal model that social mobilisation taps the inherent capacity of every person, group, and community helping various stakeholders to direct their own future. It is used intensively in programmes to assess, analyse, and generate actions, its key components are focused capacity building, specific institutional development, and strengthened organizational capability. An important element in social mobilisation, according to the SNVP-Nepal model, is the inclusion of poor or disadvantaged groups and the active involvement of community-based organizations (CBOs) and non-government organizations (NGOs). This is a prerequisite for a continuing social mobilisation process.

Social Mobilisation Process

Stages	Objectives
Appraisal and Rapport Building	Initiates dialogue
Social Analysis	Assesses the situation
Social Capital and Group Formation	Creates social capital through group formation
Social Action	Develops and implements the programme
Alliance Building	Networks and builds coalitions
Advocacy	Raises awareness toward solutions
Social Reflection	Enhances advocacy for policy and value changes

Process for Consideration during Social Mobilisation

Stage I: Appraisal and Rapport Building

Overview

Social mobilisation (SM) starts with identifying marginalised areas and people within the selected geographical areas for a given programme. It is assumed that a pre-scan has been conducted to select the area where an intervention is going to be implemented. Support or assistance is going to be provided, which will allow a community to take on an active role in their development.

Stage I can be completed in one month; however, depending on the community situation, topography, human resources, and other factors, the time needed may vary. Facilitators should adapt according to local conditions and their own insight.

Stage II: Social Appraisal and Rapport Building

- Initiates the SM process.
- Is essential for acquiring 'social' legitimacy of the SM process.
- Creates a context for generating inputs from the people at the preliminary stage of the design process.

Methodology

Step 1: Initiate dialogue and prepare a preliminary appraisal for identifying villages or settlements. Dialogue is initiated between the facilitator and the communities in the selected area. The aim is to build a good relationship with various stakeholders and prepare a summary of the secondary information on the community and area to share with the members. Where possible, try to obtain gender disaggregated data.

Step 2: Build a preliminary village profile based on a checklist. Record information using the checklist, after which obtain an agreement for Social Analysis.

Step 3: Organize rapport-building workshops. Conduct workshops with Village Development Committees (VDCs), NGOs, government organizations (GOs), and private agencies working in the area. These should bring together various stakeholders to debate, agree/disagree, and negotiate on matters related to the proposed process of SM. One must take into account the sensitive use of gender and cultural issues.

Step 4: Conduct rapport-building mass meetings in each ward. Facilitators can introduce the SM process to the people and explain and answer questions through the following activities:

- explain the objectives of the process – what the intended achievements are;
- explain the approaches – how you want to work to achieve the objectives;
- describe the SM process (briefly in preliminary meetings and in detail during orientations);

- explain how it benefits the community and what kind of work you intend to carry out in the area;
- disclose how the work is funded and the duration.
- describe what the people are expected to do;
- collect the comments and inputs, note down the points, and clarify the queries;
- incorporate the suggestions; design a preliminary process collaboratively with the people;
- do not raise expectations at the VDC and community member levels.

Step 5: Conduct group discussions at the village and settlement levels. Facilitators should establish a relationship of mutual rapport with the people. Without such a positive bond, the people, being the key players of the SM process often reject interventions that are imposed by outsiders. This is especially important if one wants to get responses from women.

Step 6: Organize informal meetings and visits. Rapport cannot be established in one meeting or interaction, but through long-term engagement with common efforts. Rapport-building is a continuous process of gaining confidence and acceptance through words and work. Facilitators should visit homes, meet people, and make informal contacts individually. A good relationship and trust between the people and facilitators are key to the success of stage I.

MOBILISING THE COMMUNITY: A PILLARS GUIDE

Source: http://tilz.tearfund.org/webdocs/Tilz/PILLARS/English

Introduction to PILLARS Guides by Isabel Carter

These guides are designed for use in small group situations where one or more people are literate and confident enough to lead others in group discussion. They aim to provide material for discussion around a subject either in isolation or as part of a regular group meeting; for example of farmers, literacy trainees or Mothers Union members. PILLARS Guides aim to increase confidence among group members, so that they can successfully manage change within their own situation without the need for outside help. They try to build on existing knowledge and experiences among the members or within their community, so that different ideas can be tried out, adapted, and then either abandoned if not found useful, or adopted if found useful.

Mobilising the Community

This guide looks at an exciting example of community mobilisation that is based on using outside facilitators and workshops. However, outside facilitators and money to run workshops may not always be available. This PILLARS guide takes the basis of the mobilisation process and shares it in a way that will help a well-organized and motivated group to use the process without outside help. It would be helpful to churches keen to support their communities or to any small groups or NGO seeking to bring changes that benefit local people.

THE INDEPENDENT CENTRE FOR STRATEGIC STUDIES AND ANALYSIS (ICSSA) MODEL

Source: http://icssa.org/Chapter%204.pdf

Process of Community Mobilisation

The social mobilisation for developing organizations at the micro-level is almost the same as followed by other rural development programmes. The most important point to highlight is that in this case the mobilisation is not carried around delivery of certain packages, but with the objective to form and then transform the village level organizations into organized representative NGOs. Any package delivered is implemented with the objective to help the community learn how to take on similar activities in the future on their own. Moreover, the organizations are not formed to shine statistics in the progress reports. The focus instead is in the interest of the communities and sustainability of the VOs. When the Social Organizers are sure that formation of VOs is not the end, but the beginning of a process on which further institutions needs to be developed, he/she will never take it for granted. Further institution building on the basic building blocks would not be possible if they are fake, consisting of just two or three accomplices in hijacking a development scheme or some other advantage from the external support programme.

The following cycle of social mobilisation needs to be carried out by the field workers/social organizers of the external support programme at the micro-level and then gradually hand it over to the meso-level organizations for keeping the communities involved in the development process on a sustainable basis. Of course, the meso-level organizations would not have to go through the initial steps of the cycle, as they would inherit well-developed grassroots institutions.

Step 1 to Social Mobilisation

Preparation

Social Organizers must prepare themselves before they can successfully stimulate self-help development in a community. They must be clear and knowledgeable about their goals; they must know about their target community; they must have the required skills; they must understand the fundamental concepts of mobilisation. Objective of this stage is to motivate, equip and train the external programme staff for the whole social organization process of developing multi-level local institutions ahead. A social organizer and programme staff has to be very clear about all the concepts and terminology used in the participatory development and social organization.

The first thing to do now is to start a diary to recording account of the day-to-day progress. An inexpensive school notebook is OK. The SOs might wish to use four notebooks or four parts in a note book and title them: *(i)* goals and Concepts; *(ii)* the Target Community; *(iii)* mobilizing Skills; and *(iv)* a Day-to-Day record. This chapter intends to focus on an SO needs to get prepared. The SOs must not, however, assume that they can get prepared 'once and for all.' The social organizers continually learn more and more about all the things mentioned in this chapter. It is a never-ending process, and we will be doomed to failure if we ever think we know it all.

1. *The Goals:* One of the slogans used in management training is, "If you do not know where you are going, then any road will take you there." This applies well to the social organizers while they are preparing for mobilizing the community for organization. As happens most of the time,

it is easy to run around, looking busy, arranging meetings, getting infrastructure projects constructed, talking to community leaders, moving advocacy groups, stimulating action, without moving forward in developing genuine representative institutions at the micro- and meso-levels. The Social Organizers need to clarify their goals, first to themselves, then on paper, then to those around them. Purposeless work or facilitation in delivery of programme packages will take the Social Organizers and their programme nowhere.

2. *The Target Community:* Another proverb that is often used in community development is, "The potter must know her/his clay." The SOs clay is the community. The SOs wants to mould and develop it into something strong. To do so, the SOs must know a lot about the community (and about the nature of communities in general). The SO must know as much as possible about its social organization, culture, economy, languages, layout (map), problems, politics, and ecology of the target community.
3. *The Needed Skills:* The skills that the SOs need are not exceptionally difficult to learn, but can be very powerful tools. They can be misused. As an analogy, one should think of the skills of a locksmith. A locksmith performs many useful and valuable services, but they can be misused for breaking, entering, and theft. As the SOs learn mobilisation skills, they should use them for the benefit of the community, not to benefit their own self at the expense of the community. Since the target group is the community as a whole, most of the SOs" needed skills belong to communication abilities? They need to learn how to be a public speaker, but not just any kind of public speaker. The kind of public speaking the SOs need to know is the kind needed for leadership and facilitation.
4. *The Basic Concepts:* To be a successful social organizer, the SOs need more than a few technical skills in public dialogue and organizing groups for action. They need to know why to use those skills. They need to know

principles. If their target is a community, then the SOs should know some sociological concepts about the nature of communities and the nature of social change (including development) of communities. This means that they need some understanding of social organization, the subject matter of sociology, anthropology, economics, politics, and the forces and processes that belong to those disciplines. It is not necessary to have a university degree, but the SOs should teach themselves the principles and knowledge of those subjects.

5. *Outside Resources:* As community mobilisers, the SOs will find that it is difficult to find a balance between resources that originate outside the community, and those from within. The SOs and the community leaders/elders will be under considerable pressure to bring outside resources into the community. Donor agencies want to help, while community members want to receive. The SOs know, however, that bringing in outside resources contributes to the dependency syndrome and reduces the chances of sustainability and self-reliance.

Step 2 to Social Mobilisation

Taking A Start

The SOs do not get the community into action until they take action to prepare it for action. The starting phase is the community's getting prepared phase. After sensitising, raising awareness among the authorities, and getting any necessary permission from the concerned authorities and elders of the community, the SOs" next task is to raise mobilising human, natural and capital resources of the target community or communities.

Raising awareness phase mainly includes: *(i)* explaining the programme goals; and *(ii)* methods; *(iii)* convincing them that they can benefit from the social guidance; and *(iv)* taking positive steps to prevent the raising of unrealistic expectations.

1. *The Mobilisation Cycle:* The mobilisation cycle is sometimes called 'The Community Participation Promotion Cycle,' or the 'Problem Solving Cycle,' or 'The Community

Development Cycle,' or 'The Social Animation Cycle.' It is a series of interventions (carried out by one or more social organizer) designed to increase the level of involvement of a community in the decisions that affect its own development. It is called a 'Cycle,' in that it is repeated, each time building on earlier successes, errors, and lessons learned.

Mobilisation cycle is a series of interventions in a logical and progressive order carried out by a legitimate, authorized and recognized social organizers. It uses the community choice of action as a means of strengthening, not as an end in itself. The cycle requires that the social organizers be informed and sensitive to community characteristics so as to promotes (encourages, advocates for, trains in skills necessary for, and supports) community participation in control and decision making of all actions affecting the community as a whole.

The main steps of this cycle are logically linked with each other and to the cycle as a whole. All steps are needed (absence of any one will seriously weaken its impact); and initiated in the following order, although there may be some overlap and continuation. Participation of all members of a target community (irrespective of biological or social characteristics) is essential to both poverty reduction and community strengthening. The key decisions to be made, and control to be exercised, include: assessing situations (needs and potentials); determining priority problems (and generating goals and objectives from them); planning actions (community action plans, project designs): implementing and monitoring them, and evaluating their results. Contributions of resources (*e.g.*, donations, communal labour, supplies), dialogue and consultation with external agencies are encouraged, although "participation – is much more comprehensive and inclusive than either 'contribution' or 'consultation.'

There is a logical and functional social process of strengthening a community. It varies in length and some details, but the pattern remains basic. The SOs" role is to initiate the process and follow it through. The Mobilisation

Cycle here is a general example followed by many development programmes. This cycle vary from community to community, from time to time, and according to the resources available, the SOs" programmes policy, and other circumstances.

2. *Paving the way:* Before the SOs begin working in the target community (or communities), they must have obtained both the needed permissions of the concerned community elders/leaders, and also the active co-operation, of the local administration and leaders responsible for the area. The SOs must keep in mind that they really have two targets (beneficiaries), not only *(i)* the community but also; *(ii)* the authorities who are responsible for the area that the community is in.

The social organizers must be recognized by authority and obtain legal status if they are not to be vulnerable to get blamed as seditious agitators, and harassed by police and others concerned with maintaining law and order. Furthermore, it is among the authorities where the most vested interest lies in maintaining the 'provision' approach and fear of the 'enablement' approach, as civil servants, officials, politicians, traditional and new leaders, and technical experts see immediate benefits of the provision approach as a means to obtain influence, popularity, votes, promotions and career advances. Sensitisation is not just a formality, but must be well planned and executed. The counteracting of rumours and false assumptions must be integral to the sensitisation strategy.

The SOs" goal for each community is to strengthen it by promoting self-help actions. The SOs" goal for the authorities is to work towards sustainability by moving towards an enabling context or environment (political and administrative) around and above the community. The SOs also have to build linkages of the local communities with different government line agencies and departments so that they may work together even when the SOs programme phases out of the area in the future.

The SOs" goal for leaders (political and informal), administrators ('bureaucrats'), and government line agencies technical experts ('technocrats') is to persuade them from being 'providers' to becoming 'facilitators of self-help by the communities.' This is not an easy task. The politicians claim that they would 'provide' (*e.g.*, any communal facility), and obtain popularity and votes. They, thus, have a vested interest in the 'provision approach.' Likewise, when administrators and technocrats claim that they would 'provide,' they look forward to enhancing their careers and obtaining promotions. They may have a vested interest in not changing to 'facilitators.' The SOs" strategy, however, is to demonstrate and convince them that they will benefit by abandoning the 'provision' approach and moving to a 'facilitating' approach.

The truth is that, if they shift from a 'provision' approach to an 'enabling' approach, in time, they will benefit. That is because every community has hidden resources that will not be identified and used so long as outside authorities are expected to provide all the resources. If the community gets the responsibility to provide its own facilities and services, and given management training to do so, many hidden resources are revealed and used. If leaders and responsible authorities shift to an enabling approach, the resulting strengthening of the communities can become the bases from which they can obtain their popularity, votes, career advances and promotions.

3. *Awareness Raising:* After the initial preparations, the SOs should start encouraging the community to take action. Before encouraging the community to act (and therefore learn and become stronger) the social organizer must make the community members aware of specific realities. During this step, it is important to avoid raising false expectations, and actively counteract the inevitable assumptions and rumours about the kind of assistance to expect.
4. *Organization:* No community is unified; there are schisms and factions in every one. The degree varies. When there is much social disparity, it is more difficult to reach a community consensus of the priority problem, and thus the priority goal. Community organization is a necessary precedent to most community mobilisation, and continues throughout the cycle as needed.

5. *Open Dialogue:* The SOs" main tool, both for raising awareness and community organization, is a public meeting in which discussion is the central feature. Here it is very important that the SOs" are thoroughly informed and conversant with their goals and the key concepts. The SOs" best role model should be that renown educator of ancient Greece, Socrates, who taught by always asking questions, never giving answers. He was a great facilitator, guiding people to think (analyse, observe) for themselves.
6. *Challenge the Community*: While the SOs want the community to develop strength, the SOs do not passively and automatically accept at first what appears to be the community's priority goal. Resistance produces strength; for instance the muscles become strong when they are force to resist in the weight lifting exercises. If the body builders" muscles never meet resistance, they will grow weak. If the SOs do too much for a community, it will not become stronger.
7. *Needs Prioritised by the Community:* Although the social organizer must first make an assessment of community resources, potentials, hindrances and needs, the strategy of the mobilisation cycle requires that an assessment be done with the community as a whole. This might not be done all at once, and may be done or continued to be done by the community executive later, after it is formed and organized. All future plans and actions in the intervention must be made on the bases of observed reality, not on the imaginings or special interests of specific factions within the community. Everyone in the community must recognize the needs and potentials.
8. *Strengthen the Community:* While there are many factors that contribute to strength, capacity, or empowerment, the one that most concerns asocial organizer is 'organization.' Other factors being equal, the level and effectiveness of organization determines the strength of a group, agency or community.

Step 3 To Social Mobilisation

Organizing the Community

It must be kept in mind that VOs are the basic building blocs of the whole rural development model proposed in this book. Therefore, all the focus should be on their sustainability right from the beginning. The SOs want the office bearers of the community organization to become stronger by being organized effectively and trained in the necessary skills. With the whole community, the SOs select and organize the office bearers. This core group of the community organization may have different names, *e.g.*, simply office bearers, executive committee, Community Implementing Committee, Project Committee, or Development Committee. Then, with this executive, the SOs make a detailed participatory assessment of conditions (including problems and resources) in the community. The sound principle is that all the community members should be involved in problems identification, prioritisation and planning phases.

Step 4 to Social Mobilisation

Implementation

At this point the community and its leaders, like the politicians and journalists, will be more interested in the actions and results (*e.g.*, the building of the water supply, clinic or school), and needs to be reminded and encouraged that monitoring and reporting must be concurrent with the action. This is where community enthusiasm can decline or be destroyed, if the action (especially in its finances) is not transparent, and made fully clear to all the community members. While the goal of the community is the finished facility, the goal of the strategy and social organizer is increased community strength and capacity, so emphasis is put on monitoring and reporting (verbal and written). Also, this is where the community becomes aware of more needed training in skills related to the action (financial and accounting skills, report writing, technical skills). By virtue of preparing the community, the SOs are already in action at this stage. Now it is time for the community to go into action. The whole community has participated in decision-making, it has formed an executive, created a community plan of action, designed a project, and an organization for acting. Time has come for it to start moving.

Step 5 to Social Mobilisation

The Mobilisation Cycle

The Social Organizers job is to stimulate a social process, which is comprised of a series of activities, (assessment, awareness raising, community organization, planning and implementation, and assessment again), which together stimulate community strengthening and increased self-reliance. The process of social mobilisation is like a cycle in a way that the SOs go back and start at the beginning again, but every time it is a changed SO and a changed community.

Community Leadership and Internal Mobilisation

The important point to keep in mind is that the key to sustaining the intervention of stimulating the community towards increased self-reliance is in the community. The community development programmes may be willing and able to replace the SOs, but their ultimate goal should be to have the community continue mobilizing on its own. The way the SOs do this is to identify persons living in the community who have the potentials to become social organizers, and the appropriate attitudes and values, and train them in the social mobilisation skills for taking over from the SOs.

Learning from Mistakes

We humans can learn from both success and failure, from achievements and mistakes. Remember that mistakes, failures and disasters are not the same. A mistake is not a failure; to err is human. A failure is not a disaster; failing to achieve something does not mean the SOs are a failure. A disaster does not mean the end of life or the end of time. When we fall down we must pick ourselves up and carry on. A day at a time. If the SOs have been successful at guiding a community to construct its own link road, or complete some other objective, then the SOs have gone one step towards making it more self-reliant. It will have not gone smoothly or perfectly.

If the SOs think it did, then they are not being honest with themselves. The Sos should analyse the process and their role in it. They need to be courageously honest in admitting their mistakes. They need to write down their analysis of the mobilisation cycle. It is necessary to be objective and neutral about mistakes and failures and not use them as an excuse to paralyse themselves with depression.

From Micro to Meso Level

The important element in the formation and subsequent sustainability of the community organizations is their own members and their interest. The interest promotion of its members is the key element to sustainability. Every organization is supposed to provide services to its members at their doorsteps; such services could be credit, employment, skills development, income generation and extension services in the field of agriculture and livestock as well as in social sector. How an organization could be nurtured and developed to provide such services to its members is the point to clearly understand by the social organizers. However, all this sounds well and makes sense on the paper. In reality, no micro-level VO can survive without the external support of an NGO or another higher level organization at the meso-level. Therefore, for sustainability of the micro-level, it is a must that there should be local, representative NGOs that should remain in the community at higher level and perform their duties like any external programme support.

Sustainability or Phasing out

The creation of a sustainable process of development is the underlying rational of Community organization. This implies that organization must itself be sustainable. Ideally for an organization to be sustainable it should develop into an institution. Practically it is possible if next level of institutions are developed after the maturity of the micro-level. The ultimate objective should be to build the capacity of community organizations to make self-managing, self-financing and self-reliant, multi-level institutions to the extent that the external programme can phase out from the area at some suitable point in time. Building the capacity of the community organizations to keep themselves informed of important issues and policies that relate to the broader development process can enable the community organizations to sustain even after withdrawal of the programme.

HEALTH COMMUNICATION PARTNERSHIP (HCP) MODEL

Source: http://www.jhuccp.org/hcp/pubs/tools/HowtoMobilize/index.html

The Field guide on 'How to Mobilize Communities for Health and Social Change' Produced by the Health Communication Partnership with support from the United States Agency for International Development, has been designed to be used by health programmes directors and managers of community-based programmes who are considering using community mobilization to improve health at the individual, family, and community level. This field guide has identified the seven steps for community mobilisation. Community mobilisation can be accomplished in seven steps. At all seven steps of a mobilisation effort – initial preparation, organizing the community for action, exploring the development issues and setting priorities, planning, acting, and evaluating together, and scaling up – external players need to keep in mind a simple rule of thumb: *community mobilisation is not just something done to the community but something done by the community.*

STEP 1: Select a Development Issue and Define the Community

One of the first things that happens in any community mobilisation effort is the selection of a development issue around which the community will eventually mobilize. Ideally it is the community itself which selects the issue. Defining the issue is an important part of selection. How the issue is defined will depend not only on the problem itself, but must also take into account how the issue is perceived by the community and externally. Programme managers need to consider the political, cultural, and social context in which they intend to work to ensure that the definition of the issue is appropriate to the setting.

STEP 2: Put together a Community Mobilisation Team

Preparing to mobilize should not be the work of one person. Before you get very far into this initial preparation stage, you will need to put together the team of people who will be working with you to support the community on this project. You may want to do this before you set about defining the development issue. This team may be made up exclusively of people from your own organization, or it may include members from partner or other organizations. Throughout this discussion, we refer to this team as the 'community mobilisation programme team' or 'programme team' for short.

How do you decide who should be on the programme team? In the end, it may all come down to practical considerations, such as who has the time or interest, or to considerations beyond your control, such as the preferences of donors or other outside organizations. If you have the opportunity to choose some or all of your own team members, you should consider the following criteria:

Expertise in the development issue

- Understanding of the political, socio-cultural and economic context (knowledge of the community and macro environment).
- Basic community mobilisation skills: communication and facilitation skills, programme design and management skills, organizational behaviour/group dynamics skills, capacity-building skills, planning and evaluation skills, knowledge of participatory methods.
- Personal attributes, such as openness, flexibility, patience, good listening skills, diplomacy, and most importantly, belief in people's potential.

As you get further into this preparation stage, you may see the need for other team members and want to add to your original team. Moreover, team composition may change as you move through the various stages of community mobilisation, with different skills needed at different times. But even from the beginning, the wider the variety of perspectives represented on your team, the less likely you will overlook important issues.

STEP 3: Gather Information about the Development Issue and the Community

After you have defined the health issue and put together your team, it will be time to explore the issue in greater detail and learn as much as you can about the people who are most affected by it and the community you are planning to work with. This knowledge will be essential when you come to the next to last step of this preparation phase: designing the overall goals and objectives of your community mobilisation plan. But you will also need this information when it comes time to develop your team, for example, to decide if you need a partner (and how to choose one), and to identify your resources and constraints. These actions cannot be carried out until you are familiar with the health issue and the community.

STEP 4: Identify Resources and Constraints

Now that you know more about the health issue and the community, you will need to do an inventory of the resources that will be available to the programme and any constraints you may face. You and your team should complete a simple worksheet where you list resources according to the following categories:

- *Financial Resources*: Project budget, income from all sources, including municipal government, the private sector, Ministry of Health funds, and nonprofit organizations.
- *Human Resources and the Types of Skills they can Contribute*: Skilled project staff, collaborating organizations' staff/ members, community members willing to work on the project, and others.
- *Material Resources*: meeting space, supplies, meals, computers, vehicles, other equipment, office space.

STEP 5: Develop a Community Mobilisation Plan

Now that you and your team have a better understanding of the health issue you will be working on, the setting you will be working in, and your resources and constraints, it's time to develop a community mobilisation plan. (If you have limited prior experience with community mobilisation, you may want to read the rest of the field guide before developing your plan.) This plan is a general description of how you and your team intend to assist this particular community to mobilize around this particular issue. For those teams working with a donor, this plan may serve as the project proposal or the basis for it if the donor requires a different format.

The purpose of the mobilisation plan you are developing is to define the overall programme goals and objectives and identify a process that will help interested communities achieve them, not to determine specific community actions or activities. As you create this plan, you should always keep the two overriding goals of community mobilisation uppermost in your mind:

- To improve the health of the community, particularly those people most affected by the issue.
- To improve the community's capacity to address its health and other needs.

At a minimum, a typical community mobilisation plan should contain the following seven elements, each of which is described in detail below.

- Background information.
- Programme goal: the overall goal of the mobilisation effort.
- Programme objectives: the overall objectives of the effort.
- The community mobilisation process: the overall process you and the community will go through to achieve the goal and objectives.
- A monitoring and evaluation plan.
- A project management plan.
- A budget.

1. *Background Information:* This section should describe the overall context for the plan, including information about the health issue, the setting, the resources and constraints, and why this particular community was selected.
2. *Programme Goal:* In some cases, the goal of the programme has been predetermined in relation to global, national, or local health priorities as identified by the donor. In other situations where communities perceive a pressing need, communities themselves may define the goal.

Alternatively, public health officials or others may identify a goal based on an analysis of community health indicators (*e.g.*, frequency and severity of specific health problems and feasibility to address them).

No matter who defines it, a clearly articulated goal that can motivate the community is one of the most important keys to an effective community mobilisation strategy. This does not mean that you should ignore what donors, public health officials, or programme staff want to achieve but to state the goal in concrete, personal terms that people will understand and want to support.

Community mobilisation goals sometimes mistakenly aim at promoting behaviours, such as 'mobilizing people to vaccinate their children', rather than emphasizing the potential benefits, such as: 'reducing the number of children who get sick or die from diseases that can be prevented by vaccination.' The *Warmi* project goal, for example, was to reduce maternal and newborn deaths, while in Vietnam the project goal was to restore malnourished children to good nutritional status.

3. *Programme Objectives:* There are many resources on how to define objectives in the context of programme design. Many discuss the characteristics of well-defined, 'SMART' objectives – specific, measurable, attainable, result-oriented and time-limited – and these are valid and useful. When mobilizing communities, however, our role is not to define the specific objectives of the overall effort because the primary actors, the community members, will do this. Instead, the plan's objectives will focus on general health outcomes and process objectives related to building community capacity and to the key underlying themes that we identified while learning about the community. Our aim at this point is to set a direction for the process so that facilitators can judge whether the programme design is effective or whether it needs to be adjusted. For those familiar with project design, this approach to setting objectives is different because it takes the setting of specific objectives out of their hands and puts it into the hands of community members.

Those who work with donors may need to explain why it is so important for community members to define and commit to their own objectives. For example, when negotiating the approval of the *Warmi* project design, donors, other programme staff and the project designers discussed at length why the project did not propose specific objectives with clearly identified indicators, as is expected with most proposals. Instead, the *Warmi* project proposal stated that the list of objectives and indicators presented in the proposal was illustrative and would be revised based on work with communities to set priorities and appropriate objectives. Fortunately, the donor was flexible and understood the rationale behind the proposal, and the project was approved with the agreement that once objectives were defined, they would be communicated to the donor.

Here are two examples of objectives, from the SECI project in Bolivia and the Bridges project in Peru. The SECI project aimed to:

- Increase communication between participating communities and health service providers through the use of a community and facility-based health information system to contribute to improved health.
- Increase participating communities' and health service providers' ability to analyze and use information to address community health problems.

The Bridges project had the following objectives:

- Increase the utilization of public health services in selected project areas.
- Improve client and service provider interpersonal interactions within health services.
- Establish mechanisms and/or systems to improve co-ordination and collaboration between health services and community organizations.

The Bridges Project went on to articulate general process objectives based on the key underlying themes identified through analysis of information gathered while learning about the community. These process objectives, stated as 'desired results,' follow on the next page.

4. *The community Mobilisation Process: The Community Action Cycle:* This field guide recommends structuring community mobilisation efforts around the five phases of the Community Action Cycle, and adds two other phases: prepare to mobilize and scale up. Accordingly, as you and your team sit down to develop your mobilisation plan, you can assume that in general this cycle is what you and the community will be going through as you carry out this effort.

Using the Community Action Cycle as a guide and keeping in mind the overall approach you wish to take and the strategies you outlined above, describe the basic tasks/activities you propose for each phase of the process. This plan does not need to be very detailed at this point, but for planning and budgeting purposes you should consider the types of activities, who will participate (approximate numbers and characteristics), and what you hope to achieve through these activities.

5. *Monitoring and Evaluation Plan:* Community participants will have the opportunity to develop their own monitoring and evaluation plan as part of the community action cycle process. However, the project monitoring and evaluation plan should meet your team's and your donor's needs for information. This section of the proposal should state, at a minimum, which health related outcomes will be monitored on an ongoing or periodic basis to determine if the objectives are being achieved. Additionally, you should consider which areas of community capacity or other process outcomes you will monitor, how and when. At this point, it may be premature to specify community capacity indicators until you have worked with the community to determine which areas they would like to strengthen. However, you may want to state how you plan to work with the community to come to this agreement. We recommend that you use both qualitative and quantitative measures and a combination of participatory and external methods, if possible, to provide a more comprehensive picture. If you do not have the

resources to afford this, you should discuss which methods you have chosen and why in relation to the overall goals of the project and in light of various stakeholder interests.

6. *Project Management Plan:* This section of your plan should state who the members of the programme team are, how they will communicate and work together, what their roles will be in relation to the project participants, and describe co-ordination mechanisms and institutional relationships if appropriate.

Staffing will vary according to your available resources (time and money), the number of communities and population you are trying to reach, and your project strategies and activities. Experience demonstrates that it is reasonable to estimate that a team of two people can work with between ten and twenty communities, even in settings that are geographically dispersed. Teams are recommended, as one person can facilitate while the other assists, observes, and documents the sessions. One person can facilitate sessions alone, but it is more difficult and is not recommended if two can possibly work together. If community capacity is such that a local person can facilitate, and having local facilitators is desirable, you may be able to have one person from your team support the effort by helping to prepare the facilitator, observe, document, and provide feedback to him/her.

7. *Budget:* Most proposals will also include a budget based on the management structure and activities proposed. It is not within the scope of this field guide to go into detail here on how to budget. However, as with all budgeting, you should consider the costs of personnel, equipment, materials and supplies, travel and transport, other direct costs for training, administration, and other project activities not previously covered.

STEP 6: Develop your Team

Once you have drawn up your mobilisation plan, it will be time to develop your team. One of the first steps in this process will be to define the role your team is going to play in implementing the mobilisation plan. Outside organizations can play a variety of different roles as mobilisers, depending on the nature of the effort and the needs of the community. Some of the more common roles include:

- *Mobiliser or catalizer:* Works directly with existing leaders and community groups to stimulate action.
- *Organizer:* Forms new organizations or brings existing organizations together in new ways around an issue.
- *Capacity-builder/trainer:* Helps to build capacity to achieve CM goals.
- *Partner:* Complements local organizations in a joint effort.
- *Liaison:* Links communities with resources and partners, builds networks.
- *Advisor:* Provides assistance to communities who request specific advice/technical expertise.
- *Advocate:* Supports community efforts to obtain resources or change policies.
- *Direct service provider:* Provides a service (*e.g.*, health care, education).
- *Donor:* Provides funding to the community to the address health issue.
- *Marketer:* Shares experience with others to expand CM.

Your team's role may change over time as both your own organization's needs and the community's needs and abilities change and as other circumstances change. It is a good idea to think through your short-term roles and plan for your long-term roles so that you may lay the groundwork more proactively. For example, if you begin work with a community as an organizer, you may want to gradually move toward being a partner and then a liaison or advisor as the community organizations' capacity is strengthened. You should continually reassess your team's role(s) and be flexible enough to respond to new community needs as the community mobilisation process unfolds. As important as defining what your role is, it is equally as important to define what it is not. Team members who understand and can present clearly what their role is and is not are better able to avoid future misunderstanding and confusion.

One of the last things you and your team will do in this preparation phase is to look again at the tasks you've set for yourselves and decide who is going to be responsible for what. Once you have done this, it will become clear as to whether your team members have the skills they need for the duties they've been assigned. If they don't, you have several choices:

- You can add people to your team who do have the needed skills.
- You can train people in the needed skills.
- You can partner with another organization who has people with the needed skills.

The size of the team is also an important question. If your team is going to be directly involved in facilitating the community mobilisation effort, the ideal size is two people for every eight to ten communities. If your team is going to play a less central role, you can have fewer members.

However you decide the question of team size and composition, you want to approach the next stage in the community mobilisation process – organize the community for action – confident in team members' ability to do the work you're about to embark on.

At this point it may also be helpful/necessary to spend some time on basic team building activities. (See Useful Tool V and references in the Resources Guide under 'Non-formal participatory learning' at the end of this chapter.)

Finally, it may help the team and the team manager to discuss and agree on the role the team manager will play in the CM effort. The team leader (usually the programme manager) should consider the following in developing his/her team:

- Create a shared team purpose with a common vision, goals, and objectives.
- Establish and model values.
- Clarify roles and responsibilities of team members.
- Create a 'learning' team (create an organizational culture to stimulate self and group assessment of individual and

team strengths and weaknesses in critical areas such as facilitation, communication, participatory methods and approaches, Non-formal education, community organizing).

- Work to prevent and/or resolve conflicts among team members.
- Encourage and reward creativity and innovation.
- Problem-solve, troubleshoot.
- Build consensus around strategies and approaches.
- Serve as institutional representative liaising with donors, partners, communities.
- Celebrate successes!

WIGNARAJA AND SIRIVARDANA MODEL

Wignaraja and Sirivardana (2000) in their edited book titled "Readings on Pro-Poor Planning Through Social Mobilisation Approach" have identified the following critical steps in social mobilisation.

1. *Efficiency and Creativity of the Poor:* The starting point: Self-initiatives of the poor form the essence of a process of participatory development, where the poor operate as conscious subjects of change. They reflect on their life-situations, and take decisions to bring about changes to improve their social and economic status. The underlying assumption, which now has a material basis is that the poor are creative as well as efficient. They are capable of taking self-initiatives for their development, but social processes have often operated to deny opportunities for the practical expression of people's creativity. A meaningful development process must lead to a liberation of the creative initiatives of the poor.
2. *From Objects to Subjects*: Conventional top-down models for development, explicitly or implicitly, treat the poor as objects of change and the relation between the intervenor and the poor often takes the form of a subject acting upon an object. It is assumed in these top-down welfare models that the poor have no knowledge-base or that their knowledge is irrelevant/unscientific, and the poor have to be told and instructed as to what they should do, or

they are merely waiting for some charity. The outcome is a paternalistic and delivery approach-that is, an attempt to bring development to the poor through deliveries of knowledge and resources from outside. It is also often a way of tranquilizing the poor. Fundamental to the initiation of a process of participatory development is the breakup of this dichotomy of subject and object, and the transformation of the relation into one between two knowing subjects resulting in a creative tension between two knowledge streams, namely poor people's experiential knowledge and the formal knowledge introduced from outside. It is a dialogical process of creating social change. This is also the essence of participation.

3. *Conscientisation and Awareness Raising:* Poor people can be expected first to investigate and analyse their reality. Then they undertake self- initiatives for change when they become conscientised, that is to say, when they become critically aware of their life-situation (the reality of life) and begin to perceive self-possibilities for changing that reality. Hence, the first step in the generation of a process of participatory development is to assist the poor to critically reflect upon, analyse and understand the socio-economic reality in which they live. Reality has to be posed to the poor as a problem to be investigated and as a challenge to transform. The reality that the majority of the urban and rural poor face is poverty and under development: in particular, low levels of production, income and consumption, and the inability even to retain a part of the surplus they generate. Hence, the problematisation of the reality must lead to an investigation and analysis of the totality of life in poverty and under-development. The assumption here is that there is considerable potential for the poor to improve their lives which remain under-utilised. Such potential for development should form the focus of problematisation and subsequent analysis by the people.
4. *Exploration of Self-Possibilities for Actions:* When the poor carry out such investigations and analysis they also begin

to perceive self- possibilities to deal with the factors in their poverty, hence to change the reality. Alternative possibilities of action will be explored and the feasibility for such actions will be examined using the poor people's own knowledge and experiences and drawing from the knowledge available from outside. Resources, requirements and constraints for each action will be carefully studied. This is a process of the poor doing their own planning at the local level.

5. *Organizational Consciousness:* In order to initiate actions, the poor need to organize themselves in a manner (as decided by them) that best suits their purposes. They may decide to build new organizations of their choice or use existing organizations over which they have effective control as instruments of action. The important point here is the availability of organizational mechanisms and support systems in which the poor have confidence, over which they have control, and which they can use for their actions. Poor women would need to build separate organizations initially, to take care of the double burden, of being women and poor, and then link into the general organizations of the poor.
6. *Initiation of Actions:* The poor tend to make a beginning with those actions which they can undertake with their own resources and which they feel could be implemented with success. They tend to start with fairly simple actions. The resources required for such actions are mobilised within the community itself, through collective actions to generate funds. The success of these initial actions gives them some experience in self-initiatives and also enhances their confidence in their abilities to bring about changes in their life-situations. They then embark upon more actions and go into larger and more sophisticated actions which involve claiming and using resources from outside. When they reach this stage, they begin to make claims and bargain for resources available from the social system (*e.g.*, extension services, credit facilities, training and infrastructural facilities) so that their own resource base

is strengthened and supplemented, thereby improving their capacity to initiate more actions. There is, then, an interaction between the poor groups and the socio-economic system with the poor making claims, bargaining for improvement in their access to social resources, while at the same time mobilizing their own resources to further the development process. As a result of this assertion, the socio-economic system will now begin to respond to the needs and requirements of the poor and to serve their interests better.

7. *A Sensitive Support System:* This is where a sensitive support system is required. As it permits the poor to expand their base and multiplies the process. The support system can be an NGO, the government, a bank or a donor agency. At present they are 'delivering inputs' to the poor. But these resources are often diverted to the rich. This is where reorientation and sensitisation of the support system comes to be another critical element in social mobilisation.
8. *From Action to Reflection:* Reflection on actions, that is, to review and evaluate the ongoing actions as a regular practice is undertaken by the poor groups themselves and constitutes an important element in a participatory development process. Reflection enhances the knowledge and understanding of the poor and helps to improve the quality of their actions. Participatory monitoring permits self-corrective actions to be taken while the problems are small. Participatory monitoring is a critical part of participatory development and cannot be separated from the total process of social mobilisation and participatory development.
9. *Capacitation of the People:* As the people's self-development process unfolds, people will begin to improve their capacities to conceive development ideas, plan, implement and manage development actions. A wide range of opportunities will be created for the practical expression and development of talents and skills that lie dormant among the poor. Leaders, intellectuals, animators,

managers, etc., will emerge from the action process reducing over a time the dependence on outside catalysts. The poor will tend to become increasingly self-reliant in their thinking and action and begin to develop autonomous capacities for action. The women's movement has raised poor women's consciousness and now the gender and equity issues have to be responded to not only at the philosophical level but also through concrete development actions undertaken collectively by poor women's groups.

10. *Diversification and Multiplication of Actions*: Initially, the organizations of the poor will naturally tend to start with the problems and issues of immediate concern to them and which they can tackle with confidence. With increasing conscientisation and experience gathered in action planning, they will tend to diversify their actions to include other aspects of their socio-economic lives. Self-initiatives are educational experiences which expand people's horizons. New problems, issues and needs will be identified for investigation, analysis and initiation of actions. The success of one action creates the possibility of undertaking another, setting in motion a flow of successive actions. Furthermore, the process tends to multiply from one group to another and from one village to another. Successful actions of one group demonstrate to others in a village the possibilities of self-development. Moreover, after a point, people's groups tend to develop an urge to expand the process among others, for they begin to realise that it is only when several groups join hands and begin to act together that they will have the strength and the bargaining power to tackle larger issues of common concern to them. The logical outcome of this process is an empowerment of the poor, the development of their capacity for self-development and the emergence of the poor as a counter-power within the socio-economic system capable of asserting their rights and claims to improve their lives. As the sensitivity of the support system increases, the total social mobilisation process becomes complete.

FUTURE GENERATIONS' SEED-SCALE PROCESS FOR COMMUNITY CHANGE MODEL

Source: http://www.future.org/sites/future.org/files/SEED-CALE%20Online%20Summary.pdf

Decades of research, field observations and application show that it is possible to use a systematic process to engage communities in determining their own futures. In the early 1990s, Future Generations and Johns Hopkins University jointly conducted a disciplined review of how to conduct community-based change. This research drew on evidence over the last century, involved UNICEF, the Rockefeller Foundation and the experience of many organizations. The focus was on what has worked in the field of development over the last one-hundred years, specifically on how to take community-based pilot projects to regional scale, and how to sustain their momentum.

Learning from this global evidence, researchers, task force members and field practioners identified key principles, steps and necessary conditions for sustainable community change and developed the SEED-SCALE process.

Overview and Objective

The SEED-SCALE process for community change attempts to answer some of the most difficult questions in community development:

- How to set the spark to ignite community energy.
- How to sustain community momentum and success, year after year.
- How to take local successes to regional or national scale.
- How to create enabling systems for ongoing equitable and sustainable change.
- How to monitor and evaluate change in a way that leads to better solutions without the overwhelming paper work.

The SEED-SCALE process of community change has two key components with two complementary objectives:

1. *SEED* (Self-Evaluation for Effective Decision-making) is a process to mobilize communities and sustain change at the local level.

2. *SCALE* (Systems for Communities to Adapt, Learn and Expand) is a process to scale-up community level change through growth in the number of participating communities and in the quality of life within those communities.

Distinction from other Models and Processes

Although SEED-SCALE builds from and draws upon many models and processes for community development, particularly from the experience of the practioners in the field of international primary health, it is distinct in its systematic and yet simple approach for sustaining and expanding community change. SEED-SCALE is distinctive for its:

- *Model:* SEED-SCALE is based on a biological model of change that allows for both adaption at the community level and exponential extension to other communities.
- *Principles:* It recognizes that there are four necessary conditions for change to be sustainable and to go to scale. These necessary conditions are referred to as the four key principles of community change.
- *Outcomes*: It recognizes that the most important outcomes of community change are not new projects or buildings, but empowered communities with skills to collaborate to improve their lives and to change collective and individual behaviour.

The Four Principles

Necessary Conditions for Change

Future Generations researchers and colleagues have been monitoring community-based development and conservation programmes worldwide to examine why some programmes have succeeded and others have failed. This research concludes that in all cases of success, in which the programme has been both sustainable and has gone to scale, four determinents can be found. In all these cases, successful community change resulted from a set of necessary conditions, which the SEED-SCALE process has described as four key principles.

Principle One: Build from Community Success

People's energy and creativity expand as they realize that they are capable of controlling the challenges in their lives.

One success becomes the stepping stone for subsequent successes and generates community confidence and forward momentum.

Building on community successes is not the customary approach to social change. Professionals, government officials (and indeed the communities themselves) typically focus on the problems, and a long list quickly develops: poverty, the bad roads, poor schools, political, ethnic, or religious factions, etc. Focusing on the problems emphasizes the deficiencies of a community instead of its existing strengths and capacity. The consequence is to beat the community down through what amounts to amassing the evidence that the community is incapable of solving its problems. The ensuing solution is for an outsider to step in and solve this litany of problems, creating a cycle of dependency.

Identifying and then building on successes, however, is an approach that focuses on building upon the existing strengths in a community. This is a forward-moving constructive effort that focuses attention on community assets rather than needs. Action is then based on an assessment of what is possible, rather than what 'needs' to be done. Costs of development go down when attention turns to building on assets, rather than attempting goals that require massive influxes of resources from outside.

Principle Two: Three-way Partnerships

Community energy seldom mobilizes by itself. Communities need help from officials, who can adjust policies and regulations to facilitate co-operation among factions and channel external resources. Communities also need help from experts who can build capacity by training, introduce new ideas, and help monitor change.

Our long-term studies of community development worldwide show that success results when communities work from the bottom up, when officials work from the top down, and when experts work from the outside in. All three roles are needed. When governments create enabling policies, change can accelerate in a cost-efficient way across entire regions. When appropriate experts are involved, development ideas are up-to-date, and fit the local ecology, culture, and economy. When communities are true partners (rather than simply being manipulated by governments or NGOs) then these communities can act more effectively to redefine their futures.

Relationships between these three partners must be flexible, and need continuing adjustment. Many projects start out working well, but then flounder because participants do not understand that their relationships need to evolve. Initially, entrepreneurial leadership is important. In the middle stages, expert-led training, monitoring, and experimentation guide the process, with appropriate midcourse corrections. Later, structured systems will better help communities expand vision and capacity. And to facilitate this phase, officials and experts must shift their roles from control to support of community action.

Principle Three: Evidence-based Decision-making

Action is effective when grounded in objective data. Lacking such data, participants will make decisions on the basis of transitory opinions. These tend to be most influenced by whoever talks most convincingly, or whoever holds more power at the moment. Lacking data from local situations, decisions are made on information from more distant situations – which may or may not be relevant. Factions polarize around differing opinions, but with accurate local data, and thoughtful guidance from officials and experts, differing community factions can find an objective common ground for working together.

While the principle of basing decisions on local data makes sense, accomplishing this goal is often compromised. The SEED process readily adjusts to local capacity, creating an easy-to-do technique by which every community each year can gather data relevant to its needs. Data gathering (especially using the key indicators of a SEED survey) is a process that can start simply and develop great sophistication over time.

Principle Four: Changes in Community Behaviour

People can come together in partnerships; they can agree on objective data; but, to achieve lasting results they must also change behaviours. While changing behaviour for the community may start simply by gaining new skills, those in positions of power – community leaders, officials, or experts – face a more challenging requirement, changing their behaviour to share power. This means giving up exclusive control, shifting to guidance that empowers rather than acting to foster dependency.

For example, at first community members must be trained how to execute their tasks. But very soon, community members must be allowed to make mistakes as part of the developing process. After that, officials and experts must rapidly let go, and not just pretend to do so. This shift is especially difficult, but it can be brought on systematically if the seven steps of the community action cycle are repeated each year.

When officials and experts show some humility, community enthusiasm becomes contagious. A feedback loop creates new expectations and standards for everyone. As one change supports another, social pressure builds, and those who do not co-operate are generally bypassed or overrun by the community's momentum. This momentum will eventually redefine the entire community's collective future.

W.K. KELLOGG FOUNDATION AND THE HEALTHCARE FORUM MODEL

Source:http://www.community-wealth.org/_pdfs/tools/cdcs/tool-kellogg-cmty-cap.pdf

The W. K. Kellogg Foundation in collaboration with The Healthcare Forum have partnered on the development of four modules designed to support Kellogg grantees in their community-based initiatives. The modules are part of the 'Sustaining Community-Based Initiatives' project which was developed to build capacity within community based organizations. Module One is organized around and devoted to five essential elements (chapters) of developing community capacity. Chapter 5 of Module 1 deals with the Community assessment – a tool for mobilizing the community and action planning. An innovative community assessment technique is a key tool for involving and mobilizing people. The approach presented involves all sectors of a community in understanding and acting upon the major issues that face them. This technique has worked in rural and urban areas, and has provided a wonderful "kickoff for community-development efforts as well as a solid base for building community support. Community assessment also serves as an effective tool for mobilizing the community and for action planning.

Overview

Community assessment and action planning are mobilizing processes in which all of the key sectors of the community can play important planning roles. Doing assessments means setting up meetings and planning sessions to be facilitated by community members. The assessment should lead to community involvement in planning, and to well-designed action plans you can implement successfully to address the issues and problems you've targeted.

How Does a Community Assessment Work?

Community assessment consists of six components: all administered by a core planning group of leaders or their delegates, who represent the sectors your assessment will target, This group decides on the assessment's objectives, on which sectors to target, on outreach strategies, and on meeting schedules, It is responsible for implementing the assessment (including facilitating meetings) and collecting the data and information produced.

The six components of the community assessment are:

(i) Community meetings.

(ii) Focus groups.

(iii) A briefing book.

(iv) Citizen surveys.

(v) A resource inventory.

(vi) Coalition expansion.

Each component of the assessment creates greater grassroots involvement in your coalition through information sharing, collaborative planning, outreach, and feedback to the community.

Stages of a Community Assessment

There are a number of stages to the process that you'll need to know about and plan for.

Organizing the core Planning Group

Your first step is to assemble your core planning group, because it will be responsible for implementing the process. This step was described in detail in Chapter 3. The group should reflect all parts of the community you want to target. Members can be leaders you know or representatives from the community that those leaders have recommended. The important thing is that each member be able to commit a good portion of his or her time during the week or two the assessment process requires. The core planning group, then, will be responsible for:

- *Deciding on Objectives and on Community Sectors to Target:* The community assessment targets organizations and their leaders within each sector and invites them to host a community meeting or focus group, which will be facilitated by one of the community planning group members. Because your planning group members represent many of these sectors, it is their task to identify which institutions to include as well as any that may be missing. For example, the ministers from the local interfaith council may host a meeting at a church.
- *Scheduling Meetings and Issuing Invitations:* You may ask community leaders and organizations to host community planning meetings *via* personal contact with the planning group member or through letters and phone calls, The planning group members will also decide on meeting sites, who to invite, and the type of meeting to organize.
- *Facilitating and Assisting at Community Meetings:* Each meeting should follow an identical format and agenda. This will be discussed in greater detail later in the chapter.
- *Collecting Meeting Data:* Community meetings are intended to involve and gain advice from participants. Planning group members should assemble and catalog this information for inclusion in reports that will be presented to the community for feedback.

Implementing a Community Assessment

Once planning group and coalition have completed the initial preparation, you are ready to implement your community assessment. Each step in this detailed process is designed to maximize community participation and ownership.

Community Assessment Meetings

- You need to answer a few questions in order to plan and conduct effective meetings.
- How many meetings should we plan?
- You should hold at least one meeting for each targeted sector of the community. The number of participants will vary depending on the response your invitations to leaders and organizations receive.

How are the Meetings Run?

All community meetings are conducted by a planning group facilitator, who is a member of that community sector or institution, Another member of the planning group should record participants' comments on newsprint in the front of the room. The meeting should be carefully planned to collect information from the participants. The discussion is guided by the following agenda:

1. Introductions.
2. Review of agenda and ground rules.
3. Problems and issues.
4. History.
5. Strengths and resources.
6. Barriers and challenges.
7. Advice.
8. Concerns and other topics.

Who can we ask to be Involved?

Identification and recruitment of participants is very important. People will attend the community meetings and get involved in the assessment process for many reasons. Among these may be that:

- The community and its issues are important to them.
- They believe they have something to contribute.

- They expect that something positive will come from their efforts.
- They have a vision of a better community and values that support that vision.

Participants at the community meetings should have knowledge and Interest or concern; something in common; diverse qualities and characteristics (age, race, gender, interest, skills, or a mix or roles and responsibilities within an organization); and a willingness to be involved in the process.

How does the Planning Group Recruit Participants?

- *Planning* group members should target individuals in existing community organizations. This includes neighborhood associations, church committees, day-care centres, and churches.
- Try to recruit as many people as possible. Personal invitations usually work better than a letter. Explain why you want them to be involved, the purpose of the meeting, and the date and place.
- Remember, if you are targeting a school, make sure you hold several meetings; one each for parents, teachers and staff, and students. For churches and other places of worship, ask members you know to recruit from within the institution.
- It is often easier to recruit friends and acquaintances, but sometimes it is more beneficial to invite strangers to participate. Think of ways you can get as many people as possible involved. Keep a list of names, addresses, and phone numbers as you build your participant 'inventory.'

What Materials are Needed for the Meeting?

Each meeting will need the following materials:

- Name tags.
- Sign-in sheets for participants (name, address, and phone number).
- Easels (two if possible).
- A newsprint pad.
- Masking tape.

- Markers (a few colors).
- The agenda.

What is the Facilitator's Role?

A facilitator is a resource person and leader, not someone with all the answers. He or she will be responsible for moving the process along and helping the group accomplish its objectives, and also for creating a climate in which people feel safe participating. Facilitators should be non-judgmental and supportive. They provide essential information but never opinions. A facilitator's role includes giving clear instructions and guidance about activities, and monitoring the meeting to keep it on time while allowing for extra discussion when needed.

One of the biggest jobs for a facilitator is to see that participants stick to the meeting's ground rules. These help keep the group in order and make participants feel comfortable when discussing their ideas. Post the rules in the front of the room. If people do not keep to them, politely mention that the guidelines are to be followed and keep the meeting on track. Always get the group's agreement on the ground rules before moving to the meeting's agenda.

What are other Roles for Planning Group Members at the Meeting?

While one member is facilitating and another recording, other members can participate by taking on one of the following roles:

- Welcoming people as they arrive.
- Introducing people to each other.
- Serving refreshments.
- Keeping track of people signing in.
- Handling last-minute logistics.
- Helping with transportation if people need assistance getting to and from the meeting.

Tasks for the Coalition

While the community planning group is working on its activities, your coalition will have some critical tasks of its own. Among these are the following:

- Selecting a facilitator and training community planning team members. The coalition should pick a facilitator, who co-ordinates the community assessment process, This person will also be responsible for training the planning group members in how to facilitate the community meetings, and for preparing them for any other tasks for which they are responsible.
- Developing the briefing book. Collect additional data on the communities you are targeting in your assessment and compile it in the briefing book. Later you can give this book to community members and use it to support whatever recommendations emerge from your community meetings. Data can include crime statistics, health and disease information, demographics, and other relevant information that forms a picture of the community.
- Creating a kickoff event. Your coalition must garner recognition in your target communities and create a feeling of excitement and expectation, The kickoff event can be a ceremony with the governor or other important elected officials, a symbolic ribbon cutting at the first community meeting site, or anything else that you feel will generate publicity.
- Be sure to generate press coverage. You want as many people as possible to know the community assessment is beginning and that you have begun this intensive effort to fully involve the community in your coalition.
- Compiling the reports, executive summaries, and recommendations. Although the planning group members will deliver the data from the meetings, it is up to your coalition members - in conjunction with the planning group - to compile this information into three documents that will be accessible to and delivered back to the communities. The reports are a compilation of all of the meeting summaries and briefing book information from that particular community. Executive summaries are the meeting summaries and the recommendations of the coalition for action based on the information gathered, Executive summaries should

also include any specific briefing book information that supports these recommendations.

- Organizing feedback to the community. When the reports, summaries, and recommendations have been compiled you need to return them to the community for feedback and adjustments. You can do this either through mailing the executive summaries, convening a special series of feedback meetings, or a combination of both approaches.
- Recruiting new coalition members and expanding the coalition. During the community assessment process, members of the community planning group and many of the meeting participants will prove to be important new recruits for the coalition, Develop strategies to enlist them in the coalition either through task forces and committees or by asking them to sit on the coalition's board of directors or main planning body.

To summarize, the seven stages of community assessment are:

- The assessment facilitator trains the members of the community planning team.
- Hold community meetings throughout the area during a one-week period.
- Bring feedback from the meetings back to the coalition and the community planning group for analysis.
- The planning group and the coalition develop recommendations to address each priority.
- Give feedback to the community at large.
- Formalize relationships and explore collaborations with community groups.
- Bring plans and recommendations to an action-planning session, where they are evaluated and possibly implemented.

MERCY CORPS' COMMUNITY MOBILIZATION APPROACH

Source: http://www.mercycorps.org/sites/default/files/Community MobilizationSectorApproach_0.pdf

Mercy Corps helps people in the world's toughest places turn the crises of natural disaster, poverty and conflict into opportunities for progress. Driven by local needs and market conditions, Mercy Corps programmes provide communities with the tools and support they need to transform their own lives. Mercy Corps believes that a community-led initiative is one that originates from and is managed by community members. Mercy Corps, as the catalyst, is wholly accountable to that community in order to achieve their vision. Community mobilization is the process of building community capacity to self-identify priorities, resources, needs and solutions in such a way as to promote representative participation, good governance, accountability and peaceful change. Community Mobilization is about making sure communities are in the driver's seat of any change process.

A number of Mercy Corps and external studies have shown that community mobilization can help meet the challenges of societies in transition by changing attitudes, norms, practices and behaviours of individuals as well as groups. As a result, communities are able to better assess their needs, identify options for addressing them, prioritize, leverage resources and create solutions. Often such processes lead to structural changes within communities, a critical transformation that supports lasting change. The diagram on the next page and the chart below further illustrate this change process and some of the many long-term benefits of community mobilization.

The community mobilization methodology, which easily adapts to diverse local contexts, calls for community representatives to work in assessing needs and responding to them through participatory project implementation and monitoring. Community mobilization programmes aim to move people across the spectrum of participation by engaging them in the leadership of the overall programme throughout its implementation and by strengthening their capacity and confidence to take on increasing levels of responsibility with each new project.

Community Mobilization....	And the long-term benefits can be...
• Increases participatory decision-making processes by bringing diverse stake holders into a common process. • Expands inclusion of often marginalized populations, such as women, youth, persons with disabilities, the elderly, and religious or ethnic minorities. • Depends on local resources, both human and Material. • Fosters stronger relationships between local government, businesses, community members and CBO/NGOs. • Ensures local ownership of development. • Promotes a more active and informed citizenry	• Communities reduce their dependence on outside aid, as they become adept at identifying and solving their own problems. • Communities can better prepare for or respond to disasters and crises because they have relationships with decision-makers and experience in quickly identifying communal needs and priorities. • Local governments gain greater credibility with their own constituencies and can better lobby national level decision-makers because they are truly aware of local need and have local support • A more stable foundation for breaking cycles of inter group tension and achieving lasting stability

SOCIAL MOBILIZATION AS A STRATEGY FOR POVERTY ALLEVIATION – EXPERIENCES FROM UNDP-SUPPORTED SOUTH ASIA POVERTY ALLEVIATION PROGRAMME IN INDIA

Background

The United Nations Development Programme (UNDP) supported a poverty alleviation project in 750 villages in three districts of Mahabubnagar, Kurnool and Andhra Pradesh in India since 1996. The project sought to demonstrate social mobilization as a effective and sustainable strategy for poverty alleviation. In this model, an attempt is made to present in brief, the strategy and lessons learnt from the project.

The project approach focused on obstacles that perpetuate poverty, with the objective of removing them and enabling the poor to overcome their conditions. Three significant elements of the approach were:

- To see the poor as subjects and partners in the effort for poverty reduction.
- To recognize the creativity of the poor, their capacity for enterprise.
- To accord the poor the respect and dignity as partners in development.

Project Strategy

The project strategy relied on the triad of:

- Social organization of the poor. This is to be facilitated through a process of social mobilization.
- Skill development to nurture inherent capacities and potentialities and widen the basket of opportunities and choices for the poor to choose for their development.
- Capital formation for improved quality of life and overcoming hunger, destitution and deprivation on a sustainable basis through judicious capital investments.

Organization-building by the Poor through Social Mobilization

Social mobilization enables the poor to build their own organizations in which they participate fully and directly and take decisions on all the issues concerning the poverty. Social mobilization is the fulcrum around which the poverty alleviation project revolves.

Conventional attempts to reach the rural poor have tried to design and improve delivery mechanisms for various developmental inputs. However, a key element has always been neglected, *i.e.*, for delivery mechanism to function properly and fulfill its objectives, there has to be a receiving mechanism at the grassroots level. The organizations of the poor offer an effective receiving mechanism. But more important than acting as a receiving mechanism, they can act as a vehicle to increase the general capacity of the poor for self-improvement. Full participation at the grassroots level is only possible if the rural poor are organized. Without this organization, participatory development will remain a mere slogan.

The organizations of the poor, especially at the village level, are meant to be self-sustaining development institutions that can enter into a partnership for development with government and private agencies. In order to achieve this status, the organization must be viewed by all parties, especially the poor, as legitimate and credible. The organization will be legitimate if it does not comprise with existing social and political vested interests. Ant it will be credible if it continues to confer benefits to its members.

To ensure that the organization remains a broad-based institution with a potential for self-reliance, two fundamental rules had to be observed at all times. *Firstly,* the organization has to meet as a general body on a regular basis. This requirement is necessary so that all members must participate in the development process in their village, in order to benefit from it. *Secondly,* all members must make savings deposits at their regular meetings. The accumulation of this equity capital is of paramount importance to the viability of the organization.

The organization has to be the necessary primary unit on which to base a programme of comprehensive development of the rural poor. It is the essence of successful development at the village level. This point needs to be emphasized because, though planners have often promoted the role of physical and administrative infrastructures in the plans, they have done so to the exclusion of what might be called a social infrastructure – a series of organizations of the poor. It is only through this infrastructure that the incorporation of the human resources of the rural areas into the planning process can be achieved.

To be viable, an organization must meet as a general body regularly and not leave affairs of the organization to be managed by a few members. The organization does elect a president and a manager, as its office-bearers. It may elect committees of members for specific activities such as: management of a tractor or machinery owned by the organization; resolution of disputes between members; enforcement of the decisions of the general body on ban on free grazing of animals; protection of common resources like pastures; forest, etc. Committees of the general body are also needed, especially to manage social welfare provision like health, education, sanitation, mother and childcare, nutrition education and family planning. However, it is through the regular meetings of the general body, which may be weekly or fortnightly and in no case less than monthly, that the supremacy of the members is assured, otherwise there is the danger of the organization being hijacked by a few, for their own benefit.

Experience has shown that executive committee has proved the bane of the co-operatives in the Indian sub-continent. The role of the lay members in keeping the organization on the right track has to be continuously emphasized. The members are urged to insist that the office-bearers keep the members informed of the accounts of the organization, savings and other matters. Where members fail to do so, either due to sheer indolence or obstinacy of office bearers the organization, makes sluggish progress. The general body meeting ensures public knowledge of the affairs of the organization and acts as a deterrent against corruption. It sits on judgement on all complaints pertaining to the members of the organization and its office-bearers.

The role of the general body in achieving equitable, productive, sustainable development and growth with social justice, at the village level, has been established beyond any doubt, in scores of rural development programmes.

The Project Experiences

The series of dialogues the project team have had with the rural poor in the project area have enabled the poor women realize the need for building an organization for themselves. The poor women in the project area bear the double burden of being poor and being a woman. It is this consciousness that induced the poor women to get organized. The project team responded to their willingness and offered social guidance to facilitate them to build their own organizations.

Formation of Self-Help Groups with Thrift as an Entry Point

The project identified thrift as its strategic entry point for organizing the poor women, for variety of factors. *Firstly,* the past experience of several projects aimed at poverty alleviation successfully used thrift as an entry point to rally the poor. *Secondly,* in impoverished households living below the poverty line, the real value of savings, however small it may be, has enormous potential to help them eke out a living. Thus livelihood security was a key concern in the poverty alleviation strategy of the project. The lead role taken by the women has to be viewed in the larger socio-cultural context of the society that tends to thrust upon women many economic responsibilities. In the project area, a woman supports the households with meager wage earnings, if the husband becomes an alcoholic and fritters away his earnings on liquor. The cultural values place the burden of children's upbringing on women's shoulders in case of desertion, abandonment or divorce by men. *Fourthly,* the project strategy views thrift as a key element for capital formation in poor households to cross the poverty line.

In the project, thrift and credit groups are used synonymously with self-help groups (SHGs). The SHG is an organization of about 15-20 poor women of same socio-economic background. The members of the group meet once in week. Typical agenda of the meeting is as follows:

- Review the action taken on the decision of the last meeting.
- Collection of savings from the members.
- Collection of loan repayments from the members.
- Scrutiny of loan applications of the members.
- Decision on the issuance of loan to the member(s).
- Fixing the repayment schedule for the loans issued.
- Discussion on the asset creation for income generation by the members and identification of problems in securing the anticipated incomes from the activities, leading to identification of forward and backward linkages.
- Discussion of primary health care, primary education, drinking water and sanitation.
- Scrutiny of the books of accounts being maintained for the group by the bookkeeper.

Majority of the groups in the project area meticulously followed group norms as detailed below:

- Regular meetings with or without facilitation by the community volunteer, mostly once in a week.
- Participation of all in the group meetings.
- Regular savings in the groups.
- Quick rotation of the group corpus by advancing loans to the mandals and recovering the same as per the recovery statement.
- Prioritization of the loans through discussion.
- Recording the transactions in books of accounts.
- Engaging a bookkeeper who is paid by the group if there is no literate member in the group.
- Presence of strong group pressure for ensuring prompt recovery of loans advanced to the members.
- Resources generated from within and accessed from outside are pooled as group corpus.
- Collection of interest on all loans.
- Fixing of clear repayment schedule through discussion with the borrower.
- Maintenance of nearly 100 per cent recovery rate.

Genesis of a Village Organization as a Federation of the SHGs in Each Village

As the SHGs mature in to self-managed units, they realized that there are many things which cannot be handled by small groups. All the SHGs in each village are federated into a village organization (VO) (there are about 5-10 groups in each village when the VOS are formed). The VOS in the project area symbolize the collective strength of the poor. They have the critical mass to give visibility to the organization of the poor. The project team take care to see that there is role clarity between the SHGs and the Vos. The Vos do not impinge on the autonomy of the SHGs in decision-making. The Vos focus on the issues which the SHGs are not able to handle at the SHG level. All the members of the SHGs in the village are the members of the VO which meets once in a month. Some of the responsibilities of the Vos are:

- Monitor the functioning of the small groups and assist the weaker groups to improve their performance.
- Formation of new groups and their capacity-building.
- Capacity-building of the groups by organizing training, etc.
- Provide audit services to the groups.
- Provide linkages with the banks and line departments.
- Assert the for rights and entitlements of the poor.
- Mobilise community action for securing basic minimum amenities for the poor in the village.
- Enhance access of the poor to education and health.
- Take greater role in identification of the poorest of the poor for the anti-poverty programmes of the government.

VOs as village Financial Intermediaries

One of the strengths of the project is the development of the VOs as village financial intermediaries. The availability of seed capital (micro-capital assistance) of the programme helps the project to develop the Vos as financial intermediaries (VFI). The VO secures bulk loan from outside and lends to the SHGs. The SHGs, in turn, lend the capital to the members. The VO earns some interest margin to meet it's running cost and also to pay for the services of the village level specialists. The VOs have demonstrated the capabilities of the poor to manage this function most prudently. All the VOs initiated into financial intermediation have shown sound credit discipline and prudent financial management. The recovery performance has been near 100.

Given the multiplicity of the SHGs in each village, linkages of all the SHGs with banks is far fetched. The banks would find it convenient to deal with just 10-12 VOs (there are about 10-12 villages in each service area of the banks). The transaction costs also would substantially come down for both the borrower and the lender.

Building Catalysts: Village Activists and Village Specialists

Organizations of the poor have thrown up leaders who are sincere, committed and dynamic. Such leaders of the community-based organizations are called village activists.

Village activists are those who act as catalysts in the process of social mobilization, taking leadership in building participatory organizations. The project has been identifying such human resources and started building their capacities which is yielding rich dividends. Village level activists facilitate the functioning of the grassroots people's institutions.

While organizations of the poor embarked on new initiatives or searching for new opportunities, the project found enlightened members of the poor within the village who are well informed, and who can contribute to the reservoir of functional knowledge. They are called village specialists. Their contribution lies in guiding the people. The village specialists have been assisting people in areas like watershed as watershed specialists, and in animal husbandry as livestock specialists (barefoot professionals), or in primary health care as community health activists. The project recognizes the vital role of village specialists and seeks to equip them with new information and skills for effective role performance. The village specialists are paid service charges by the VO. This will ensure sustenance of the service provision.

Thus village specialists identified and supported by the community-based agencies themselves, are a reservoir of knowledge and skills built through the capacity-building efforts of the project in key sectors such as agriculture, animal husbandry, watershed management and primary health care. The village level specialists will offer locals on-the-spot technical and educational support for the poor instead of they running to Mandal and district headquarters to redress minor problems at huge cost and agony. The vision is an active self-reliant village with all expertise available within and managed by people's institutions at a low cost.

Lessons in Social Mobilization

Planning and implementation was a process of continuous learning, unlearning and relearning for the project team. The experiences, the strengths and the limitations offered several lessons to the team engaged in the innovative task of alleviating poverty through social mobilization. It was gratifying to discover the tremendous determination, tenacity and self-management capacities of the rural poor though weighed down heavily by years of subjugation, impoverishment and illiteracy. Notable lessons were:

- People are basically willing to get organized. The process of social mobilization has to induce. It is not spontaneous.
- There is tremendous potential within the poor. The potential is harnessed by organizing them.
- People have inherent conviction and confidence in merits of social mobilization.
- Availability of a large number of activists in villages. They are committed, and sincere and dynamic leadership emerged from the most disadvantaged and even most illiterate men and women.

Andhra Pradesh in India has been able to demonstrate an approach of poverty reduction encompassing over 10 million rural poor families comprising, nearly 45 million people which has no parallel anywhere in South Asia. Andhra has found the solution to rural poverty comprising:

- A three-tier institutional grassroots framework of Self-Help Groups (SHGs), Village Organizations (VOs) and Mahila Mandal Samakhyas (MMSs).
- An independent and autonomous sensitive support organization like Society for Elimination of Rural Poverty (SERP) for fostering a statewide 3-tier grassroots institutional framework.

In 1991, South Asian Association for Regional Co-operation (SAARC) had set up an Independent Commission for Alleviation of Poverty. The Commission made an overarching recommendation which the SAARC Summit in its meeting at Dhaka in 1993 endorsed, namely, that Social Mobilization should be the centrepiece for all poverty reduction strategies of the governments of the region to be achieved by setting up independent and autonomous support organizations to mobilise rural poor men and women.

7 SUMMATION

Poverty is a multi-faceted phenomenon, defined (and explained) as a situation in which a person lacks the necessary capabilities and entitlements to satisfy his or her basic needs and aspirations. From this point of view, the fight against poverty must consist in establishing entitlements that will allow the poor access to the material, social, and spiritual means to develop their capabilities. Facilitating access to productive resources-ranging from land and water, to infrastructure – for the poor is not a one-time event, but an institutional process, requiring permanent adaptation to changing circumstances of power, economics, and culture. Thus, it becomes necessary to focus on empowerment of the poor as the crucial requirement for a sustainable solution to poverty and hunger. Empowerment is understood here as the ability of people, in particular the least privileged, to: *(a)* have access to productive resources that enable them to increase their earnings and obtain the goods and services they need; and *(b)* participate in the development process and the decisions that affect them. These two aspects are related; one without the other is not empowerment.

A key requirement for any escape from poverty and hunger is access to productive resources. For the rural poor, land and financial resources are of foremost importance, but technology, seeds and fertilizer, livestock and fisheries, irrigation, marketing opportunities, and off-farm employment are also essential. Facilitating access to productive resources – ranging from land and water, to infrastructure – for the poor is not a one-time event, but an institutional process, requiring permanent adaptation to changing circumstances of power, economics, and culture. Without the participation of the rural poor in the implementation of programmes, and without the establishment of effective organizations of the rural poor that act as countervailing forces to vested interests, it is unlikely that much progress will be made in increasing the access of the poor to productive resources.

Participation is the fundamental element that defines the demand-driven development approach. Individuals and communities are empowered to influence and control the decisions and resources that affect them. Traditionally, decisions were made by 'government experts', but participatory approaches have demonstrated that governments can allocate local investments based on the needs and preferences expressed by the community itself. *Community obilisation, capacity building* and *participatory planning* are key activities to ensure meaningful and inclusive participation.

Community mobilisation is an integral part of the participatory development process. The community mobilisation in a broader sense means organizing people living in the same community with a specific purpose. Community mobilisation is a capacity-building process through which community individuals, groups, or organizations plan, carry out, and evaluate activities on a participatory and sustained basis to improve their livelihood and other needs, either on their own initiative or stimulated by others. Communities lead or participate in all stages, from start to finish.

Community mobilisation aims to organize and improve community participation. Motivating all member of a community provides the opportunity to utilize a variety of skills and abilities, which improves ownership and increases sustainability. The aim of community mobilisation is to build the capacity of the local community and that of its grassroots organization structures to enable them to undertake their own desired and aspired, self-owned and managed development.

Community mobilisation process ensures putting development resources, skills, responsibilities and authority into the hands of the community of stakeholders.

Community mobilisation, a key strategy for increasing demand for and use of various public services, is a process that helps communities to identify their own needs and to respond to and address these needs. Gaining the participation of community members can help providers raise awareness both of developmental issues at the community level and of social and cultural issues that may promote or inhibit use of information and services, as well as improve clients' understanding of the methods or services being offered. Specific barriers to service access and use can be addressed and service utilization increased. For the community development projects, community mobilization is important in linking public service institutions and structures to communities, fostering greater access to and equity in development outcomes.

Promoting community mobilisation and empowerment builds community and village institutions that are organized, transparent, and that can manage their own development priorities. Experience shows that this approach leads to more sustainable outcomes and helps programmes reach sufficient scale to reach more of the poor. Mobilized and empowered community organizations enable the poor to develop linkages with the financial sector and markets, and allow them to become credit and investment worthy. When communities organize and begin to manage their own projects, their self-esteem and confidence grows. As their experience builds, the groups can take over most of the functions performed by project staff and/or other functionaries.

Community mobilisation acts as a catalyst for organizing the members of a community to take group action by sharing their problems and seeking their own solutions by pooling their own resources, obtaining external help and participating actively in the decision-making processes that shape their lives as individuals and as members of households and the local polity. The process of community mobilisation creates energy/

force. If constructive, this force can be used to enhance social capital (Laws and Regulations, Respect for Laws, Monitoring, Evaluation, and Accountability), human capital (Knowledge, Skill etc.,) and Physical capital (Community building, Drinking Water, Irrigation, Sanitation, Hydro Power, other physical infrastructure) in the society, which raises the welfare of the people.

It is generally agreed that in society, people are willing and have the potentiality to do many things by themselves for their own well-being and the well-being for their family and their society/community. The aim of community mobilization therefore, is to harness the dormant potentiality and willingness of people to help themselves. However, people need social/technical guidance to harness their potential. Such guidance is essential for following purposes:

- *To get organized* for pooling of resources, cutting down overheads, achieving economy of scale, etc.
- *To identify genuine leaders/cadres/activists* from amongst themselves from the community. It is only these cadres and not outsiders that can bring out the willingness and harness the potential of the people.
- *To identify and prioritize* what people are willing to undertake in terms of opportunities and needs.
- *To assess the feasibility* of identified opportunities and needs in terms of peoples' capacity, willingness, equity, sustainability, requirement of resources from within and outside.
- *To arrange, secure and facilitate* the flow of required resources to the community.
- *To monitor, lobby and establish linkages* between communities and other development agencies.

Community mobilisation approach has generally been very successful in unifying once-unorganized members of the communities, raised their levels of awareness, built capacity and improved the livelihood conditions of the people with whom they work. It has also increased people's access to resources/loans, fostered habits of saving, and created opportunities for participation in training and employment.

The strategy of community mobilisation has helped the poor and the disadvantaged in forming self-help groups, in working together towards common goals, in psychological empowerment through these processes, and in bringing subtle improvements in the livelihoods of those mobilized. Though the community mobilisation process has created a forum and opportunity for the poor and the disadvantaged to raise their voices and articulate their choices through their own organization and to mainstream their priorities, it has tended to limit the inclusion of the ultra-poor in its efforts largely because of three factors: limitations in defining/assessing extreme degrees of poverty; the social distance of the ultra-poor from the mainstream of the local population; and the absence of a focused strategy/design for involving the ultra-poor within a holistic approach that also regards the non-poor as members of community organization. The fact that targeted programmes are often unsustainable, leading to tensions within the community, suggests that targeted programmes should be built into holistic social mobilization efforts. This kind of approach, complemented by horizontal and vertical linkages covering the entire country, can become the most effective medium for empowerment at the grassroots level. It is also crucial to strengthening the decentralization process because it integrates grassroots initiatives with meso and macro-level policies and institutions. It is also important to make the community mobilisation campaigns more accountable and transparent so as to sustain capacity-building as a mechanism of empowerment at the grassroots level. Apart from a 'residual' approach, no strategy has been developed for inclusion of the ultra-poor. Their integration requires an 'affirmative action' or 'positive discrimination' policy, along with strategic steps to involve them through enlarging their assets and opportunities at the household level, together with appropriate capacity-building. Ways and means should be explored to increase resource mobilization though building real partnerships with other agencies currently working to improve livelihoods at the grassroots level, whether in gender concerns, legal aid or other specialized fields. From a policy perspective, the main challenge remains to replicate and upscale the best practice models to ensure that the scale of intervention matches the existing scale of neglected outreach.

With community mobilisation, the role of the implementing agency shifts from a more traditional one of teacher/advisor/ leader to that of facilitator. A more comprehensive definition of community mobilisation suggests that it is a dynamic and participatory process of empowering people, especially the poor and the socially excluded, for their socio-cultural, political and economic upliftment in a sustainable manner. It causes a transition and a feasible environment for a change to take place in the society. Empowerment of the poorest of the poor is, thus, an effective outcome of this process or instrument of change called community mobilisation.

Effective mobilisation can generate positive social capital that not only helps communities work collectively to address their development problems, but also strengthens community level governance. Some examples include:

- The participatory identification of the poor is a public process involving all villagers and the results of which are voted on in a public forum (gram parishad, etc.,) by all villagers.
- Social Audit Committees within village organizations monitor the activities of the organization's leadership, the procurement practices, and the financial management.
- Grievance systems (sometimes referred to as communication trees) provide an avenue to community members to report corruption at the local level.

The community mobilisation process helps people move from the passive status of welfare recipients to that of citizens who possess vital knowledge of their communities and localities and therefore know best how to effect – and direct – change at the local level. Few strategies so fully embody the human development paradigm in all the dimensions of empowerment – the socio-cultural, economic and political. Community mobilization thus enhances both individual and group capabilities, widening people's choices and enlarging the range of things they can do and be. Unlike social engineering attempts by external experts from above – often paternalistic and usually unsustainable – community mobilisation processes place the values, priorities and agency of citizens at the grassroots level at the centre of development efforts. Though a useful – indeed, necessary – instrument of any broad-based development strategy, it usually requires supply-side input and support to work effectively and sustainably. As a vehicle of organizational capacity building, community mobilisation functions primarily as a mechanism of empowerment.

Community mobilisation is a process which relies on external stimulants and support, however, it is rarely achieved effectively through only the efforts of external consultants or community workers. This is because, although outsiders to the community can get to know the community well, they are unlikely to have the same insights and gain the same levels of trust of as an 'insider'. Also, by definition, external consultants are usually only visitors to the community and are restricted in how often they can make visits because of the limited available resources (for example, to pay for transport costs), their available time, and by natural conditions. A mobiliser who is from and lives in the community, is, on the other hand, more accessible to community members and more able to manage their mobilisation work on a flexible basis.

Agencies facilitating community mobilisation should guide communities through a step-by-step process that includes: *(i)* a big-picture assessment of the community's issues, needs, and resources; *(ii)* community exploration of issues and priority-setting; *(iii)* community action planning; *(iv)* implementation of community action plans; and *(v)* monitoring and evaluation of community mobilization. The main role of the community mobilisers will be to initiate and develop a social process within the target communities for collective analysis of community needs, collective action leading to solutions of those problems, and to make the process self-sustaining and self-managed. Self-management will be channelled through the formation of groups (SHGs/CBOs), with the mobilisers playing an important role in identifying potential group members and catalysts.

The skills that the community mobilisers need are not particularly difficult to learn, but can be very powerful when put to good use. They need to learn how to be a public speaker, but not just any kind of public speaker. The kind of public speaking the community mobilisers need to know is the kind for leadership and facilitation. The community mobiliser must learn how to draw information and decisions out of groups, which requires a full understanding of the goal and relaxed confidence in front of people. They must be able to recognize preaching, lecturing and making speeches and avoid those styles. The technical skills they need as mobilisers thus include public speaking, planning, managing, observing, analyzing and writing. Along with these skills, community mobilisers also need to develop a personal character that is honest, enthusiastic, positive, tolerant, patient, and motivated.

The community mobiliser must know how to listen and understand when people talk, and they have to know how to:

- Ensure that information is accurate.
- Illustrate a point and make it interesting to a listener, especially in terms of the local context.
- Encourage dialogue and open speech, and discourage rhetoric and 'sermons'.
- Be sensitive to gender considerations.
- Acknowledge rights and speak out when rights are being oppressed.
- Ensure all voices are heard and avoid discussions being dominated by one or two individuals.

Since the community mobiliser will help organize community groups and form executive committees, they also need some organizational skills in terms of basic management competency, ability to use basic computer programmes and research on the internet, draw simple project designs, and be able to maintain accurate records, including basic financial reports.

Community mobilisation activities should strengthen and develop referrals and linkages with services. It is important to meet increased demand with supply. The community mobilization process can raise expectations as well as create demand for public services; if facilities do not have the capacity to cope with demand, this can create discouragement and disenchantment. Gaining donor support and partnership in the process is critical. Projects have been able to balance community and donor needs by assuring that community mobilization goals and efforts are consistent with strategic objectives and are directed at achieving the same results as donors. In terms of demonstrating results, indicators for monitoring and evaluating community mobilization tend to be process-focused rather than impact-focused. Programmes often face the challenge of demonstrating the value and results of community capacity building.

While capacity-building usually refers to knowledge transfers to individuals or groups, community mobilisation enables people to fuse what they themselves know with external information and techniques so as to carry out particular activities. For disadvantaged groups in particular, this transformation increases their power relative to that of other groups in their socio-economic and political environments. Empowerment in this sense is thus an outcome of both the capacity-building of people and a reform of the rules and practices that oppress them. Community mobilisation reduces poverty because it is based on the premise that the poor are willing and able to carry out a number of functions themselves to improve their situations, given encouragement to form their own organizations for promoting their development through their own efforts and participating actively in decision-making that enhances their livelihoods. The scope of community mobilisation reaches well beyond pooled savings, training effort, literacy or hygiene campaigns or even choices concerning basic livelihood opportunities. It concerns not only improving project performance by making claims on external resources but also demands accountability from powers that be. In itself, it educates citizens politically in the art of governance and the pursuit of rights and civic roles. In its broadest sense, then, social mobilization is a dynamic, participatory process of for their sustainable socio-cultural, economic and political advancement; the sustained nature of the outcome – whether in livelihoods, literacy or any other realm – brings about change in the existing power structure that mitigates poverty, reduces the risks of social conflict and encourages smooth transitions in the community or society in which the effort takes place. At the individual level, people may experience immediate psychological empowerment – increases in self-respect, self-esteem or self-confidence and capacity – that evolves from collective action. At the community level, this empowerment allows individuals and groups to mobilize themselves towards the goals of socio-economic and political change that they themselves define.

Community mobilisation and participation projects do not follow a 'one size fits all' model – each scale-up area requires a local adaptation of processes and methods. Strategically linking community mobilization with marketing and promotion activities can have increased effect. Important lessons learned from a number of on community mobilisation campaigns suggest the following conditions for successful outcomes.

- Allow adequate time for the process.
- Define who participates and how.
- Recruit effective leaders, community representatives, and volunteers.
- Have skilled facilitators.
- Understand socio-cultural context.
- Use culturally accepted methodologies.
- Develop community mobilization activities in the context of larger social reforms.
- Accommodate unanticipated consequences.
- Demonstrate mutual respect and non-hierarchical relationships.
- Where possible, work with established networks, drawing on existing local-level associations.
- To optimize mobilization, involve local service providers and community representatives in collecting information, analyzing information, and advocating the method or service.

BIBLIOGRAPHY

Adams, Dale W., Douglas Graham and J. D. Von Pischke, eds. (1984). *Undermining Rural Development with Cheap Credit*. Boulder and Colorado: Westview Press.

Adato, Michelle, Timothy Besley, Lawrence Haddad, and John Hoddinott. (1999). 'Participation and Poverty Reduction: Issues, Theory and New Evidence from South Africa'. Background paper for *World Development Report 2000/2001*. International Food Policy Research Institute and World Bank: Washington, D.C.

Alinsky, S. D. (1971). Rules for Radicals. A Pragmatic Primer for Realistic Radicals, New York: Vintage. 196 + xxvi pages.

Alkire, S., A. Bebbington, T. Esmail, E. Ostrom, M. Polski, A. Ryan, J. Van Domelen, W. Wakeman, and P. Dongier. (2001). Community-driven Development. In *PRSP Source Book*. Washington, D.C: World Bank.

Amarsinghe. (2001). Mobilizing Rural Women for Development: Experience of Social Mobilisation Programme in The Hamabantota District, Sri Lanka Personal Communication.

Ambrose, Yvon. (1992). Empowering the Poor: Animation for Social Change. Caritas India, New Delhi.

Anderson. No. Martinez. E., Cerrato F Morales, E. and Ledogar, R. (1989). 'The use of Community-based Data in Health Planning in Mexico and Central America'. Health Policy and Planning 4(3), 197-206.

Askew, I. (1986). The Community Participation Approach in Family Planning Programmes, London: IFFP.

Barua, Jayanti. (2001). *Social Mobilisation and Modern Society*. New Delhi: Mittal Publications.

Binswanger, H. and S. Aiyar. (2003). Scaling up Community Driven Development: Theoretical Underpinnings and Programme Design Implications. Draft. World Bank, Washington, D.C.

Carl Tjerandsen. (1980). *Education for Citizenship: A Foundations Experience,* Santa Cruz: Emil Schwarzhaupt Foundation, Inc., p. 240.

Channell Katherine. (2000). 'The Social Mobilisation Approach: A Participatory Model for Local Resource Mobilisation', *Canadian Journal of Development Studies*. Vol. XXI.

Cohen, A. P. (1985). *The Symbolic Construction of Community.* New York: Tavistock Publications and Ellis Horwood Limited.

Cohen, Sylvie I. (1969). 'Mobilising Communities for Participation and Empowerment', Chap. 13, from the Book' Participatory Communication For Social Change', Ed.by Sam Dave Beckwith and Randy Stoecker, *Community Organizing: Soul and Substance,* forthcoming.

D'Souza, Fr. Frederick. (2012). Fostering Animation, Caritas News India today, Issue 53, October 2012.

Durning, A.T. (1989). Action at the Grassroots: Fighting Poverty and Environmental Decline, Washington, DC: Worldwatch Institute.

Eller, Cynthia. (1995). *Living in the Lap of the Goddess: The Feminist Spirituality Movement in America*. Boston: Beacon Press.

Ernesto Cortes, Industrial Areas Foundation, as quoted in: Harry C. Boyte. (1980). *The Backyard Revolution: Understanding the New Citizen Movement,* Philadelphia, Temple University Press, p. 44.

Fellin, P. (2001). *The Community and the Social Worker* (3rd ed.). Itasca, IL: F. E. Peacock Publishers.

Forrester, Simon. (2012). Community Mobilization for Empowerment of Vulnerable Women and Men: Guidebook. Joint Integrated Local Development Programme (JILDP). Moldova.

Freire, Paulo. (2007). Pedagogy of the Oppressed. New York: Continuum.

Ganj, Marshall. (2005). What is Organizing? 32 (1) Social Policy 16 (Fall 2002), Kennedy School.

Goodman, Robert M. *et al*. (1998). 'Identifying and Defining the Dimensions of Community Capacity to Provide a Basis for Measurement', *Health Education and Behaviour* 25(3): 258-78.

GRAAP. (1985). Pourune Pedagogie de I' Autopromotion, Nouvelle Edition pourles Animateurs Villageois, Burtkina Faso, Africa: GRAAP.

FAO. (1997). Participation in Practice: Lessons from the FAO People's Participation Programme, Rome, Italy. http://www.fao.org/Participation/ourvision.html accessed on 20 Marche 2004.

Grootaert, Christiaan, and Deepa Narayan. (2000). 'Local Institutions, Poverty, and Household Welfare in Bolivia'. Local Level Institutions Working Paper 9. Social Development Department. World Bank, Washington, D.C.

Grootaert, Christiaan, Gi-Taik Oh, and Anand Swamy. (1999). 'Social Capital and Development Outcomes in Burkina Faso'. Local Level Institutions Working Paper 7. Social Development Department. World Bank, Washington, D.C.

Henry Allen. (1998). 'Organizing, Power, and Public Policy: One Foundation's Road to Supporting Community Organizing'. *Shelterforce*, September/October, p. 31.

IFAD. (2003). Transforming Rural Institutions In Order To Reach The Millennium Development Goals, Roundtable Discussion Paper for the Twenty-Fifth Anniversary Session of IFAD's Governing Council.

IFAD. Empowerment of the Poor. http://www.ifad.org/events/past/hunger/empower.html

Ishmael Mkhabela (2011). Community Mobilisation: Constraints and Opportunities for Change and Development Done By the People, Not To People. *A Paper Presented by Ishmael Mkhabela to the Leadership Forum Convened at Spier Estate Conference Centre on 9 and 10 February, 2011.*

Jacqueline B. Mondros and Scott M. Wilson. (1994). *Organizing for Power and Empowerment,* New York: Columbia University Press.

Jan, Abid Ullah. (2000). Community Organizing: Community Change Participant's Manual. HRD Center Sarhad Rural Support Corporation, Peshawar, Pakistan.

Jan, Abid Ullah. (2001). Developing Meso-Level Institutions. Integrated Regional Support Programme - Pakistan. http://commdev.ca/books_meso_level.php.

Jimenez, Emmanuel and Vicente Paqueo. (1996). 'Do Local Contributions Affect the Efficiency of Public Primary Schools'? *Economics of Education Review* 15(4): 377-86. World Bank, Washington, D.C.

Jimenez, Emmanuel, and Yasuyuki Sawada. (1998). 'Do Community-Managed Schools Work? An Evaluation of El Salvador's EDUCO Programme'. Impact Evaluation of Education Reforms Paper 8. Development Research Group.

Joshi, Anuradha and Moore, Mick. (2000). The Mobilizing Potential of Anti Poverty Programmes, IDS Discussion Paper 374, accessed from the website.

Lam, W. F. (1998). Governing Irrigation Systems in Nepal: Institutions, Infrastructure and Collective Action, Oakland, *California*: ICS Press.

Mattessich, P., Monsey, B., and Roy, C. (1997). *Community Building: What Makes it work: A Review of the Factors Influencing Successful Community Building.* St. Paul, MN: Amherst H. Wilder Foundation.

Mike Miller. (1985). Organize Training Center, as Quoted in Sally Covington and Larry Parachini, *Foundations in the Newt Era,* Washington, DC: The National Committee for Responsive Philanthropy.

Moulik, T.K. (1977). 'Techniques of Mobilizing Rural People to Support Rural Development Programme', Working Paper No. 171. *Indian Institute of Management*, Ahmedabad.

Musisi, Christine. (2002). 'The Role of Civil Society in Local Governance and Poverty Alleviation: Concepts, Realities and Experiences'. May.

Narayan, Deepa, Raj Patel, Kai Schafft, Anne Rademacher, and Sarah Koch-Schulte. (2000). *Voices of the Poor: Can Anyone Hear Us?* Washington, D.C.: World Bank and Oxford University Press.

Nettle, J.P. (1967). Political Mobilization: A Sociological Analysis of Methods and Concepts, London: Faber and Faber Ltd.

Nina Wallerstein. (1992). 'Powerlessness, Empowerment, and Health: Implications for Health Promotion Programmes'. *American Journal of Health Promotion,* (6): 197-205.

Oakley, P. (1991). Projects with People: The Practice of Participation in Rural Development. Geneva: International Labor Office.

Pandey, Kalyan. (2002). 'Social Mobilization: Concept and Application for Poverty Reduction and Self-Governance'. Paper for Regional Workshop on Promoting Effective Participation of Civil Society in Local Governance and Poverty Alleviation in the ECIS Region – Challenges and Good Practices – May (2002). Proceedings of the Regional Workshop on Promoting Effective Participation of Civil Society in Local Governance and Poverty Alleviation in the ECIS Region – Challenges and Good Practices – May.

Raju, K. (2001). 'Social Mobilisation as A Strategy for Poverty Alleviation – Experiences from UNDP – Supported South Asia Poverty Alleviation Programme in India', in Mini-Scale Rural Infrastructure Development, Asian Productivity Organization, Tokyo.

Reddy, G.N. (2001). Social Mobilisation and Empowerment of Women through Self-Help Groups – The Case of Peddamangalaram Village, in 'Mini-scale Rural Infrastructure Development, Asian Productivity Organization, Tokyo.

Rana, Madhukar S.J.B. (2001). 'Culture, Democracy and Development in South Asia', Edited by N.N. Vohra, *India International Centre,* Delhi: SHIPRA Publications.

Ravallion, Martin. (1999). 'Is More Targeting Consistent with Less Spending'? *International Tax and Public Finance* 6(3):411-19.

Rootaert, Christiaan. (1999a). 'Does Social Capital Help the Poor? A Synthesis of Findings from the Local Level Institutions Studies in Bolivia, Burkina Faso, and Indonesia'. Social Development Department. World Bank, Washington, D.C.

SAPNA. (2001). The Regional Poverty Eradication Programme for South Asia, Progress Report No. 8, Sri Lanka.

Sara, Jennifer, and Travis Katz. (1997). 'Making Rural Water Sustainable: Report on the Impact of Project Rules'. United Nations Development Programme (UNDP) and World Bank Water and Sanitation Programme, Washington, D.C.

Sarachild, Kathie. (1973). *Conciousness-Raising: A Radical Weapon.* Excerpts from a speech at the First National Conference of Stewardesses for Women's Rights in New York City, March 12, 1973. Retrieved from:

http://library.duke.edu/rubenstein/scriptorium/wlm/fem/sarachild.html.6 Jan 2012.

Sen, Armartya. (1999). Development as Freedom. New York: Alfred A. Knopf.

Seth Borgos and Scott Douglas. (1996). 'Community Organizing and Civic Renewal: A View from the South', Social Policy.

Shor, I. And Freire, Paule. (1989). Pedagogy of liberation. Granby, MA: Bergin and Garvey. Seneares, Thomson L. Jacobsonb, Shigley a. White, Sage Publication, Delhi. *Development Journal of the United Nations Development Programme in Kyrgyzstan* (Issue No. 1, October 2001). 'Social Mobilization'.

Stone, J., and Mennell, S. (Eds.). (1980). *Alexis de Tocqueville on Democracy, Revolution, and Society: Selected writings.* Chicago: University of Chicago Press.

Swarts, Heidi J. 12 Feb. (2010). "Organizing Nationally to Win Locally: Faith-Based Community Organizing's New Frontier." *Shelterforce*. Retrieved from: http://www.shelterforce.org/article/print/1869

Tang, S. Y. (1992). Institutions and Collective Action. Self-Governance in Irrigation. San Francisco: ICS Press.

UNAIDS. (1997). *Community Mobilization and AIDS*, UNAIDS Best Practice Collection, Geneva, Switzerland.

UNDP. (2002). Social Mobilization, http://www.undp.org/mainundp/propoor/civil.htm, accessed on 26 Dec.

UNICEF. (1986). Community Participation: Assignment Children. Report No. 59. Geneva, Switzerland: UNICEF.

UNICEF. (1997). Social Mobilisation for the Elimination of Child Labour: Issue Paper, International Conference on Child Labour, Oslo, 27-30 October, UNICEF, New York.

Whyte, A. (1986). Guidelines for Planning Community Participation in Water Supply and Sanitation Projects, ETS/83.8 (Offset Publication No. 96). Geneva: World Health Organization.

Venkatamaran, Arjunamurthy and Julia Falconer. (1999). 'Rejuvenating India's Decimated Forests Through Joint Action: Lessons from Andhra Pradesh'. Project brief. World Bank, Washington, D.C.

Wignaraja, Ponna and Sirivardana (eds). (2000). Readings on Pro-Poor Planning through Social Mobilisation in Asia, Vikas Publishing House Pvt. Ltd., New Delhi: Sage Publications.

Wignaraja, Ponna and Akmal Hussain (eds). (1989). The Challenge in South Asia: Development, Democracy and Regional Cooperation, New Delhi: Sage Publications.

— (2001). Towards The Theory and Practice of Strategic Pro-Planning And Social Mobilization For Poverty Eradication. Inaugural address in the National Seminar on 'Planning for Social Mobilisation', 21 March, 2001, NIRD, Hyderabad, India.

Will Parks and Linda Lloyd. (2004). Planning Social Mobilization and Communication for Dengue Fever Prevention and Control: A Step-by-Step Guide. World Health Organization Geneva.

Women's Health and Safe Motherhood Project-Partnerships Component (2000), A Project of the Filipino People Financed through a Partnership between the Government of the Philippines and the European Union. Community Health Development Package, Module 7. Community Organizing and Community Development for Health.

World Bank. (2000). *Word Development Report 2000/2001*. Washington, D.C.

Index

O

P

****